Educating Voters

for

Rebuilding America

With

National Goals and Balanced Budget In This Decade

JACK E. BOWSHER

AUTHOR: EDUCATING AMERICA

Avoiding an Economic Depression
and
Financial Meltdown of U.S. Federal Government

Educating Voters for Rebuilding America
National Goals and Balanced Budget

iUniverse books may be ordered through booksellers or by contacting:

iUniverse
1663 Liberty Drive
Bloomington, IN 47403
www.iuniverse.com
1-800-Authors (1-800-288-4677)

ISBN: 978-1-4620-1488-0 (sc)
ISBN: 978-1-4620-1490-3 (hc)
ISBN: 978-1-4620-1489-7 (ebk)

Printed in the United States of America

iUniverse rev. date: 09/12/2011

TABLE OF CONTENTS

OPPORTUNITY TO ASSESS KNOWLEDGE
PRIOR TO READING THE BOOK

The reader should think of this book as an education session providing the knowledge to make good decisions on which candidates and political parties will rebuild America rather than lead our country into another economic depression. As in other education programs, it is always good to have an assessment to determine what one knows about a subject prior to investing the time to learn more. The assessment at the end of the book will show the reader how much knowledge he/she has gained. Use a piece of paper or your electronic reader to answer the following questions. Store the information in your book or electronic reader until you complete the 25 questions at the end of the book.

1. What do you consider to be the five most important issues facing our federal government?
    1.
    2.
    3.
    4.
    5.

2. What year would you predict the United States government will have a financial meltdown if the borrowing and spending continues?

3. Which political party is most responsible for the mountain of debt that has been created during the past 30 years?

4. What four areas of the federal government have caused the growth in annual deficits and national debt?
   1.
   2.
   3.
   4.

5. Do you believe the federal government can create and implement systemic changes in this decade to reduce the size of the annual debt and the growth of the national debt?   Yes   No

6. What are the national goals of the Republican Party?

7. What are the national goals of the Democratic Party?

8. What are the most important changes required to reduce the cost and improve quality of health care in this decade?

9. What should the federal government do to generate millions of new jobs in order to reduce unemployment to 5% or lower?

10. Do you support an increase or decrease in military and homeland security spending?

11. Do you support a greater financial investment in American education systems?

12. Do you believe Social Security should be means tested for certain income levels?
   Families earning in excess of $1 million
   Families earning in excess of $250,000
   Families earning in excess of $100,000

13. What income tax deductions should be abolished to reduce the deficit and debt?

14. How much (in billions of dollars) should the federal spending be reduced?

15. Do you believe the federal budget can be balanced by 2020?

16. Do you believe millions of educated voters will reduce the uncivil language and meetings that have existed in recent years as the major challenges of our country are discussed?

17. Do you believe that Social Security and Medicare are the heart of the deficit and debt problems facing our nation in 2012? Yes   No

18. Do you believe that a split government where one political party controls the Congress and another party controls the White House will control spending better?   Yes   No

19. Do you plan to vote in the 2012 election?   Yes   No

20. Do you believe the War on Terror is affordable?   Yes   No

INTRODUCTION AND OVERVIEW

It is unbelievable what has happened to our country in a ten-year period. The United States had almost full employment in the 1990s and today there are millions of unemployed and underemployed workers. The Federal Reserve had projected over a $5 trillion surplus for the first decade of the 21st Century and it appears our country will have a national debt of $16 trillion by 2012 and estimated to be over $20 trillion by 2016. How could a nation go from balanced budgets during 1998, 1999, 2000 and 2001 with surpluses totaling $560 billion to annual deficits exceeding a trillion dollars year after year? How could a nation be borrowing around 40 cents for every government dollar spent? These are the questions every American should be asking Presidential and Congressional candidates in 2012. Voters also need to ask what plans each political party has to return this nation to sound financial management and a balanced budget by the end of this decade.

The amount of borrowed money required to keep the federal government afloat is almost incomprehensible. For example, in 2010, the United States had to borrow $7.054 trillion to merely repay debt that came due plus $1.294 trillion for the 2010 deficit which amounted to borrowing $8.348 trillion. On average, in a 50-week period, more than $100 billion is borrowed weekly. Keep in mind up to 1974, the largest amount of borrowed dollars for a deficit in a given year was $25 billion which did not include any transfer of Social Security trust fund money. As this mountain of debt was growing, there was little or no discussion of this potential financial crisis in elections during the past ten years.

When I was a member of the Comptroller General's Advisory Board during the years 2002-2006, I heard in-depth briefings on our federal government's overall financial system. The Comptroller General is the chief executive officer of the Government Accountability Office (GAO) which reviews all the major areas of the federal government and renders reports on the effectiveness of their various departments and programs to Congress and the White House. These presentations informed us that expenses were far exceeding revenues. In fact, the annual deficits were increasing each year in the General Fund (all revenues and expenses other than Social Security and Medicare). In addition, we heard discussion about how the "baby boomers" would eventually cause a financial crisis due to the increased volume of Americans who would receive Social Security and Medicare benefits. Most of the attendees did not view this as a near-term financial crisis due to the trillions of dollars in the entitlement trust funds and the reassurance by the President and Vice President that with the multi-trillion-dollar U.S. economy, the debt was manageable. The Comptroller General, David Walker, appeared to be a lone voice as a government financial executive who was concerned about the size of the expanding national debt and annual deficits.

Today, Americans are scared . . . . and they have every right to be as leaders of all political parties are ringing the alarm bell about the size of annual deficits and the mountain of national debt. Our federal government is headed for a financial meltdown that could make the 1930s Great Depression pale in comparison. For most Americans, their standard of living has been slowly decreasing for years, but it could go into a freefall in this decade if competent Presidential and Congressional candidates are not elected in 2012. Americans need to be educated on the facts and potential solutions to avoid the financial debacle. There must be intelligent and knowledgeable voters in the 2012 general election. There are five major reasons for writing this book.

First, there is an unbelievable amount of inaccurate information about the budgets, deficits, and the national debt sent to Americans each day in their e-mails, faxes, and by some misinformed members of the press which greatly confuses potential voters. The barrage of illusions, exaggerations, and false information has reached such a level it is nearly impossible to hold an unbiased election in our country.

Second, Americans simply do not have sufficient knowledge about the federal government's financial system to make independent decisions on which political leaders have realistic solutions to avoid a financial crisis. Most citizens do not even have the knowledge to ask penetrating questions for candidates to answer.

Third, neither political party has articulated national goals to build strategic and action programs to avoid a financial crisis. Nor do they have a realistic plan to reduce the size and cost of government.

Fourth, there are groups in Washington, D.C. and state capitols who are developing requirements for a number of new taxes or tax increases to add revenues rather than reduce expenses. If Americans take-home wages are greatly reduced due to tax increases or elimination of tax deductions, the economy could fall into an economic depression due to a major reduction in consumer spending.

Fifth, the proposed solutions are often built around sharing real financial pain, thus further reducing the American standard of living and morale of our country.

Therefore, there is a requirement for another document to explain *how* the federal government can reduce the size and cost of government, return the country to a balanced budget in this decade, and rebuild our country to have a rising standard of living. To create this document, a five-step management system is utilized by the author.

Step One: Recognize There Is a Leadership Crisis

It is always difficult for financial executives in an organization to declare there is a leadership crisis because quite often they have been part of the management team creating the financial crisis. This is true in corporations as well as government. This document will clearly identify which Presidents were great spenders and which were fiscal conservatives. Both parties have fiscal conservatives and big spenders. There must be a new emphasis on cost containment and financial management by leaders of all political parties.

Step Two: Identify the Main Causes of the Annual Deficits

It is not difficult to identify the major areas of excessive spending by comparing the actual spending of Fiscal Year 2000 to Fiscal Year 2010. It becomes clear there are six areas of spending and the unaffordable tax cuts that have caused the large trillion-dollar-plus annual deficits which increased the national debt and interest costs to an unsustainable level. Here is a short briefing on all six areas that far exceed their affordability levels.

First, there is an increase of nearly a half trillion dollars in loss of income tax revenue and increase in unemployment benefits (welfare, unemployment insurance, food stamps, etc.) due to the Great Recession of 2008. Neither political party has a realistic plan to restore millions of jobs for unemployed and underemployed citizens. One political party is completely against any economic stimulus. There is no chance to balance the budget without putting our country back to work.

Second, the Defense, Intelligence, Homeland Security, Veterans' Affairs and Pensions, Military Medical expenses, plus interest on the debt of $5 trillion of borrowed funds for the War on Terror that now exceeds their 2000 budget by $500 billion a year. In fact, this spending consumes almost all the personal and corporate income taxes collected last year. American political leaders have raised the cost of war to a level where it will bankrupt even the world's richest nation. The United States can only remain the "policemen of the world" if Americans are willing to accept at least a 25% surtax on their income tax. If not, there must be an end to the wars in Iraq and Afghanistan and our nation must change its foreign policies and reduce the budgets of these organizations. It becomes clear that peace and prosperity are two essential goals of our country if it is to return to a balanced budget in this decade.

Third, the health care industry, which includes Medicare, Medicaid, HMOs, Institute of Health, etc., has created an unaffordable health care system costing twice as much as other countries who provide health insurance to all their citizens from the day they are born to the day the die. There must be major changes in our health care system that go far beyond the 2010 Affordable Care Act.

Fourth, the education industry that includes the K-12 public schools, institutions of higher education, and workforce training has had an annual increase in expenses even exceeding health care. New instructional and management systems in education are essential if a balanced budget is to be achieved at both the federal and state levels.

Fifth, most government agencies and programs have far exceeded their 2000 year spending levels throughout the decade ending in 2010. Agency budgets must be reduced on average by 20 percent during the years 2013 to 2016 if a balanced budget is to be achieved, because revenues only increased by seven percent during the ten-year period between 2001 to 2010.

Sixth, the baby boomer generation is retiring and there is no money in the Social Security Trust Fund which means benefits must be adjusted or revenues increased so Social Security does not require funds from the General Fund, which will be in debt by an estimated $16 trillion by 2013. Social Security needs to be a self-funding organization.

In addition, presently both political parties are buying votes from taxpaying citizens and corporations with tax cuts that are not affordable. Political leaders also solicit millions and billions of dollars worth of funds for campaign expenses based on tax cuts. This has to stop. Only when there is a long-term surplus should tax cuts be approved by Congress and the President.

A reader will learn what leadership decisions are necessary to bring all these excessive spending areas under control and how to explain the requirement to restore some of the tax cuts from the first decade of the 21st Century to have a balanced budget in this decade.

Step Three: Establish a Vision and National Goals

To "Rebuild America" and solve the financial crisis over an eight-year period, there must be a vision supported by a vast majority of Americans with national goals returning the country to a balanced budget and a rising standard of living. Listed below are the proposed national goals.

1. **Peace With Strong Defense and Homeland Security Systems**
2. **Prosperity and a Rising Standard of Living With High Employment**
3. **Adequate and Affordable Health Care System for All Citizens**
4. **Superior and Affordable Education Systems**
5. **Efficient and Affordable Government**
6. **Decent Retirement for Senior Citizens**

A reader will learn how each one of these goals can be achieved and which senior government executives are responsible for managing their government agency to reach the goal.

Step Four: Implement a Change Management System

Today, large and complex organizations are using research-based methodologies to create systemic changes and new paradigms improving organizational performance as well as containing costs in future years. Reengineering studies are essential and benchmarking procedures are additional tools to achieve more work using fewer resources. All of this change is discussed in the book. A multi-year phased approach is utilized to achieve the financial objectives rather than a one-year budget cycle. The public sector is as capable as the private sector in utilizing all these methodologies and management systems.

Step Five: Overpowering Communication Strategy Is Essential

The President and Congress who are elected in 2012 must have an overpowering communications strategy that is pro-active rather than re-active on how their congressional members with a large majority will return the United States to a balanced budget in this decade, a rising standard of living, a much higher employment level as well as how they will achieve the six national goals and the vision of "Rebuilding America." Voters must be convinced that leaping from one political party to another every two-or-four years as they did in 2008 and 2010 will not be successful because that results in a "do nothing" Congress and keeps the excessive spending programs in existence.

Every political party agrees borrowing and spending trillions of dollars in the 2001 to 2012 time frame cannot continue without hitting a long-term and deep economic depression. If the debt level and interest payments become so great where a country cannot pay its bonds when they come due or pay annual interest payments, a "bond crisis" comes crashing down on a nation. This book describes three strategic options our political leaders must select from in 2013 to 2016 after the general election.

Option One: Continue the Civil War Between the Political Parties With Continuous Borrowing and Spending

This is the option currently being used today after the 2010 mid-term election. This option leads to Option Two when financial institutions reduce the credit rating on Treasury Bonds which could happen after the 2012 general election. This move could drive up interest cost by hundreds of billions of dollars and eventually bonds may not be purchased later in the decade. Then there is no other course of action but to have emergency meetings in Congress as were held in 2008 over the financial Wall Street crisis, except the nation will not be able to avoid a financial crisis by borrowing trillions of dollars as they did in 2008. Option Two then takes over.

If voters do not become knowledgeable about the serious issues facing our country, the 2012 general election will result, once again, in a "do nothing" government no matter which party is in charge of the Senate or White House, because the minority party will be able to stop almost every bill proposed in the Senate with a filibuster. Spending will continue with more than a trillion-dollar deficit for each year in the 2013 to 2016 administration. The national debt will be at least $20 trillion by 2016, and there will be no plans to reduce spending which could lead to an economic depression in this decade.

Option Two: Major Tax Increases and Benefit Reductions

This option is now being considered in Washington, D.C. and includes the potential of large number of tax increases and the elimination of tax deductions that amount to tax increases. The "take home" pay will be greatly reduced and our country could slide into an economic depression similar to the 1930s due to a substantial decrease in consumer spending. In addition, this option will, no doubt, lead to serious class warfare demonstrations on college campuses, in state capitols, and Washington, D.C. by citizens who feel political leaders are inflicting financial pain on them when they did not create the financial crisis. Eventually, there will a major decline in the standard of living to a level where the United States will have a second-class way of life below citizens in leading European and Asian countries.

Presently, one political party has a 2012 strategy at all three levels of government (federal, state and local) to campaign on a financial pain strategy for all Americans except wealthy citizens. Somehow, they believe Americans will vote for a lower standard of living and an economic depression that comes with supporting Option Two.

Option Three: Implement Major Systemic Changes To Minimize Tax Increases and the Elimination of Tax Deductions Under the Banner of Rebuilding America

This book provides knowledge on how political leaders can create major systemic changes within the six spending machines and how to recharge the private enterprise system to increase employment. Action programs must be tied to achieving the six national goals. The leadership crisis must be ended by electing qualified candidates in the 2012 election who will provide changes in our defense organizations, education, health care, Social Security, and government agencies to reduce their budgets to affordable levels as well as increase employment by millions of jobs.

The hope is for at least one political party in 2012 to adopt a pro-active and positive vision with national goals for "Rebuilding America" minimizing the financial pain on Americans. This strategy is the opposite of tearing down the federal government with machete cuts in the budget greatly lowering the American standard of living which could drive the country into a long-term and deep economic depression. There is no requirement for means-testing Social Security or Medicare. The nation must not retreat on the march to achieving health insurance for every American from the day they are born to the day they die. Unemployed citizens must be returned to meaningful jobs. The student learning crisis must be solved and costs must be contained at institutions of higher education. The American workforce must be retrained to be the most competitive workforce in the world. Our government must be efficient and affordable. Our Defense and Homeland Security Systems must protect our country from Terrorism. All this and a balanced budget is possible with great leadership in Option Three. To make all this happen, knowledgeable voters must send a strong message to the winning political party that Rebuilding America is the vision they expect in the 2013 to 2016 administration.

The book summarizes all the potential spending reductions in a lesson explaining how our country can return to a balanced budget by 2020 which was accomplished in the late 1990s and 2000. Once again, this approach minimizes the amount of revenue required through tax increases and the elimination of tax deductions. Listed below is a preview of those figures. The following estimates are the amount of expenses that could be reduced on an annual basis by 2016 based on a four-year phased-down of expenses and an increase of some revenues.

With a return to prosperity:

Increase tax revenues from higher employment	$250 B
Decreases in unemployment expenses	<u>250</u> B
Assumes an unemployment of 5 percent	$500 B
Reductions in the operations of defense and intelligence	$300 B
Reductions in health care (Medicare & Medicaid)	100 B
Reductions in other government agencies/departments	100 B
Better tax collection	130 B
Reduced Earmarks	10 B
Restore income tax on $250,000 incomes and above	100 B
Restore tax on $50,000 to $250,000	135 B
Increase income tax on $25,000 to $50,000 earners	<u>25</u> B
Total with all tax cuts restored	$1,400 B

As one reviews this list, it becomes clear the return to a balanced budget is dependent on peace and prosperity as well as containing costs within the health care systems. The lessons in the book explain how these reductions could be achieved. This list of revenue increases and reduced expenses enables the United States to achieve a balanced budget in this decade, and it shows how deep our financial crisis is to reach that goal.

As an American born at the start of the Great Depression in the1930s, I never thought I would live through another economic depression due to ineffective leadership by political and business leaders. In the month I was born, 30 American banks in the Chicago area went through bankruptcy, and took the savings of Americans who were reduced to high levels of unemployment and poverty. Unemployment reached as high as 40 percent in some cities. Millions of Americans lost their homes. There was no unemployment insurance. Families had to move into the homes of other family members or become homeless. Begging for food became a major occupation in our country. Having read Liaquat Ahamed's book *Lords Of Finance*, describing the Great

Depression in detail, one realizes an economic depression is the result of ineffective leadership by business executives, central bankers, and political leaders. We must never let this situation happen again to our country. That is why Americans must be educated to elect qualified candidates in the 2012 election. The book provides a reader with a complete listing of spending by government agencies.

I was raised in one of Chicago's middle-class neighborhoods. The Democratic Party managed the city affairs during my upbringing. As a young adult, I voted for Democrats because they were improving the American standard of living. Like millions of Americans, I believed they were the political party that would avoid another economic depression. But the excessive spending for both the War on Poverty and the Vietnam War under President Johnson made me question the party's strategies of tax and spend. Like many other Democrats, I voted for President Reagan because he advocated a smaller government, less taxes, and the prosperity of the free market system. Later we moved to San Diego and I joined the Conservative Order of Good Government. For a number of years, I was an officer and even President of COGG. I have always been a lifelong fiscal conservative who believes in a balanced budget and manageable debt. But with the excessive spending and the two questionable unpaid wars under President Bush and Vice President Cheney, and their Congressional leaders, I believed that the Republican Party had left me as well. Today, I am an Independent and a concerned citizen, trying to determine which candidates and political party will return the country to sound financial management and prosperity as President Clinton did in the 1990s with an efficient and affordable government plus a balanced budget. He achieved four out of the six national goals and tried his best to solve the student learning crisis and the healthcare problems.

A number of people have asked why did I devote a year to writing this book? The answer is quite simple. Like many Americans, I am in shock over what happened to this country in the past ten years. Therefore, I decided to take a "helicopter view" of the mistakes made by leaders of the private and public sectors who created this financial crisis. One thing I have learned over time is usually leaders who are responsible for a crisis rarely develop a strategy and vision to end the crisis. Futurist Joel Barker stated that important shifts in new paradigms will not often come from a person who has been entrenched in the existing paradigms. As the author, I do not have to defend any past decisions or programs; nor do I have to support any basic beliefs of a political party or political leader. My income is not dependent on any stock. Therefore, I can provide a true independent analysis of what has caused this crisis and what must be accomplished to avoid an economic depression. As an educator, this book provides a series of unbiased lessons for voters. I am not endorsing any candidates at this time. It is up to educated voters to decide which candidates to support.

As I started to do research for how I would vote in 2012 to rebuild America, it became clear how much information all of us need to fully understand where each political party will take this country. There is never a perfect candidate or perfect party, but all Americans should vote for candidates and a political party that will best achieve our national goals and a balanced budget in this decade. This book can be read on a business trip or over a weekend. You do not need a college degree in finance or accounting to understand its messages. Any American with a high school education can comprehend the knowledge in the 15 lessons. I chose the word "lesson" rather than chapter because this book is really an education course to become an educated voter. Some editors told me Americans do not read any more due to their focus on electronic gadgets. That statement is simply not true. Today, bookstores are larger than many small town libraries. Millions of Americans read books and millions of citizens have electronic readers.

This book will educate readers on the issues and challenges related to these questions:

-Who will help create jobs for the unemployed?
-Who will help bring back the values of our homes?
-Who will reduce excessive government spending?
-Who will protect our Social Security benefits?
-Who will phase down and end the wars?
-Who will return our economy to prosperity?
-Who will achieve a higher quality of health care at lower costs?
-Who will protect our Medicare health insurance?
-Who will solve the student learning crisis in our schools?
-Who will help reduce the cost of a college education?
-Who will reduce the cost of energy and ensure an adequate supply?

My great hope is this book will also be read by members of the press, candidates for Congress, campaign staff members, national state and local political leaders, the White House staff, budget and finance executives, senior military and defense executives, health care administrators, education administrators, energy company executives, and corporate senior executives. The subjects discussed in this book will have a major impact on all these individuals, as well as on millions of concerned American citizens and voters.

This book can also serve as the framework for town meetings, debates, coffee club discussions and conversations among friends, with the questions voters should be asking their candidates, which are listed in the final lesson. It is time for Americans to have more civil discussions about the major issues facing our country rather than disruptive meetings that have taken place in recent years. Candidates should not give us months of negative ads trying to destroy the image of their opponents with multi-million-dollar budgets and at the same time, providing little or no insight on how they would vote if elected. This book has been written prior to the primary elections which determine who the candidates will be in the general election with the hope the messages in this document will influence the campaign strategies of both political parties. Many events can occur in 2012, but the major challenges facing our nation will probably not have major changes prior to the general election. Hopefully, this book will motivate leaders of both political parties to offer detail plans on *how* to rebuild America with a minimum of financial pain. Americans want a rising standard of living. In this book, I have compiled the best thinking of many government financial executives, public policy experts, and elected officials to help all of us become more informed voters in 2012. Remember, an educated voter is usually an outstanding citizen. May our country have a successful and prosperous future based on the performance of our voters in 2012.

PART I

REQUIREMENT FOR GOALS AND FISCAL RESPONSIBILITY

Our country cannot continue to be the world leader in peace and prosperity with the highest standard of living unless our federal government returns to policies and practices of fiscal responsibility as well as establishing national goals for the 21st Century. This section of the book provides a reader with summary lessons on how close our nation is to a financial meltdown of the federal government as well as a basic understanding of the federal financial system. It is important for Americans to know how our government descended into this financial crisis and how our country will emerge with new national goals to obtain a vision resulting in a bright future for our children and grandchildren.

LESSON 1

A WARNING ABOUT A FINANCIAL MELTDOWN

Early Ringing of Alarm Bells

In 2004, Peter G. Peterson, the former Secretary of Commerce in President Nixon's administration and the former Chairman of the Federal Reserve Bank in New York, wrote a book entitled *Running On Empty: How The Democratic and Republican Parties Are Bankrupting Our Future And What Americans Can Do About It.* Peterson stated, "When George W. Bush came into office in 2001, the ten-year budget balance was officially projected to be a surplus of $5.6 trillion. But after three large tax cuts, bursting of the stock market bubble, and the devastating effects of 9/11 on the economy, the surplus had evaporated, and the deficit was expected to grow to $5 trillion over the next decade."(1) While they were in office, Vice President Cheney claimed President Reagan proved 'deficits don't matter' and President Bush claimed that deficits were just numbers on paper.

The purpose of Mr. Peterson's book was to use hard facts to refute these comments because deficits do matter. He focused on entitlements and tax cuts as the two major reasons why the federal government would eventually go bankrupt. He listed ten partisan myths that both political parties use to justify passage of entitlements and tax cuts. He did not address the massive build-up of military expenses because it had not happened at the time he wrote his book.

Peterson's book was aimed at raising public awareness about the economic, political, and even geopolitical perils of living beyond our country's means. He urged the President and Congress to reform Social Security and Medicare. He advocated means-testing which entailed the middle class losing some of their benefits and the wealthy losing almost all benefits. At the time, he thought 401k accounts would be much higher in value and no one was predicting the 2008 meltdown of our financial institutions and the stock market. He also promoted several reforms in the overall healthcare system and he supported political campaign funding reforms.

Mr. David M. Walker served as the seventh Comptroller General of the United States from 1998 to 2008. In this role, he served as the CEO of the Government Accountability Office (GAO). This is a 15-year presidential appointment with the consent of Congress. He left the office in 2008 to become President and CEO of the new Peter G. Peterson Foundation. In 2009, he wrote *Comeback America: Turning The Country Around And Restoring Fiscal Responsibility.* His book is essentially a continued ringing of the alarm bell that was started by Pete Peterson. He provides more facts and figures. Of course by 2009, the massive build-up of the military budget was a fact resulting from the two pre-emptive wars in Iraq and Afghanistan as well as from American military groups trying to prevent the spread of terrorism in other countries.

He discusses in detail the $56 trillion government debt which includes the accrued payments for entitlements such as Social Security and Medicare. This debt works out to $483,000 per citizen, an alarming figure to say the least. He forecasted this accrued debt would grow to $63 trillion by September 30, 2009. His book also informs us that in 1990, foreign countries held 19 percent of our national debt. Currently, they hold over 50 percent of our debt. He also forecasts our interest payments that could exceed a trillion dollars becoming the largest single expenditure in the federal budget by the end of the decade.(2)

Mr. Walker agrees with Mr. Peterson that the solution is to raise taxes and reduce entitlement benefits to middle-class and wealthy Americans. He also advocates downsizing our military organizations. He supports a single pay government health plan like Medicare for all Americans, but with a limit on what can be spent on health care. His book contains practical suggestions for increasing revenue to the Social Security program, and he makes several practical suggestions on how to reduce Medicare costs. He also proposes a VAT tax to provide health care. He ended his book with a series of penetrating questions for politicians.

There are many other books that are also ringing the alarm bell predicting a financial meltdown. Most of these books have been endorsed by former senior financial and political leaders within our federal government, including:

-Former Chairmen of the Federal Reserve
-Former Senators and political leaders
-Former Secretaries of Treasury
-Former Presidential candidates
-Famous economists
-Famous media and press members

So far, though, this bell ringing has not motivated American citizens enough to speak out against runaway government spending. The exception is the Tea Party advocates who want to tear down large sectors of the federal government. However, they cannot agree on which sectors to eliminate. Most Tea Party members support expensive pre-emptive wars, massive military organizations, Social Security, Medicare, farm subsidies, etc. Increased spending in these areas will not solve this financial crisis. Former government financial executives do not want to tear down the government.

In addition, several full-length motion pictures have been produced on climate control, student learning crisis in the public schools, the Wall Street meltdown of financial institutions, greed of corporate America, and the growing national debt. All of these films do a great job of defining the severe problems facing our country, but the solutions shown are often incomplete, sometimes not even accurate, and rarely is there a precise plan of action. Therefore, these films have not motivated systemic change and our country continues to throw massive amounts of money at problems resulting in only minimum change. Compare this to the action plan President Kennedy and Congress implemented successfully to create the NASA organization that landed a person on the moon within one decade.

There is a need to educate the vast majority of Americans who view our national debt the way they viewed the Soviet Union's nuclear bombs during the Cold War. They know the debt exists just as the bombs did, but they simply cannot conceive of our federal government going bankrupt. Somehow, they believe there will be a bailout or something else that will prevent this economic debacle.

How Serious Is the Potential Meltdown of Our Government?

In the past decade, federal government revenues increased by 7 percent and expenses grew by 108 percent, creating a $1.4 trillion deficit by 2009 and trillion-dollar deficits for several years. Simply put, the United States is in the most serious financial trouble in its history. Readers of this book will learn in Lesson 3 how one political party is more responsible for creating the mountain of federal debt, the record annual deficits, and the national debt that is heading towards $16 trillion by 2012 and could reach nearly $20 trillion by 2016. The interest costs for this debt could increase to almost $500 billion (a half-trillion) within a few years.

Each political party wants the other political party to raise taxes, reduce Social Security and Medicare benefits and eliminate significant tax deductions to reduce the deficit. These changes, which will decrease the take-home pay, will not happen because whichever political party does all this will be voted out of office for decades. Therefore, both political parties will continue blaming each other for the fiscal problems. As the civil war continues between Democrats and Republicans, the spending train will continue to move full steam ahead. Eventually, there will be a federal government meltdown which will destroy the American standard of living for years to come.

The Peter G. Peterson Foundation has sponsored A Committee For A Responsible Federal Budget comprised of 34 members including former Federal Reserve Chairmen, Secretaries of Treasury, Comptroller Generals (GAO), former Cabinet Secretaries, Economists, Chief Executive Officers, Members of Congress, Pentagon Secretaries, and Directors of Management and Budget. These leaders believe that the stunning financial projections for the United States mandate reforms because the country's fiscal policy is on an unsustainable course. The U.S. government must make adjustments in its spending and tax programs. This committee predicts that, by the end of this decade, the national debt will be at a level equal to the percent of GDP at the end of World War II. The Baby Boomer generation will push retirement benefits to record levels. In its April 2010 paper entitled "A Preventable

Crisis: Exploring Fiscal Crisis Scenarios For the United States," the committee documented six different crisis scenarios. However, the paper did not forecast which scenario would cause the meltdown or in which year it would occur.

Future Options for the United States

To deal with this fiscal crisis, the United States has three options:

Option One: Continue the Civil War Between Political Parties

Under this option, voters flip-flop between political parties every two or four years with minor changes taking place within our foreign policy, defense strategies, health care, energy, education, etc. The Republican Party calls the Democratic Party a "tax and spend" party and blames them for our deficits, debt, and cost of interest. The Democratic Party calls the Republicans a "borrow and spend" party and blames them for the pre-emptive wars, the mountain of debt, record annual deficits, and the unsustainable interest costs. Except for $38 billion reduction in the 2011 budget, both parties continue to spend as if there is no immediate financial crisis. That is why our national debt has grown from less than a trillion dollars in 1980 to nearly $16 trillion in 2012, and will approach $20 trillion in 2016. Also under this option, companies in the free enterprise system will continue to lose market share, triggering high unemployment for years to come. This option is like the frog in the pan of hot water story where the temperature gradually keeps rising, but the frog does not realize the danger until he expires.

If the United States continues to borrow and spend, it will reach a debt level that will discourage other nations, individuals, pension plans, foundations, and insurance companies, from purchasing United States government bonds. Interest rates will escalate from record lows to record highs within a few days or weeks just as they did in Greece and Portugal. In 2011, Portugal was paying 9.3 percent interest on 10-year bonds. If that happens in the United States, our interest expense would be $1.5 trillion each year which would consume all our personal income taxes. At that point, the United States will be selling bonds just to pay interest on debt. Our economy will most likely go into a severe recession followed by a long-term depression. The government will no longer have funds to stimulate the economy or to bail out financial institutions. Major tax increases will be required, and benefits for entitlements will be greatly reduced. Millions of Americans will lose their jobs and there will be absolutely no funds for expanded welfare, unemployment insurance or other safety net programs. The military services will have to be downsized by several hundred billion dollars. This option will be like a bolt of lightning that can strike any year prior to 2020 if our excessive spending continues.

Somehow, a majority of voters in the 2010 midterm election decided that a "do nothing" government that has a gridlocked Congress would reduce spending. There will be some budget reductions. But, the high speed spending train will continue at even a faster speed due to the continuation of all tax cuts that became unaffordable when the country entered into the War on Terror in 2001.

Option Two: Major Tax Increases and Benefit Reductions

England's Conservative Party is implementing Option Two by choice. Other European countries are being forced by external organizations to adopt Option Two because they stayed in Option One to the point where a "bond crisis" descended on the country. If the United States continues in Option One by borrowing and spending trillions of dollars, our country will eventually be forced to transfer from Option One to Option Two as the British did, but the extension of the Bush Tax Cuts for all Americans rejected this voluntary move to Option Two. It is clear the United States will remain in Option One in 2011 and 2012 based on the bipartisan agreement to borrow close to $900 billion in both years to maintain tax cuts as well as provide stimulus funds for 2011 and 2012. The size and cost of the U.S. government will continue to expand for at least two years.

While there has been and will continue to be a great deal of discussion about Option Two and the various reports, neither political party will probably not implement the recommendations for fear of not being elected for one or two decades. Americans will never forget which party raised their taxes, reduced their Social Security and Medicare benefits, and eliminated their key tax deductions. Option Two, if implemented, would significantly reduce the American standard of living and, undoubtedly cause a long-term economic depression resulting from decreased consumer spending.

In April, 2011, the rating agency of Standard & Poor's warned the United States it could lose its coveted status as the world's most secure economy if lawmakers did not reduce the federal deficit and amount of borrowing that has existed for several years. S & P changed its outlook on the United States from "stable" to "negative" and threatened the AAA rating.

If the "bond crisis" does descend upon the United States, the financial crisis of 2008 and 2009 will be repeated. Once again, the very wealthy will lose billions of dollars, the rich will lose millions of dollars, the middle class will lose thousands of dollars in a relatively short period of time. The stock market will plunge. Taxes will be increased and large tax deductions will be eliminated. The military budget will be downsized by 75 percent. Unemployment will rise rapidly. Housing values will fall steeply. Foreclosures will hit new highs. Senior citizens will have reduced pensions, and most important, there will be no opportunity to borrow trillions of dollars for a grand recovery plan that was available in 2009, 2010 and 2011. A "bond crisis" will result in a long-term and deep economic depression for Americans and a significant reduction in our standard of living.

Option Three: Major Systemic Changes to Minimize Tax Increases

The only possible way to avoid the potential financial meltdown of Option One and Two is to move quickly to Option Three in the 2013 to 2016 time period after the 2012 general election. Under this option, the President and Congress will implement major changes in our foreign policy, defense strategies, national energy plan, health care, education, financial institutions, and Social Security programs. They will also adopt a laser focus on cost containment in all government agencies to reduce spending by over a trillion dollars. These changes will enable the United States to remain a world leader within the global economy and to keep its vastly superior defense organization. A series of programs will also be implemented to recharge the private enterprise system so it can achieve prosperity and full employment. The results of these efforts will be an efficient and affordable federal government that will minimize the amount of new increased taxes on our citizens while achieving a balanced budget before the decade's end. This book explains what must be accomplished in order to implement Option Three.

Other Countries That Have Experienced Financial Meltdowns

In 2010, Greece became the great case study of Option Two on how fast a government could experience a financial meltdown. An associate professor and director of the International Studies Program at Alliant University in San Diego, David Felsen wrote on April 30, 2010, "The current Greek public finance debacle began in November, 2009. Shortly after coming to power, Greece's new government revealed that the country's public finances were in worse shape than had previously been reported. The projected annual deficit for 2009 was revised upward to twice the amount originally stated. This announcement did untold damage to Greece's financial credibility and adversely impacted the cost of borrowing." Virtually overnight, the yield on Greek two-year government bonds went from a little over 5 percent to nearly 15 percent. The national debt in Greece bulged to 120 percent of Gross Domestic Product, an unsustainable level to say the least.

Austerity measures were immediately announced and implemented by the Greek Government. No longer will Greeks retire at 55 years of age; they will now retire at 65 years of age and their pension will be reduced. All public sector employee pay was frozen, and for many jobs, was reduced. The Greek stock market declined by 25 percent within 30 days. Tax increases equal to 15 percent of Greece's economy will be imposed over the next four years. Stunned by these emergency measures, Greek citizens took to the streets in ugly demonstrations where some protestors were killed or seriously injured. Rampant fear spread that the Greek government would default on its bonds. Greece will now enter a severe recession because consumers will be afraid to spend.

As a result of the Greek crisis, the euro fell to $1.2176 against the dollar from its high of $1.60 in 2007. The very future of the euro was suddenly at stake. It took a European version of the 2008 TARP bailout of U.S. banks to save the euro. In an unprecedented move, the European Union joined forces with the International Monetary Fund to pledge up to 750 billion euros (925 billion dollars) for Greece and other European countries with serious financial problems. Ireland and Iceland are also receiving bailouts from the European Central Bank. Some predict that Portugal, Spain and perhaps Italy will require bailouts as well.

The Greek financial crisis proves to all nations, including the United States, that a financial meltdown can occur within a few weeks when investors decide that a nation will not be able to pay the interest or even the capital on its bonds. Remember how the Lehman Brothers collapse caused a meltdown on Wall Street. The Greek crisis did the same thing to the mighty European Union.

Why Americans Are Worried About the Future

A recent Gallop poll found that only one in seven American citizens think it very likely that today's children will have a better life than their parents. We are now living through the most wrenching period since the end of World War II except perhaps the 1960s when the country was more divided than at any time since the Civil War. That is how Robert J. Samuelson started his January, 2011 NEWSWEEK column, "The Shadow of The '60s and The Turmoil of Today."(3) Samuelson further stated, "What frightens people today is that we've experienced setbacks that were so completely unpredicted and unimagined (financial panic, major bank failures, General Motors' bankruptcy, huge budget deficits, collapsed housing values) that they raise dark doubts about our institutions and leaders. The political order seems unequal to the challenges. The stridency of debate reflects fears that one political crowd or the other will yank the country in a disastrous direction. With time, luck, and leadership, America has the capacity for self-repair." It is time to rebuild America.

How This Financial Crisis Evolved

It has been seven years since Pete Peterson released *How The Democratic And Republican Parties Are Bankrupting Our Future And What Americans Can Do About It.* Near the end of the book, Peterson wrote, "To today's young Americans, I say, you have a right to be angry about the financial encumbrance your elders have collectively placed upon you. But you also have reason to be understanding. Your individual parents and grandparents did not intend to saddle you with this debt. They didn't vote to pick your pocket. Instead, they were misled by various experts and politicians—some of them high-minded, some of them craven—into supporting policies that turned out to be based on false premises."(4)

The theory of "supply side economics" promised lower tax rates that would yield higher tax revenues. What it produced instead were record deficits and major increases in the national debt, which could result in high interest rates in the coming years.

Americans supported the War on Terror after the terrible attack on 9/11/2001, but no one told us it would cost nearly five trillion dollars in borrowed money by 2014. Worse yet, over 5,000 Americans have been killed, tens of thousands have been wounded, and the sheer number of terrorists has increased due to our occupation of Islamic countries.

Social Security has enabled three generations of senior citizens to have a decent standard of living in their retirement years, but some political leaders have tried to blame the deficits and debt on Social Security. Since 1983, the program has provided $2.4 trillion in surplus funds which have been diverted to cover General Fund expenses such as defense, the War on Terror, tax cuts, and other government agency budgets.

Some political leaders have tried to scare Americans about socialized medicine. The reality is Medicare represents one of the most successful government programs ever because it is a single pay system operating in all 50 states at a very low administrative cost. In the meantime, the cost of private insurance plans has increased far more than inflation. Health care will drive up the deficits and debt in future years if major changes are not made to improve the quality and to lower the costs.

In early 2008, voters were told the nation's economy and the stock market were fundamentally sound. After the stock market crash in the 1930s, most Americans adopted the following rule of thumb: don't invest any money in the stock market that you cannot afford to lose. Then came a few decades of a rising and safe stock market, prompting the rule-of-thumb to change to: "invest almost all your savings (down payment for a house, college educations, retirement, etc.) in the stock market." Americans never expected Wall Street to risk their deposits and mortgages so that a small group of Americans could become billionaires which resulted in a 2008 meltdown of several major investment and commercial banks. In the fourth quarter of 2008, savings plunged by 40 to 65 percent as a result of this Wall Street meltdown.

The Six Major Problems Causing Annual Trillion-Dollar Deficits

There are six areas of the General Fund that are simply out of control due to excessive spending during the past decade and lower revenues due to tax cuts that are not affordable, but essential to avoid an economic depression.

1. Military costs due to the War on Terror
2. Health Care due to new pharmacy benefits in Medicare and the growing cost of Medicaid.
3. Education due to falling tax revenues in state and local government budgets requiring funds from the federal government.
4. Low growth economy resulting from the severe 2008 Great Recession that led to high unemployment costs and reduced tax revenues.
5. Many government agencies received increases in their budgets during the ten-year period when there was almost no growth in revenues.
6. Due to the transfer of Social Security tax revenues from the Trust Fund to the General Fund, the Social Security System requires increased revenues.

All six major financial problems will be discussed in Parts II, III, and IV of this book with specific recommendations for reducing expenses, and at the same time, achieving the six national goals as reviewed in Lesson Five. The crisis in leadership that has existed in the past decade by members of both political parties must be ended. The President and Congress who are elected in 2012 must have a grand vision for "rebuilding America" and concrete plans for implementing systemic changes to accomplish the vision. This book will help them develop both their vision and implementation plans for major changes. Our leaders must do more than merely throw multi-billions or trillions of dollars at our major problems with only a hope costs will be reduced and/or performance problems solved. Leaders within our health care systems, our education systems, and the military must realize that taxes are not going to be increased so they can continue to receive annual increases in their budgets. The crisis in leadership within the private enterprise system must also be solved to return our country to prosperity and full employment.

A Necessary Education for 2012

Americans need to understand the important issues that affect government spending, taxes, and budgets. Many persons want to ring alarm bells. However, few people and documents truly explain the issues facing our government and what options our leaders should consider to prevent a financial meltdown of our federal government and our future standard of living. That is the purpose of this book. We must be educated on these issues so we can vote for responsible political leaders in 2012 and beyond. The President elected in 2012 must be a bold and strategic leader who is capable of reducing government spending by over a trillion dollars. The goal for this decade must be a balanced budget by 2020. To achieve this fiscal objective, major changes must take place within several large areas of the federal government outlined in this book. We must demand an efficient, honest, and affordable federal government that supports our high standard of living in future years.

To make this demand, we need to have a fundamental understanding of how our federal financial system operates. That is the subject of the next lesson.

NOTES FOR LESSON 1

1. *Running On Empty*, Peter G. Peterson, Farrar, Straus and Giroux, 2004, page 7
2. *Come Back America*, David M. Walker, Random House, 2009, pages 3, 4, 8, 18
3. "The Shadow of The '60s and The Turmoil of Today," Robert J. Samuelson, NEWSWEEK, SAN DIEGO UNION-TRIBUNE, January 17, 2011, page B5
4. *Running On Empty*, Peter G. Peterson, Farrar, Straus and Giroux, 2004, pages 227 to 234

LESSON 2

<u>A BASIC UNDERSTANDING OF THE FEDERAL FINANCIAL SYSTEM</u>

The Secretary of the Treasury, in coordination with the Director of Management and Budget (OMB), is required to submit annual financial statements for the United States Government to the President and Congress. The General Accountability Office (GAO) is required to audit these financial statements.

A Message From the Secretary of the Treasury

"Over the past two years, the Administration, along with Congress and financial regulators, implemented emergency policies that ended the worst recession since the Great Depression and put the nation on a path to economic recovery. Yet today, the country still faces significant and persistent challenges: the need to create millions of new jobs, build a new and stable foundation for prosperity, and address a medium—and long-term fiscal situation that could undermine future economic growth."

"While the Government's immediate priority is to support economic recovery and combat unemployment, we must also address the nation's significant fiscal challenges. In FY 2010, the deficit decreased as a result of increases in tax receipts and a decline in outlays. Yet persistent growth of health care costs and the aging of the population remain key causes of long-term deficits. The Affordable Care Act marked an important step in controlling health care costs and has the potential to significantly lower the long-term growth trend for Medicare and Medicaid costs. The Affordable Care Act will also drive critical innovations in the health care system that will help improve quality and further constrain costs over the long term."

"Today, we must balance our efforts to accelerate economic recovery and job growth in the near term with continued efforts to address the challenges posed by the long-term deficit outlook. The Administration's top priority remains restoring good jobs to American workers and accelerating the pace of economic recovery. Two key pieces of legislation signed by the President, the American Recovery and Reinvestment Act of 2009 and the Hiring Incentives to Restore Employment (HIRE) Act of 2010, have helped further this goal by creating or saving over three million jobs. But as we combat unemployment, we must also address the challenge of bringing future debt down to sustainable levels. The work of the National Commission on Fiscal Responsibility and Reform has emphasized that to sustain economic growth in the medium—and long-term, we need to make difficult choices to reduce deficits and the national debt."

"The Administration has already taken common-sense steps, such as proposing a three-year freeze on non-security discretionary funding, calling for a two-year pay freeze for federal civilian workers, and restoring the rule that the Government pays for its priorities to promote fiscal responsibility. These efforts must continue in the months and years ahead."(1)

Signed—Timothy F.Geithner, Secretary of the Treasury

Difference Between Cash and Accrual Accounting Systems

Businesses, not-for-profit organizations, and governments once utilized a cash accounting system. Under this system, cash receipts or expenses were recorded when they occurred. This accounting system required fewer bookkeepers and was adequate for small family owned businesses. They knew, on an informal basis, if they signed a contract for future expenses that they would need cash as those expenses came due. Profit and loss statements, balance sheets, and budgets were all based on the cash accounting system.

When businesses and not-for-profit organizations expanded in the early 20th Century, many organizations converted to the accrual accounting system to show future commitments (income or expenses). After so many bankruptcies and failures in the Great Depression, the Securities and Exchange Commission mandated the accrual system for corporations that sold shares of stock to owners outside their organization. Accordingly, banks mandated organizations that wanted to borrow money to use the accrual system.

However, the federal government never shifted from a cash accounting system. The federal budget is currently based on what receipts in dollars are to be received within a fiscal year (October 1ˢᵗ to September 31ˢᵗ of the next year) as well as what cash expenses are incurred in that fiscal year. The fiscal year 2011 actually starts on October 1, 2010 and ends on September 31, 2011. Therefore, Congress can pass a benefit such as Social Security in the 1930s that has expenses every year, but the only expense recorded in the government's books is the cash expense of benefits for one year matched against the cash receipts for the same year. This accounting system enables Presidents and members of Congress to commit funds for many years without recording any long-term debt. In recent years, Congress and the administrations have begun accruing expenses for veterans' benefits and for future pension benefits to federal employees. This approach is referred to as a modified cash accounting system.

Two Methods To View Federal Financial Statements

George Will of THE WASHINGTON POST wrote an article on May 10, 2010 entitled—"Frugality Theater of the Absurd." Will stated, "62 percent of federal spending goes to entitlements (56 percent) and interest on the national debt (6 percent). Both will be growing portions of future budgets and both are immune to any vetoes. Defense and homeland security are 21 percent of the budget and will be almost entirely immune to change. So the line item veto that Presidents Reagan, Clinton, and Obama asked for would be at most 17 percent of the budget. What about earmarks? If all 9,499 of last year's had been vetoed, this would have saved $15.9 billion or a small half of one percent of spending."(2) The percentages changed in 2010, which are reviewed in Lesson 14.

When members of Congress, the press, and political candidates hear these numbers, they usually leap to the wrong conclusions and make errors in judgment. For example, many people are now claiming the financial deficit can be reigned in by reducing Social Security and Medicare benefits to senior citizens who paid into these programs for 30-to-50 years through payroll taxes. Such statements send a terrible message to workers that our government is treating payroll taxes as a second income tax on American employees and employers. If this approach is taken, there will be lower or no benefits to young and middle-age workers when they retire. Americans are simply not going to buy into this transfer of Social Security and Medicare benefits in order to pay for the reckless spending of Presidents and members of Congress over the past 30 years. Lesson 3 will explain which Presidents were the biggest spenders during these years.

To avoid past mistakes, voters in 2012 will need to know how our country could have sunk into this big deficit hole and accumulate this mountain of debt. The first four lessons of this book will explain how the United States ended up in this financial mess.

In the late 1960s, President Johnson unified all federal budgets to help reduce the overall federal deficit caused by both the War on Poverty and the Vietnam War. All Presidents and members of Congress have continued to use the Unified Budget, but it should not be the only financial presentation made to the public.

There is a better way to see a total financial picture of the government than through the traditional Unified Budget system. The federal government has four major sources of income:

-Income taxes from individuals
-Income taxes from corporations
-Social Security payroll taxes
-Medicare payroll taxes

Social Security and Medicare entitlements created surpluses of $2.4 trillion up until 2010. Therefore, it is fundamentally wrong to blame our current financial crisis on Social Security and Medicare. These surpluses were forecasted to last longer, but increases in unemployment and early retirements by baby boomers reduced payroll tax income to the point where the General Fund will be required to help pay benefits in future years. No doubt there will be changes to these entitlements because there is no cash in the Social Security and Medicare Trust Funds which is explained in Lesson 7. The deficits clearly stem from the General Fund budget where all government expenses except for Social Security and Medicare payments are recorded.

Understanding the Fiscal Problems in the General Fund

The overview section of the 2010 Secretary of Treasury's report stated, "Government revenues decreased $454 billion from 2007 to about $2.2 trillion during 2009 and 2010 due in great part to the effects of the recession and tax changes associated with the 2009 stimulus package. Individual income tax revenues decreased by 13 percent and corporate tax revenues have decreased by 51 percent since 2007. Corporate and income taxes account for the majority (nearly 90 percent) of total revenues to the federal government for the General Fund."

The Statement of Net Cost shows 2010 expenses at $4.163 trillion. (3) The major areas of spending are:

Department of Defense	$889 billion
Department of Veterans Affairs	235
Homeland Security	<u>50</u>
Subtotal for Defense and Security	$1,174
Department of Health and Human Services	858
(Includes Medicare, Medicaid, National Health)	
Social Security	754
Interest on Debt Held by Public	215
Department of Treasury	373
Department of Agriculture	131
Department of Transportation	80
Department of Education	89
Department of Labor (unemployment expenses)	179
Department of Housing and Urban Development	55
Department of Energy	25
Department of Justice	31
Office of Personnel Management	25
Department of the Interior	18
National Aeronautics and Space	22
Department of State	22
Railroad Retirement Board	9
Department of Commerce	14
Environmental Protection Agency	12

Agency for International Development	10
Federal Communication Commission	9
National Science Foundation	7
Small Business Administration	5
Smithsonian Institution	1
U.S. Postal Service (Surplus)	(8)
All other federal government entities	<u>47</u>
Total Net Cost	$4.163 Trillion

In summary, the federal government has $2.2 trillion in revenues and $3.5 trillion in cash expenses resulting in an annual deficit of over $1.3 trillion. As previously noted, the deficit stems from the General Fund not from Social Security and Medicare entitlements.(4) The difference between $4.163 trillion and $3.5 trillion is accruals.

Lesson 6 will discuss how the runaway costs of health care can be contained in future years and how the quality of care can be increased simultaneously.

Lesson 7 will explain the changes needed to stabilize Social Security and Disabled benefits for decades.

Lesson 8 will explain why the military, intelligence, homeland security, and veterans' affairs budgets must be restructured for peacetime defenses.

Lesson 9 will explain why in the fourth quarter of 2008 President George W. Bush and the Democratic Congress had to join in a bipartisan effort to prevent a complete meltdown of the American financial system. This lesson will also discuss the reason why increased regulation is needed for financial institutions and other organizations that are "too big to fail," including Social Security and Medicare.

Lesson 10 will discuss what the President and Congress must do to recharge the private enterprise system in order to have an adequate tax base for defense and other General Fund departments as well as provide adequate employment for Americans.

Lesson 11 will discuss what the federal Department of Education must do to contain costs in the United States' overall education system in order to avoid another federal entitlement that taxpayers cannot afford.

Lesson 12 will explain why the country needs a cost-effective, nationwide energy system which will stop the flow of U.S. dollars to Middle Eastern countries that sponsor terrorism, making our country independent of their oil.

Lesson 13 will explain why Americans must have an efficient and affordable government that provides all the necessary services for the world's leading economy, provides the highest standard of living for its citizens, and operates within a reasonable tax system.

All of these lessons will be based on a new vision for an economic recovery that includes a strong defense organization and an efficient government. These national goals for the 21st Century will be described in Lesson 5.

Two Spending Areas Requiring Major Changes

One does not have to be a Certified Public Accountant or Budget Director to know which two areas of the General Fund are far exceeding the budgets and cannot be sustained in the future. By analyzing the growth from 2000 to 2010 in the General Fund, the picture becomes quite clear in which expense areas the President, the cabinet, and members of Congress must make major changes.

Lesson 8 will discuss the military budgets in more detail. The War on Terror will cost our country somewhere between $4 and $5 trillion in borrowed money from 2002 to 2014, with a current rate of borrowing approximately over half a trillion dollars each year. A volunteer military was affordable in peacetime, but the defense costs have accelerated significantly during the ten war years and are simply not sustainable without a large surtax on income tax in future years. Lesson 8 will also discuss the changes needed in our foreign policies, defense/wartime strategies, intelligence agencies, and homeland security programs. These three budgets currently represent 31 percent of our total financial expense.

The Department of Health and Human Services now represents 21 percent of the total federal unified budget. This expense area includes Medicare, Medicaid, the Children's Health Plan, the Center For Disease Control, major research grants, and national health hospitals. In 2000, these costs totaled $393 billion. In 2010, the total costs were $923 billion, a 135 percent increase. Again, this cost escalation is not sustainable. Lesson 6 discusses what must be accomplished to bring quality controls and best practices into the health care field, to control costs, and to improve the world's finest medical system.

Cost Containment Focus Throughout Government

At the current spending rate, all other government departments represent approximately $1,152 billion which includes stimulus funds in 2010. This figure does not include interest on public debt. The national debt is now over $14 trillion, and is estimated to be close to $20 trillion by 2016. Therefore, it is imperative for the President and Congress elected in 2012 to mount a formal cost-cutting program throughout all government agencies as was done in the 1990s.

Lesson 13 will discuss practical plans that will enable government agencies to do more with a smaller budget in the future. These agencies need to engage in strategic downsizing that does not damage their employees' performance.

Lesson 14 proposes a plan to reduce spending and to increase revenue so that a balanced budget can be achieved by 2020.

Why This Book Does Not Focus on GDP

In the past, political leaders have been able to mask the growing annual deficits, the mounting national debt, and the increasing interest on the debt by expressing every budgetary line item as a percentage of the Gross Domestic Product (GDP) which is the measure of economic progress. Most Americans have no idea what the GDP stands for. As a result, they cannot understand the true budget issues when GDP is constantly used to describe how much is being spent in a given area. For example, as the national debt expanded every year from 2001 to the present, Americans were assured the country could afford the debt because of the size of its GDP. Another problem in using GDP as a budget measurement is the fact that GDP goes up almost every year, even when revenues decrease due to tax cuts and a major recession.

One Presidential candidate recently stated the Defense Budget is 3.8 percent of GDP and it should be 4 percent. Actually, the Defense Budget was 4.3 percent in 2008 and is now close to 5 percent. Four or five percent doesn't sound like very much money, but it actually represents nearly $900 billion out of one trillion dollars of cash received to pay for all expenses besides entitlement programs. In other words, the cost of military spending and veterans' benefits are far exceeding our income. The ten-year War on Terror and three tax cuts have exploded our debt, not Social Security and Medicare.

Furthermore, the Gross Domestic Product is based on estimates and assumptions. In 2008, French President Nicolas Sarkozy launched the Commission for the Measurement of Economic Performance and Social Progress chaired by Joseph Stiglitz. This commission is trying to develop a better definition of GDP.

Potential Pain of Government Financial Decisions

Senior citizens have suffered a 60 percent loss in interest on their bonds and in dividends due to the 2008 Great Recession. Political leaders are now discussing the possible reductions in Social Security and Medicare benefits. Many citizens have also lost their company health care benefits.

Middle-aged workers have paid large sums of payroll taxes into the Social Security and Medicare Funds. They have lost money in the value of their homes and investments. Most company pensions have disappeared, and other fringe benefits have been reduced. Workers will not support a large surtax on their income to pay for past mistakes by former Presidents and Congresses. They also must have full Social Security and Medicare benefits in future years.

Young adults, who are now ready to enter the workforce, are facing high unemployment and underemployment. They need government investment to recharge the private enterprise system. Needless to say, they are scared by the new taxes being discussed. They fear they will not be able to make major purchases and save for life's basic requirements such as furniture, automobiles, home, college educations for their children, and retirement. They also fear they will not be able to repay their own college loans.

American voters in 2012 should demand plain facts based on cash receipts and cash expenses to determine how viable the candidates' plans are to restore fiscal responsibility in federal, state and local government agencies. The next lesson will reveal which Presidents were good fiscal managers and which were big spenders.

NOTES FOR LESSON 2

1. "Fiscal Year Financial Report of the United States Government," Secretary of the Treasury, Washington, D.C., February 2011, page 1 of Overview
2. "Frugality Theater of the Absurd," George Will, THE WASHINGTON POST, May 10, 2010, Opinion Page
3. Same as #1—pages 40 and 41
4. Same as #1, page 4 of Overview

LESSON 3

WHO IS RESPONSIBLE FOR THIS FINANCIAL CRISIS?

The National Debt From 1776 to 1945

Few Americans cared about the size of the annual deficits, the growing national debt, and the expanding cost of interest until one political party raised the issue in 2009. Both political parties have tried to blame each other for the mountain of debt that will exist at the end of 2012. Voters are confused over who is responsible for this financial crisis. Voters want to know which Presidents far exceeded their budgets, increased the national debt, and the annual cost of interest. This lesson addresses that topic.

In the 1920s, the Republican Party controlled the White House for 12 years (1920-1932) with three different administrations. During those years, there were periods of great prosperity with few regulations on business or financial institutions. There were millions of small businesses and only a few large corporations. Income taxes were low, so the rich became very wealthy. Workers had almost no benefits and minimum job security. It was a period of small government, small businesses, and low taxes.

The 1920s started with an economic downturn in 1920 and 1921 with numerous layoffs and bank failures. This bleak period was followed by the most spectacular economic boom our country had ever seen. Materialism flourished like a religious cult. On October 24, 1929, the stock market suddenly plunged and the 10-year Great Depression started. Between late October and mid-November that year, stocks lost more than 40 percent of their value.

In 1928, the federal government budget was $4 billion. The entire government spent only $3 billion which provided a 25 percent surplus of $1 billion. If you stand in front of the White House, you will see why the government was so small. To the left of the White House is the Department of Treasury. To the right is the Eisenhower Executive Office Building that housed the Departments of State, Army, and Navy. The Capitol and two other office buildings housed the members of Congress. There were a few other buildings for Indian Affairs, Agriculture, Commerce, etc. President Hoover did not believe the federal government should be responsible for the economy, the stock market, the financial system or the unemployed. He did not help the banks, so when they closed, thousands of Americans lost their savings, homes, farms, and businesses to foreclosure.

By 1931, President Hoover and the Republican Party decided the government had to help the private sector rebound. Their economic recovery programs resulted in deficit spending of over $3 billion. By this time, 27 percent of Americans were out of work and millions lived in poverty. Hourly wages had dropped by 60 percent and millions of Americans did not have enough food for their families. A new President, Franklin D. Roosevelt, took office in 1933. He used the power and wealth of the federal government to recharge the "dead in the water" private enterprise system, created a middle class, rebuilt financial institutions, and created jobs. He implemented the Federal Deposit Insurance Corporation, Social Security, and other stimulus programs. (1) He created many public sector jobs through the CCC (Civilian Conservation Corps) which provided 2.5 million jobs for young men, and through the PWA (Public Works Administration) which put thousands of Americans to work on bridges, highways, tunnels, hospitals, government buildings, post offices, dams, and world fairs. The WPA (Works Progress Administration) also created thousands of jobs on smaller projects. Through other programs, Roosevelt brought electricity to farms and small towns. He also had a grand recovery plan entitled the NRA (National Recovery Administration). Republicans opposed most of these programs and called Roosevelt a Socialist, Communist, and a dictator. After the 1936 reelection of Roosevelt, he reduced his recovery programs which caused a double dip recession in 1937 and 1938.(2) Prosperity and high employment started to return in 1939 just as World War II was breaking out in Europe. During the war years, every American who wanted to work had a job including 18.2 million women. By 1945, the national debt was $260 billion, a great deal of money at that time. After 170 years of U.S. history, which included many recessions, the Great Depression, the War of 1812, the Civil War, the Spanish American War, World War I and World War II, the national debt was manageable, but large compared to previous years.(3)

Post War Years of 1945-1960

Americans feared another Great Depression after World War II because over 16 million servicemen had to find jobs within the peacetime economy. Voters reelected Harry Truman in 1948, the fifth consecutive presidential victory for the Democrats. Americans still blamed President Hoover and the Republican Party for the Great Depression. President Truman was regarded as a successful President because he moved the country from wartime production to a peacetime economy with four years of surpluses totaling $22 billion. These surpluses are even more impressive when you consider that he funded the GI Bill, the Marshall Plan for Europe, and the creation of the UN and NATO during those years. But in 1950, Truman committed the United States under the UN banner to a civil war in Korea that was originally forecasted to last less than a year. The Chinese Army came into the war in 1951 on the side of North Korea, leaving no hope for a grand victory. By 1952, Truman was so unpopular that he could not run for office in that year. Raising taxes and reinstituting a military draft had devastated his poll numbers.

In the 1952 election, the Republican Party decided they could only win if they had a candidate that was not aligned to President Hoover or to the negative opposition to the Roosevelt economic recovery programs. They selected a World War II hero, General Dwight D. Eisenhower, who could have run as either a Democrat or a Republican. With leading business executives from the East coast ensuring adequate financial campaign support, Eisenhower ran as a Republican. One of his key campaign messages was, "I will go to Korea and try to end the civil war." The Republican Party decided not to nominate fiscal conservative Senator Taft because they believed voters would view him as another Hoover who would return the country to an economic depression. Eisenhower was a moderate Republican who not only ended the Korean War, but achieved peace (by avoiding a civil war in Indochina to help France which later became Vietnam) and prosperity during the 1953-1960 period. He believed in a strong central government that could accomplish major projects such as the national interstate highway system. By ending the Korean War, he was able to produce surpluses in three years that totaled $83 billion. Over the eight years that he was in office, he added $18 billion to the national debt mostly due to the 1951 recession. He ended his career by warning Americans to beware of a military-industrial complex taking over our country because he had witnessed how such a complex had bankrupted and ruined Japan and Germany. Later, a military-industrial complex would destroy the Soviet Union. He once stated the only way a nation could win a third world war was to prevent the war.

1960-1980: Vietnam and Watergate Years

Vice President Nixon ran against Senator John Kennedy for what would have been President Eisenhower's third term. Nixon was the first true conservative since President Hoover on the Republican ticket and he lost by only a narrow margin. Americans still feared the Republican Party could not successfully manage the economy. Senator Kennedy was a better communicator who sold voters that the United States was on an economic plateau. Kennedy pledged he would get the United States back to a growing economy. Even though President Kennedy achieved peace and prosperity during his three years in office, he added $15 billion to the national debt due to the tax cuts he implemented to stimulate the economy.

President Johnson won the presidential election in 1964 easily after the assassination of President Kennedy. Senator Goldwater of the Republican Party scared voters with his talk about more war with the Communists. President Johnson turned out to be a real agent of change with civil rights, equal opportunity for women and minorities, and education reform. He had prosperity on his side, but he made a fatal mistake with his massive military buildup to achieve a victory in Vietnam. What was originally forecasted to be another quick victory turned into an eight-year civil war with no victory or end in sight. The military draft instituted for the Korean War still existed, enabling a fast buildup in Vietnam. The cost of the war could have turned voters against the war, had President Johnson not convinced Congress to unify the federal budget. By using the surplus in the Social Security trust fund, Johnson was able to mask the increased cost of the war. In fact, he told Americans we could afford both the Vietnam War and the War on Poverty. He added only $48 billion to the national debt because, in 1968, he also added a surtax to the income tax to pay for the war. President Johnson became so unpopular due to the failure of the Vietnam War and its high casualties that he decided, like President Truman, not to run for a second term in 1968.

Former Vice President Nixon ran for a second time in 1968 and won mainly because he stated he would bring peace to Vietnam. It had been 36 years since a true conservative Republican had been elected President. Unfortunately, President Nixon never told Americans his phase-down of the Vietnam War would take over four years rather than the six months that President Eisenhower needed to end the Korean War. Nixon continued to use the surplus money in Social Security, Medicare, and the other trust funds as Johnson had with the unified federal budget to finance the Vietnam War, but government expenses increased each year of the war. President Nixon was re-elected in 1972 due to the country's economic prosperity and his phase-down of the Vietnam War which ended in 1973 under a successful plan by Secretary of Defense Mel Laird. They also ended the military draft of young men.

Extending the Vietnam War for four years proved to be very expensive during the eight years of Presidents Nixon and Ford. An additional $200 billion was added to the national debt while 40,000 more troops were killed and hundreds of thousands more were wounded. Watergate forced President Nixon to resign in 1973. His successor President Ford appeared to be a fiscal conservative, but he did not decrease the overall expense budget after the Vietnam War ended. In fact, his last year of spending was 87 percent higher than his first year in 1974. Inflation accounted for much of this growth.

Governor Jimmy Carter won election in 1976 because Americans were still upset over the Watergate debacle. President Carter was not a big spender, but he did not reduce spending either. His final year in office in 1980 was 28% higher in expenses than his first year, but inflation was also high during that period. President Carter added $228 billion to the national debt which proves when spending and inflation get out of control, it is difficult to reduce the budget. The Iran Hostage Crisis made Carter look weak against an inferior foe. He could not reduce the high interest and inflation rates which contributed to low economic growth rates. He did appoint Paul Volcker to be the Chairman of the Federal Reserve, but Carter was not willing to risk a deep recession to break the rate of inflation. Carter dwelled on problems rather than on opportunities, so he could not inspire Americans to believe they still had the greatest country in the world. The nation began looking for a great leader.

Even with two wars (Korea and Vietnam), several recessions, and the Watergate crisis after World War II, the United States had only $930 billion dollars of federal debt in 1980 when Republicans regained control of the White House under President Ronald Reagan. The 1980 deficit was $59 billion, a far cry from the $1.4 trillion deficit President Obama inherited in 2009.

1980-2000: Reagan, Bush, and Clinton Years

Like President Roosevelt, President Reagan sold "hope" to American voters and raised their self esteem. Both Roosevelt and Reagan were great communicators. Reagan also sold himself as a "true" fiscal conservative by stating the size of the government was the problem. He promised to reduce the federal budget, the annual deficits, and the federal debt so he could provide meaningful tax cuts to voters. He also promised to eliminate the Departments of Energy and Education.

At the outset, he had to reduce the high rate of inflation and high rates of interest (over 20%) that Nixon, Ford, and Carter had not been able to handle in the 1970s. Paul Volcker, Chairman of the Federal Reserve Board, made these reductions happen, but only after a severe recession in the early 1980s with very high unemployment (10.4%). Fortunately, prosperity had returned for the 1984 election due to large government spending to build up the military and due to additional spending by consumers resulting from the tax cuts. By the time the tax cut law was enacted, it contained hundreds of pages. The tax cuts proved to be good policy, but much of the law was designed simply to gain votes. These tax cuts resulted in a trillion dollars of future government revenue given away without any corresponding reductions in government spending. From 1982 to 1987, President Reagan approved several tax increases due to increases in spending.(4)

31

President Reagan sold Americans on having a greater trust in individualism and markets and having less dependency on government. However, President Reagan failed to reduce the size and cost of government. In fact, the federal government grew substantially under his leadership. He added $1.6 trillion to the national debt which was more than all previous Presidents combined, and he accomplished this feat during eight years of peace. David Stockman, Reagan's own budget director, eventually declared Reaganomics to be a failure, but Jack Kemp and other conservatives went to their graves believing that supply-side economics was a success story. By 1986, the OMB (Office of Management and Budget) announced that annual revenues would be $660 billion less than had been originally forecasted due to tax cuts.

To save the federal government from a financial problem, the Greenspan Commission was created to solve the looming financial crisis in the Social Security trust fund. It had been close to 20 years since President Johnson had unified the federal budget, and during that time, hundreds of billions of dollars had been transferred by both political parties to the General Fund of the federal budget. By making these transfers, political leaders created a future shortage in the Social Security and Medicare Trust Funds. Few people outside of the government understood how this money had been transferred from Social Security and Medicare to pay for the Reagan tax cuts, the massive buildup of the military, and the ever-growing size of the federal government.

The bipartisan Greenspan Commission created a record increase in payroll taxes (up to 13.7%) to insure that there would be adequate funds in the Social Security Trust Fund for the "baby boom" generation. This new surplus money would also be transferred out of the Social Security Trust Fund and into the General Fund through IOUs that would probably require tax increases in future years to repay the IOUs.

In 1988, George Bush, Sr. won what was essentially the third term of the Reagan administration. During his August nomination acceptance speech in New Orleans, he made his famous pledge: "Read my lips: no new taxes." Soon afterwards came the Savings and Loan crisis that cost several hundred billion dollars of borrowed money that with interest has since inflated the national debt by half a trillion dollars. Saddam Hussein invaded Kuwait, but much of the funding for the resulting Gulf War came from allied countries. With the war, the S & L crisis, carryover of large annual deficits from Reaganomics, and a recession with reduced revenues, President Bush added $933 billion (nearly a trillion dollars) to the national debt in just four years. Eventually President Bush (41) was forced to raise taxes. Almost overnight, both political parties labeled him a failure as a fiscal conservative, but he deserves credit for increasing revenues and implementing PAYGO for cost containment of government expenses. By trying to be a true fiscal conservative, he lost his bid for a second term to Governor Bill Clinton.

President Clinton and Vice President Gore became fiscal conservatives due in part to pressure from Wall Street, the Secretaries of Treasury, and Chairman Greenspan at the Federal Reserve. In 1993, President Clinton and his fellow Democrats passed a major deficit reduction tax increase package without a single Republican vote. This legislation helped Congressman Newt Gingrich advance his "Contract With America" campaign which, in the Fall of 1994, enabled the Republican Party to take both houses of Congress for the first time in 40 years.

Clinton and Gore, with some help from Republicans reduced government spending, reduced the size of the federal government by downsizing the military after the Cold War, and reduced the annual deficits as well as the federal debt. Vice President Gore led a program to re-systematize many areas of government to reduce expenses. On top of all this work, President Clinton achieved eight years of peace and prosperity with the following unbelievable set of positive statistics:

- The 1992 federal deficit that was nearly $300 billion at the end of President Bush's (41) administration, transformed into a surplus of $200 billion at the end of President Clinton's administration. This financial miracle to achieve a $500 billion (half a trillion dollars) change in spending enabled Clinton to balance the budget within six years.
- Over 200 million new private sector jobs were created.
- Unemployment fell from 7% to 4%.
- Inflation remained low while GDP grew at an average rate of 3.4% per year.
- Productivity growth averaged 2.5% each year between 1995 and 2000, a level not seen since the early 1970s.

- The surpluses in future years could have repaid the Social Security and Medicare Trust Funds after over $2 trillion had been transferred to the General Fund by both political parties.
- The defense budget of $287 billion was fully funded by tax receipts for the first time in 34 years.
- Poverty rates dropped significantly.
- The cost of welfare and safety nets had been substantially reduced.
- The bull stock market was at an all-time high.
- In the first five years of the Clinton administration, there was $750 billion in deficits as he tried to get spending under control and in the final three years there were $400 billion in surpluses. Therefore Clinton added $350 billion to the national debt over eight years.
- The Iraq military expansion had been contained.
- All the world leaders, including China and Russia, respected the United States.
- There were prospects that the $980 billion federal debt in 1980 could have been paid off by 2003.

It was a grand period of peace and prosperity from 1993 to 2000. President Clinton also continued the PAYGO process where new government spending could only be approved if some existing programs were eliminated, a process started by the first President Bush near the end of his administration. Nearly everyone predicted Vice President Gore would win the third term of President Clinton, but he did not run an effective campaign. In addition, he talked about putting all the surplus tax dollars into a government lockbox to pay back the Social Security and Medicare Trust Funds. Governor George W. Bush told voters he would continue to run the country as well as President Clinton did, but he would give the voters a large tax cut. American voters fully understood the meaning of a tax cut. They did not fully understand the "lockbox" strategy. Labeling himself a compassionate conservative, Governor Bush promised he would have a bi-partisan administration that would not engage in foreign nation building. Gore eventually lost the election in the Supreme Court. The federal debt was now around $5 trillion ($3.4 trillion in public debt and $2.2 trillion in trust fund debt). Keep in mind, the first President Bush (41), House Speaker Gingrich, President Clinton, and Vice President Gore had all worked hard to get the federal budget under control after the failure of Reaganomics, but it took ten years to go from a large deficit to a surplus. The nation's economic history proves that wars, recessions, the Great Depression, and tax cuts caused deficit spending, not Social Security and Medicare.

2001-2008: The Bush-Cheney Administration

Early in their administration, President George W. Bush (43) and Vice President Dick Cheney pushed through major tax cuts arguing that the surplus generated during the Clinton years really belonged to the people and should be returned to them. They also ended the PAYGO law which ensured no new programs would be implemented unless there were extra funds. In an attempt to end the first recession he faced, President Bush decided to use hundreds of billions of dollars for a stimulus program. It soon became clear he was following the advice of Vice President Cheney who once stated, "Deficits are unimportant, which was proven by President Reagan." The Bush-Cheney administration immediately moved the government from a surplus to a deficit position. Under their watch, the federal government had seven consecutive years of deficits and established new records for spending and borrowing during some of those years.

The Bush-Cheney administration used the September 11, 2001 terrorist attack to justify unlimited spending for defense, homeland security, and veterans' benefits. Like Truman in the Korean War and Johnson as well as Nixon in the Vietnam War, Bush-Cheney believed the two pre-emptive wars in Iraq and Afghanistan would be over in months. It is now clear that the Iraq War will be a nine-year war and Afghanistan will last at least 12 years and perhaps 15-to-20 years depending who is elected in 2012. President Bush never included the wars in the Defense budget, but they were included in the 2009/2010/2011 federal budgets. The record shows Defense spending had grown from less than $300 billion to $889 billion. Veterans' benefits have soared as well. An entirely new organization called "Homeland Security" now has one of the largest budgets within the federal government and it too grows annually. In round numbers, the growth of these three budgets plus the reduced revenues from the Bush-Cheney tax cuts will result in approximately trillion-dollar annual deficits through 2012, irregardless of who was elected President in 2008. Furthermore, at least two trillion dollars will be added to the federal debt in the years 2009 to 2012 just for the War on Terror.

One reason why the Defense Department budget grew so much was the decision to use the volunteers of the regular military services, the active reserves, and the National Guard units rather than ask Congress to draft the young men and women from the ages of 18 to 26. The Bush-Cheney administration knew they would have lost the 2004 Presidential election if they had passed a $500 billion tax increase and a draft to fight the two civil wars that had no end in sight. They were determined not to duplicate Truman's mistakes. By giving generous increases, allowances, and re-enlistment bonuses, the Bush administration avoided a draft of both young men and women, but also created a financial crisis.

In 2004, the Bush-Cheney administration convinced Congress to pass a Medicare Drug benefit that is going to cost $399 billion with no corresponding increase in taxes. The Bush-Cheney administration also pushed through the $288 billion farm bill to ensure votes for the elections. Billions of dollars in earmarks had set new records by members of Congress to buy votes. The multi-billion-dollar energy bill was well received by the energy corporations. Education received billions of incremental dollars as well.

During the Bush-Cheney administration, the federal government responded inadequately to Hurricane Katrina after it struck New Orleans. The Homeland Security Secretary admitted to the Senate Committee that he and his department failed to respond adequately to the disaster, suffered lapses in management, bungled the delivery of relief supplies, deployed staff improperly, and moved much too slowly to evacuate people who were packed into the Superdome and the convention center. In an attempt to make up for this horrendous performance, the administration implemented an "open" checkbook policy that has cost between $40 and $50 billion to restore New Orleans gradually back to a livable city. There were several other examples of mismanagement during the eight years that led to massive spending which were not in the budget to make up for the problems that were highlighted in the press. For instance, by not solving the immigration crisis, the federal government now needs to employ over 20,000 border agents.

In 2007, a second recession occurred. It was not officially recognized as a recession until 2008 when the Bush-Cheney administration implemented another stimulus program. The 2008 recession looked eerily like the 1929 to 1939 Great Depression.

- Very wealthy Americans lost billions of dollars.
- Rich Americans lost millions of dollars.
- Upper middle-class Americans lost tens of thousands of dollars.
- Lower middle-class Americans lost thousands of dollars.

In addition, these same problems that existed in the 1930s Great Depression resurfaced which is why many economists believed the fourth quarter of 2008 was the start of another depression.

- The Dow Jones had a 53 percent meltdown that wiped out $10 trillion of retirement savings and college funds. In 1952, only 4.2% of Americans owned stock, but by 2008, the vast majority of Americans had invested and lost money in the stock market.
- With sub-prime mortgages and hedge funds in severe trouble, American financial institution foundations crumbled. Investment banks were merged with commercial banks because they were technically bankrupt.
- Only the 1930's FDIC deposit insurance program saved the entire banking system from a total meltdown. $700 billion of borrowed money was used to save banks.
- Family net worth dropped by 20 percent to $51.48 billion due to the lower value of stocks and homes.
- The national poverty rate rose to 13.2% meaning 39.8 million people were now living below the poverty line. These numbers increased again in 2009 due to higher unemployment.
- Corporate profits declined by over 80 percent with a record number of bankruptcies. Multi-billion-dollar

government bailouts were required for General Motors, AIG, and other companies.

- The unemployment rate approached ten percent. If the underemployed had been added to the number of people who were seeking a full-time job, the rate would have exceeded 15 percent.
- Foreclosures rose 70 percent in 2007 and spiked another 81 percent in 2008 and were higher in 2009 and 2010 for millions of households.
- Construction of new homes and condos were at their lowest level since the Great Depression. The price of housing fell between 10 to 40 percent, depending on which city or state was measured.
- For the first time since the Great Depression, there was deflation in prices rather than inflation.

President Bush's proposed 2009 budget of $3.1 trillion was over 66 percent higher than when he took office in 2001. At that time, the federal budget was under $2 trillion. This budget included a stimulus program of $168 billion due to the recession that started in 2007. Expenditures under Bush (43) and Cheney rose from $1.8 to $3.5 trillion in just eight years.

With the meltdown of the financial institutions and the economy in the fourth quarter of 2008, it was no longer possible for the Bush-Cheney administration to have a payback plan for the Social Security and Medicare Trust Funds. The taxes of the General Fund will now have to fund any excess payments over the income of those two programs until the program is modified to spend only what it receives in payroll taxes. There will be no more surplus funds from Social Security and Medicare to offset the deficits of the General Fund.

President Obama Inherits Major Financial Problems

No matter who had been elected in 2008, the new President would have had to choose from only two basic economic strategies.

One strategy would be to avoid a ten-year depression as the country experienced from 1929 to 1939. To accomplish this feat, the President had to implement programs to merge and bail out financial institutions like the nearly trillion-dollar ones implemented just prior to the 2008 election to save Wall Street. To save Main Street and prevent unemployment growing close to 20 percent, a $787 billion stimulus program was needed in 2009 and 2010 to help state and local governments to save jobs, to create new jobs, and to save a few corporations such as General Motors and Chrysler. To save the housing market from a complete meltdown, bailout money was provided for Fannie Mae, Freddie Mac and mortgage adjustment funds. Two trillion dollars of borrowed money was also needed to phase out the Iraq War, to continue the Afghanistan War, and to finance the very enlarged Defense Department, Homeland Security, and Veterans' Benefits budgets.

By the end of 2012, the national debt is forecasted to be $15 to $16 trillion if no new programs are added by the new President and Congress. President Bush not only left a $10 trillion debt, but he also ensured that the debt would reach $15 to $16 trillion four years later based on his decisions to reduce taxes, to fund two pre-emptive wars, and to have excessive spending for eight years in nearly every area of the federal budget. The Chairman of the Federal Reserve, Alan Greenspan, also deserves a great deal of credit for the size of the deficits and the debt as well as the huge cost of interest and the severe economic conditions of 2008.

The other strategy that the new President in 2008 could have followed was exactly the same program and decisions made by President Hoover from 1929 to 1932:

- Freeze all federal spending except for defense, veterans' affairs, and homeland security (the fastest growing areas of the federal budget).
- Provide no federal financial assistance to state and local governments, insurance companies, or corporations which would have meant many more bankruptcies and massive layoffs in the government sectors. The layoffs in the private sector would also have doubled. All total, unemployment could have exceeded 20 percent and the nation would have plunged into a ten-year depression which was a warning from the Secretary of the Treasury.

- More tax cuts that would have driven up the deficit, the debt, and the cost of interest.

For obvious reasons, this alternative strategy was not implemented by President Obama, and it is doubtful Senator McCain would have either.

What Really Caused the Mountain of Debt?

By now it is clear that recessions, depressions, unemployment, wars, and tax cuts are responsible for the large national debt that had been under control until the year 2000. The national debt has not been caused by Social Security and Medicare.

One political party has been talking about reducing the size and cost of the federal government, while it has occupied the White House for 28 of the past 40 years. During that period, not one of this party's four Presidents has been able to reduce the size and cost of government. In fact, their leadership and decisions resulted in the vast majority of the accumulated debt. Accordingly, they have been nicknamed the borrow and spend party. The other political party that inherited a tax and spend reputation from the 1960s was the only party that managed their years in the White House as fiscal conservatives. Republicans voted eight times to raise the national debt by $5.4 trillion just in the 2001 to 2008 time frame alone. With all the financial problems in the fourth quarter of 2008 and the Great Recession, the federal debt ceiling has now surpassed $15 trillion. The votes for raising the debt ceiling were virtually guaranteed of passing because the government cannot issue checks once the debt ceiling is reached, but many members of Congress threatened to destroy the economy and the federal government by refusing to raise the debt ceiling.

President Obama is not going to be able to reduce the deficits in his last two years of his administration which are due to commitments in the two wars, the decision to keep the tax cuts in place, and high unemployment based on the civil war in Congress. No one can predict if President Obama will be elected for a second term, or whether he will greatly reduce government spending to avoid major tax increases, benefit reductions and important tax deductions eliminations. No one can predict either if the Republican Party will move from the illusion of small government and reduced spending that they have successfully sold for 40 years but never achieved, to a real plan of reducing the size and cost of government. Both political parties did pass some budget reduction legislation in the Congress, but this will not achieve a large reduction in government spending. Voters in the 2012 election must demand practical and realistic plans from both political candidates before they cast their vote. One key message from this lesson is there are fiscal conservatives in both the Republican and Democratic parties as well as great spenders in both parties who have contributed to a mountain of debt. This book will help voters evaluate the financial plans of both political parties. The country must have a great strategic leader and a fiscal manager as President from 2012 to 2016 to avoid a major financial meltdown of the federal government and a long-term economic depression.

We have reviewed the facts about the financial crisis, gained a basic understanding of the federal financial system, and learned which administrations were big spenders. With that knowledge, we can move on to the next lesson which discusses the feasibility of creating and managing change within the federal government that the presidential candidates can use.

NOTES FOR LESSON 3

1. "Hard Times:1930s," LIFE MAGAZINE Decade Issues, 2000
2. *Great Depression*, T. H. Watkins, Little Brown and Co., 1993, page 340
3. Historical Statistics Tables, U.S. Treasury, 2009, "Federal Debt At The End Of The Year," pages 133-134
4. "Tear Down This Myth," Will Bunch, FREE PRESS, 2009, page 126

LESSON 4

IS SYSTEMIC CHANGE FEASIBLE WITHIN GOVERNMENT AGENCIES?

Nine Challenging Situations Requiring Potential Tax Increases

What makes this financial crisis different from other recessions and depressions? First, there are nine key problems that need to be solved rather than just one or two.

1. There is a limit of debt that individuals, pension plans, insurance companies, foundations, financial institutions, and foreign governments will buy through American government bonds. The Congressional Budget Office has stated that at $20 trillion of debt, investors might stop buying U.S. Treasury bonds. In that case, interest would escalate rapidly to well over a trillion dollars per year. Interest rates could far exceed 10 percent. Keep in mind that at $10 trillion of public debt, every one percent of interest increase adds $100 billion more of annual interest expense. At $20 trillion of public debt, interest would increase by $200 billion for every one percent increase. This situation would force the government to implement annual increases in income tax rates to pay for the privilege of living beyond our means these past decades. Government spending must be reduced or taxes must be increased by 2016 to solve this situation.
2. Except in World War II, there has never been an expense for defense and veterans' affairs that requires $500 billion in borrowed funds each year like the Iraq and Afghanistan wars. This spending will require at least a 20-to-25 percent surtax

on income tax or the two wars must be ended and the military downsized to an affordable level.

3. For the first time ever, revenues for Social Security payments are not adequate, which means money from the General Fund will be required every year to pay Social Security benefits. This amount will grow each year due to the number of baby boomers who will be retiring. Thus, an annual increase in taxes may be needed for Social Security unless age adjustments are made in the benefits.

4. The severe recession has caused unemployment rates that have increased the cost of unemployment insurance, welfare payments, Medicaid payment, and other "safety net" expenses. At the same time, income tax revenues have decreased. Normally, the government would borrow funds during a recession and pay back these loans in periods of prosperity. If loans at a reasonable interest rate are not available, a surtax on income tax could be needed which will deepen and extend the recession.

5. Our private enterprise system is not growing at an acceptable GDP rate, and hiring is not adequate. The government must invest taxpayer funds to create public sector jobs and/or to stimulate the private sector until it starts hiring at a rate of 300,000 new jobs each month for a few years. Again, more income taxes could be needed for this challenge.

6. The cost of health care is expanding more each year at a rate that far exceeds inflation. A laser focus must be applied to reducing health care costs or an annual increase on income and/or Medicare taxes could be needed for that areas as well.

7. Without a national strategic plan to reduce American dependence on gasoline and fuel, the price of gasoline and oil could escalate to the point where it will have the same impact as the severe recession. The government will be forced to grant financial aid to the unemployed and the working poor to pay their fuel bills, another subsidy that will require more income taxes. Some political leaders want a large federal tax on oil and gasoline to motivate Americans to drive fuel-efficient automobiles and to live in smaller houses that require less fuel.

8. Over 40 of our states are in serious financial trouble. They simply cannot pay the operating costs of their Medicaid programs, the judicial/prison systems and their overall education systems due to their balanced budget laws. They already received bailout funds in 2009 and 2010. Education has become another entitlement that the federal government simply cannot afford. Again, the federal government may have to raise income taxes to provide an annual bailout to state governments each year for a much larger contribution to education. The worst case scenario is a municipal bond default in large states such as New York, Illinois or California which would also require a bailout from the federal government.

9. For decades, either by raising taxes or more recently by borrowing tens of billions of dollars, every branch of the federal government has asked for an annual increase in operating budgets. They continue to operate under the mentality that there is going to be an annual cost-of-living increase due to inflation which requires more taxes. The private sector gave up cost-of-living increases after the inflation rate stabilized to a few percentage points each year.

For 30 years, one political party has convinced Americans that they can receive multi-billion-dollar tax cuts because the government is too large. This party then spends and borrows like there are no revenue problems. The other political party has now adopted a similar strategy of tax cuts and borrowing record amounts of funds for increased spending and reduced revenues. Too many political leaders claim to be fiscal conservatives, but only a few members of Congress are serious about reducing the size and cost of government. Deregulation decisions made during the Bush-Cheney administration resulted in an emergency meeting with leaders of Congress, Cabinet Secretaries, and the President. The crisis was so large and so immediate that a $700 billion bailout had to be agreed to within 24 hours to keep our government and banks alive. There may very well be more meetings like that one in future years.

No one bipartisan task force can solve all nine problems the way the one crisis (shortage of Social Security revenue) was handled in the 1980s. There are committees inside and outside of the government that met in 2010 and 2011 to consider numerous tax increases, benefit reductions, and tax deduction eliminations to return the country to a balanced budget like the ones it had in 1998, 1999, 2000, and 2001. These committee reports will have some influence on political leaders who will realistically only have three options to select from to prevent a meltdown of the United States federal financial system as described in Lesson 1.

Decades of Additional Employees and Funds To Solve Problems

Whenever a major problem or crisis arises, the typical answer is: add whatever money and additional employees are necessary to solve the problem or crisis. This approach is adopted when a war does not go as planned; the government sends in thousands of extra troops which cost tens of billions of dollars. With the student learning crisis in the public schools, our federal, state, and local governments doubled and tripled the education operating budgets in order to add more teachers, aids, and administrative personnel. When institutions of higher education do not control costs, billions of dollars in scholarships and financial aid are added to the government budget. Annual increases in health care require large sums of incremental funds each year. When environmental problems arose in New Orleans and the Gulf of Mexico, federal aid poured billions of dollars into these crises until the press went home and there were no longer negative stories on the evening news. When Wall Street had a meltdown, trillions of dollars were used to stabilize our financial institutions. A spike in unemployment requires tens of billions of dollars to help Americans survive a major recession.

All of these financial interventions are good for those who receive government money, but this method of solving problems can last only as long as our country has a superior credit rating and nearly an unlimited amount of borrowed money available from Treasury Bonds as was the case in the 20th Century. However, in the 21st Century, our country has borrowed so much money over the years that there is a real possibility the borrowing of incremental funds may come to an end. What will happen when an insufficient number of persons, foreign countries, and financial institutions quit purchasing U.S. Treasury bonds?

The United States must then do what it should have been doing during the past 30 years. The government agency responsible for containing or solving the crisis will be forced to fix the problem with a comprehensive solution that does not require a massive amount of new government funds. Every one of the country's major problems can be solved, because they usually have been caused by ineffective leadership in past administrations, by outdated programs or regulations, or by laws that have become barriers to progress. Entirely new paradigms for operating government agencies will be required. Of course, creating and implementing new paradigms is hard work compared to throwing money and additional employees at a problem.

How Does a Government Agency Create and Implement Change?

Anyone, including political leaders, can talk about change. In practice, very few chief executive officers, school administrators, hospital administrators, executive directors of community-based organizations, church leaders, high ranking military officers, and political leaders ever *create* change and even fewer are able to *implement* change. Why is this? The fact is that there are many people who will fight against change because they fear the unknown or they believe a new vision will not benefit them, and very few executives have been trained on how to create and manage major changes in their organizations.

About 20 years ago, a few consulting firms performed extensive research on *how* to create and manage change effectively. In 1987, Dr. Joel Barker wrote about change in a book entitled *Discovering The Future: The Business Of Paradigms*. A number of management consulting firms developed methodologies to create and manage change. All of this knowledge enables leaders to be outstanding performers at creating and managing change once they have studied the methodologies that have been proven during the past 20 years.

Below is a brief overview of a five-phase process:

Phase 1: Develop an Overpowering Case for Change

This phase is usually quite easy to accomplish. In a political campaign, a candidate often talks about the need to change. Unfortunately, the message is too often a statement of general information. The message needs powerful statistics and stories of *why* change is absolutely essential. The story should be so compelling that voters are in full agreement that change is a "must do" instead of a "nice to do" requirement.

Phase 2: Create an Exciting Vision and Establish Goals

Too many visions are merely statements of good intentions that have little value or motivation. Sometimes a successful vision is only one sentence, such as: "By the end of the decade the United States will land a person on the moon." Sometimes, the successful vision is a paragraph. For example:

The (name of the school district or the state department of education) is organized, staffed, and funded to develop successful learners in a safe and enjoyable environment based on an integrated curriculum of lessons that meets the state and school district learning standards. With the assistance of parents and community leaders, all children, except for those who have serious physical, mental or language challenges, will be successful students at the proficient level (Grades A & B) in their appropriate grade level during the kindergarten through high school years. Graduates will be prepared to enter the workforce or be able to enroll at institutions of higher learning without the assistance of remediation programs, and they will have the necessary knowledge to become good citizens and lead productive lives. To achieve this vision, (name of school district or state department of education) will implement proven learning, assessment, administrative, and management systems that focus primarily on learning and cost containment.

A final sentence could be added to show how much of a stretch goal this is. For example, the vision could state that it will require a 100 percent improvement in the number of successful students at their appropriate grade level and a 90 percent reduction in the number of high school dropouts.

There would then be four or five specific goals that clearly indicate to everyone when the vision has been achieved.

Phase 3: Develop a Blueprint for Change and Implementation

This phase is the most difficult one in creating and implementing change. To make Social Security fiscally sound, for instance, Congress and the President have about four or five decisions to select from:
- Increase the payroll tax to fund Social Security
- Require citizens to pay the payroll tax on a higher percent of income

- Move the date to receive full benefits from 67 years of age to 68 or 70.—Early retirement would be moved from 62 years of age to 65
- Change the cost-of-living adjustment

Within a few weeks or months, a bipartisan commission could make a recommendation. Congress could subsequently approve or modify the recommendations so that the President could sign these recommendations into law.

In areas such as defense, education, health care, infrastructure rebuilding, and homeland security, phase three will be much more complex and it will require months or years to develop an implementation plan that includes the following components:

- Strategies (that outline how a goal will be achieved over several years)
- Action Plans (what will be accomplished each year to implement the strategy)
- Budget for change (how will the change be funded)
- Organization chart (accountability of those in charge of change)
- Staff responsibilities (tasks for each team member)
- Project manager (when will the work be completed and who is responsible)

The vision of landing a person on the moon by the end of the decade required seven years in Phase 3, but it was a great success story of how government could achieve fundamental change. The implementation plan for occupying Iraq and Afghanistan as well as accomplishing the related nation-building projects there have been failures. The No Child Left Behind vision also suffered from a failed implementation plan in Phase 3.

Phase 4: Achieving Proof of Concept

In the corporate world, Phase 4 is absolutely essential because a senior management team does not want to "bet the company" on a new vision until it has first had a successful pilot project. Unfortunately in government, Phase 4 is often ignored altogether. That is why there are often massive mistakes on funding required for Medicare and Medicaid. Another example is our military did not know how to occupy one Islamic country successfully before it invaded a second Islamic country. The cost estimates are often many times higher than the original forecasts, and in this case, the government missed the cost objectives by trillions of dollars.

Phase 5: Institutionalize Change Throughout the Organization

When the federal government makes major changes in education or healthcare, it will be essential to have a plan to expand the successful pilot project created in Phase 4.

A comprehensive implementation plan is required to phase in the new paradigm over several years with funding estimates for each year of implementation.

Who Is Responsible for Creating Change?

The following individuals and groups must be identified with clear responsibilities for creating change.

– **Change Agents**
  Dr. Martin Luther King and his followers were change agents in the Civil Rights movement. The media and press are often change agents, but change agents have no authority to implement change.

– **Sponsoring Executive and Legislature**
  President Johnson and the Congress were the sponsoring executives of the Civil Rights laws that ended segregation. They had the power and the funds to implement these changes.

– **Director of Change**
  The Director of the Civil Rights Commission was responsible for implementing the new laws in all companies, schools, hospitals, and not-for-profit organizations. The Human Resources Vice Presidents within each organization were in charge of implementing the law.

- **Change Team**
  The personnel in the federal government's Civil Rights
  Commission and the equal opportunity staffs within
  Human Resources Departments actually did the work
  associated with the implementation.
- **Changing Personnel**
  All the managers and executives in corporations,
  government agencies, and not-for-profit organizations
  who were responsible for implementing the equal
  opportunity laws turned out to be the people who
  eventually implemented the change to end segregation
  and to provide equal opportunity in the workplace.

Has the Government Been Successful With Major Changes?

There have been many successful government programs that have
contributed significantly to the American standard of living:

- State and local governments created the finest public
  schools system early in the 20th Century.
- The federal government created the finest system for
  expanding higher education with the Land Grant Act which
  helped form hundreds of new state universities. Later, the
  federal government created the GI Bill that elevated the
  number of college graduates from approximately 5 percent
  to over 25 percent of the population.
- The federal government was responsible for the waterways
  canal system, the transcontinental railroad system, and the
  finest airline service in the 19th and 20th Centuries. The
  national interstate highway system is another example of
  a successful government program.
- Federal and state governments worked with farmers to
  raise the quantity of food products while simultaneously
  lowering the price of food for all American citizens.
- The top tier of medical schools and hospitals resulted from
  successful government grants, support, and leadership.

- The space program, including the Man-On-Moon project, was the result of successful government leadership through the NASA agency.
- Our military services are considered the finest in the world and have protected the United States for centuries.
- Social Security is certainly another example of a well-run government agency that changed the American standard of living.
- The national parks system provides enjoyment for millions of families every year.
- Rural Electrification was another successful program.

No one can say the United States government cannot accomplish great visions and goals. Unfortunately, in recent years, there have been too many political leaders telling voters that our government cannot solve the major problems facing our country. It is the political leadership that is the problem. Voters need to elect better government leaders.

A former managing director at Lazard Freres & Co. and the 1975-1993 chairman of the Municipal Assistance Corporation in New York State that helped resolve the financial crisis in New York City, Felix Rohatyn wrote a book in 2009 entitled *Bold Endeavors: How Our Government Built America And Why It Must Be Rebuilt Now*. It shows how important a partnership between government and the private free enterprise system has been in past years and how important it must be in future years to maintain our standard of living.

Requirement for Goals, Strategies and Implementation Plans

Many people are documenting the size and scope of our financial crisis, but we need to spend more time and effort developing national goals and strategies to reach these goals. We also need implementation plans that actually achieve these goals. Most of this book is dedicated to accomplishing our goals so voters can ask more penetrating questions of their candidates in the 2012 elections. The next lesson deals with the development of national goals that will maintain or enhance the American standard of living and our continued leadership within the world.

LESSON 5

NATIONAL VISION AND GOALS

Cannot Create Systemic Change Without a Vision and Goals

It is important for Americans to understand that their country was heading for a long-term and deep economic depression like the 1930s during the fourth quarter of 2008 and the beginning of 2009. The President and Congress had to stop the descent into the economic depression which they accomplished. Now the challenge is to rebuild America because it has been badly damaged over a ten-year period. Because there has been no vision or national goals, the extreme left and right pundits as well as the press scream that every step along the road to recovery is either insufficient or too much. Americans need to have a vision where each political party will take this country over the next four-to-eight years. Voters should demand to know what are the national goals and strategies to achieve the goals and vision before they vote in 2012. Depending on their votes, the nation will sink into an economic depression or have a recovery as it did in the 1990s.

An American Vision Is Required

As the old saying goes, "If you don't know where you are going, any road will get you there." Unfortunately, this adage describes our country in recent years. Americans need to develop a vision of where they want their country to be in future years. Political parties can then develop and implement the strategies and programs that, over a four-to-eight-year period, will achieve the vision. This vision will motivate voters to support the fundamental changes that are necessary to achieve the vision. Ken Blanchard, author of *The One Minute Manager*, states: "A vision is a picture of the future that produces passion, and

53

it's this passion that people want to follow. An organization without a clear vision or goals is like a river without banks—it stagnates and goes nowhere."(1)

If you ask the average American what are the goals of our country, they would make a list of problems to be solved rather than goals that would rebuild our country. In the past, Americans have been united around several visions that gave them faith in the future of our country and a belief they would have a rising standard of living which was realized during the 20th Century. There was the "New Deal" in the 1930s, and later the "Great Society" and the "New Frontier." President Reagan had "Freedom From Government." All of these visions have come to an end. Neither political party has communicated a vision for our new decade. Millions of Americans are losing their sense of optimism. They do not believe they or their children are going to live better in the future. They see a declining standard of living with millions of Americans looking for a job or a better job; many for one and two years. Those that are over 50 years of age believe they may not work again at a job with benefits or a decent income commensurate with their education and experience. The vast majority of our citizens think the country has been on the wrong roads during the past decade. Americans need a new vision and national goals. Below is an example of a vision that most Americans would get passionate about for the future:

> *Americans want to live in peace and be able to support themselves financially throughout their adult years with at least a middle-class standard of living. During their lifetime, they will need affordable health care and excellent education systems. There should be an honest, efficient and affordable government that is dedicated to improving their standard of living and to providing an economy that achieves a high level of employment. In their senior years, retired Americans should be able to continue living an independent life with the help of a government pension plus the income they can earn from their investments. Americans will always enjoy the personal freedom that the United States Constitution guarantees all citizens.*

A vision must have supporting goals that the government can aim for and reach. Listed below are six potential national goals that would achieve the vision.

Goal: Peace With Strong Defense and Homeland Security Systems

For centuries, leaders of countries have tried to conquer other nations. A classic example was the military and fascist dictatorships that rose prior to World War II. The end result was the defeat and destruction of both dictatorships in Japan and Nazi Germany. It took decades for those two countries to rebuild their governments, their industries, and their societies. World War II killed over 65 million people, and wounded millions more. Millions of people lost their homes, tens of millions lost their jobs, and trillions of dollars were spent on destroying other people and their countries. No one wants to repeat World War II.

Citizens of every country want peace. Parents do not want their sons and daughters going off to war to be killed or seriously wounded. Spouses and their children are devastated when a husband, wife, mother, or father is killed or gravely wounded in battle. Families are disrupted and too often devastated by wartime service.

When is war our only option? If another country tries to invade the United States, our citizens will join the military services to defend our country. If another country bombs our country, the United States should retaliate with sufficient force to eliminate hostile action by that enemy country. The United States and other leading industrial countries, with the help of the United Nations, have prevented a World War III since 1945. At this time, no other country has the military organization to start World War III, nor is there any country trying to take over major areas of the world with military force.

However, there will always be rogue and ruthless leaders in some countries who cause great harm to their citizens. The world will always have some messy and unstable situations. The vast majority of Americans do not want to spend trillions of taxpayer funds on pre-emptive wars, or on civil wars with no end in sight. They do not want the American military services turned into the world's policemen trying to impose our religious beliefs, our way of government, our economic system, or our education system on other countries. If other countries want to have different religions, economic systems, and methods of government, we should leave them alone as long as those countries do not plan to bomb or invade our nation. If they do, our Navy and Air Force should be able to bomb them into decades of poverty. The United States must have a strong defense organization, but the country must be prudent as to when to send its military forces thousands of miles away to fight in civil wars. Our country needs to avoid committing ground troops for invading other countries, occupying other countries, and implementing multi-billion-dollar nation-building projects. In some situations, such as the Gulf War when the United States and our allies quickly forced Iraq to retreat to its own borders, ground troops may be necessary for a few weeks or months. But American troops should not occupy hostile nations for years. The United States must avoid multi-year civil wars like the ones in Vietnam, Iraq and Afghanistan.

Terrorism is completely different from one nation attacking another country, like Japan did to the United States with the bombing of Pearl Harbor in 1941. Terrorists can come from any of over 50 countries, or they can even be American citizens who are religious fanatics recruited to become deadly terrorists. The illusion that a multi-year war in the Middle East, Asia, or Africa involving thousands of American soldiers will prevent terror attacks in our country is no longer believable. Therefore, the Department of Homeland Security working in conjunction with the FBI, CIA, Coast Guard, Border Patrol personnel, Passport and Immigration Control, and local police forces must be our first line of defense against terrorism.

Our foreign policy strategies must be directed toward building friendly relationships with every possible nation. Our country should stop trying to create regime changes in other countries and should stop declaring some countries as enemies in order to justify a massive military organization. With the existing and growing national debt, our country cannot afford to spend trillions of dollars waging war in far-off lands.

Goal: Prosperity and a Rising Standard of Living With High Level of Employment

After World War II, when most other countries lay in ruins, our large corporations transformed into multi-national organizations that helped rebuild the world. Our major companies were leaders in producing automobiles, trucks, airplanes, appliances, electronics, textiles, steel, clothing, food, furniture as well as construction, transportation, financial institutions, and health care. All this production led to full employment, annual raises, employer health care benefits, company pensions, and few unexpected layoffs. Americans bought homes, automobiles, and took great vacations. Americans lived the good life for decades. They were able to pay for their children's college educations at state universities without requiring financial aid. Promotions were frequent.

Senior citizens and older middle-age Americans grew up in this environment. This prosperous way-of-living represented normal life.

How life has changed. In a majority of households, it now takes two people working at least two full-time jobs to maintain the standard of living that their parents or grandparents enjoyed. The standard 35-to-40 hour work week is now a 50-to-60 hour work week for many Americans. Weekends and vacation days are no longer rest periods; they are now extensions of the work week through cell phones and computers. If a family has young children, it faces the challenges of day care, pre-school, and child care during the late hours of the day in elementary and middle-school years. Weekends and evenings are filled with an endless list of chores for house cleaning, maintaining the landscape, preparing meals, and other household projects. There just never seems to be time to rest and enjoy life.

On the job, there is the constant threat of sudden unemployment, loss of health care benefits, and loss of a home, automobile, vacations, or college educations. Layoffs today often have nothing to do with job performance; a company is downsizing or outsourcing jobs to another country simply to increase profits. There are fewer promotions because companies are often losing rather than gaining market share in the global economy. Worse yet, there are fewer wage increases. Managers are not as respectful to employees (and vice versa) because they constantly live in fear of being fired, so working conditions are often poor. Except in government jobs, there usually is no union to help protect an employee's job, working conditions, or dignity. In this severe recession, there are sudden wage reductions. Employee morale is at an all-time low in many corporations. Customers are not happy because customer service is also at an all-time low. As a result, customers are often rude to employees.

Americans want to know what our government can do to return our country to a level of prosperity where we have job security, hope for increased promotions and raises, and a rising standard of living rather than a declining one.

Time between jobs is becoming longer which is why more homes are being foreclosed, more automobiles are being repossessed, and health care benefits are being lost. These losses are another reason why two incomes are necessary in most households today. Surveys show that the average American will change jobs five-to-ten times during their 40-to-50 year careers. Even five job changes can cause great financial and emotional stress. With the disappearance of unions, Americans are depending more on government because private enterprise companies no longer feel obligated to provide full or life-time employment nor a safety net of benefits. For this reason, Americans are turning to their government for solutions on how to bridge the gap from one job to another without going bankrupt.

Nearly half of American adult citizens suffer from debt stress. According to an Associated Press poll, approximately 46 percent of those surveyed state they are suffering from debt-related stress, and half of that group describe their stress as "great deal or quite a bit." On the other hand, approximately 53 percent claim they feel little or no stress at all. People are whittling down their debt. The average credit debt is now $3,900 compared to $5,600 last year. Of course, only people with the most stellar credit are able to obtain loans. Ken Goldstein, an economist at the Conference Board (a research group that keeps close tabs on consumers) states, "It is people's individual circumstances that shape their confidence and their stress over debt."(2)

Goal: Adequate and Affordable Health Care System for All

With few exceptions, Americans require health insurance from the day they are born to the day they die. The country needs a formal program to improve the quality of our health care system and to lower the cost of studying and implementing the best medical practices. Americans must be able to select their own doctors and hospitals so they can obtain correct diagnostic determinations and optimum care for their illnesses. An affordable medical system needs to be developed for our unemployed and homeless populations as well.

Goal: Superior and Affordable Education Systems

The Secretary of Education and the 50 Chief State School Officers must develop a new instructional and learning system for the American public school system to achieve the goal of the No Child Left Behind law that requires over 90 percent of students to be A or B performers in their K-12 years of public school. The high school dropout rate must be reduced by over 90 percent. The vast majority of Americans must achieve a real high school education that prepares them for the job market or for additional education at institutions of higher learning. Institutions of higher learning must develop an affordable education method that enables middle-class students to earn a college degree without incurring large debts. Student aid should be needed only by students who are living below the poverty line. Through their trade associations, major industries must provide superior job training that will enable American employees to be a competitive workforce that knows more and produces more than their overseas competitors. Life-long learning must be made available to all Americans.

Goal: Efficient and Affordable Government

Government services are often taken for granted. Few citizens think about the roads, sidewalks, storm sewers, waste sewers, street lights, traffic lights and signs, water, gas, electricity, police, fire protection, emergency medical service, schools, libraries, and parks that are all provided by local government. These facilities and services require planning, funding, construction, and maintenance. Few citizens would want to give up these local government projects, because if they did, they would lower their standard of living.

At the state level, citizens have their judicial and prison systems that protect them against criminals. Institutions of higher education provide their children with college educations. Medicaid and welfare services are provided to those who are homeless or living in poverty. There are state parks and rest areas. State police provide safety throughout a state.

The state funded National Guard units are available for drastic storms, riots, and other emergencies.

The federal government funds the country's large defense organization and the important veterans' benefits for those who have served our country. Social Security pensions, Medicare for senior citizens, agriculture support for farmers, regulations of financial institutions, and FDIC insurance to protect our savings are also provided at the federal level. The safety of our airlines, railroads, and buses is maintained by the federal government. Public housing for people living below the poverty line, homeland security, the Supreme Court and Department of Justice, the Treasury Department, and the Federal Reserve are all federal institutions. Federal dollars also fund the national parks, the Department of State that implements foreign policy to prevent violent military wars and trade wars, the Securities and Exchange Commission that regulates the stock market, the postal service, the Small Business Administration, the Federal Communications Commission, and the Pell Grants to universities. The National Science Foundation, the National Aeronautics and Space Administration, FEMA for terrible storms and other disasters, and the Department of Health and Human Services are also federally funded institutions. Simply put, Americans cannot maintain their standard of living if a financial meltdown occurs within our federal government.

Only the most radical Libertarians and Tea Party members want to abolish the federal government. In reality, only 1-to-2 percent of our wealthiest citizens could exist without any help from the three levels of government. These people have their own jets. Their cars are fully paid for as are their million-dollar homes. They do not need financial aid, because they can afford the most expensive colleges and universities for their children. They could rebuild their home if it was ruined by a storm and they could afford hundreds of thousands of dollars in medical bills. Their children can attend private schools and their businesses can operate independently of government regulations. The rest of us, the remaining 98-99 percent of Americans, want an efficient and affordable government at all three levels. We have every right to get upset when there is waste, corruption, or incompetence in government.

We also need our government to develop a nationwide energy plan that provides us with affordable and sufficient energy to heat our homes, provide power for our automobiles, and supply electricity throughout the country. The threat of insufficient energy supplies resulting from hostile foreign governments or from inflated prices must be minimized.

Goal: Decent Retirement for Senior Citizens

With Americans now working 40-to-50 years and retiring in their late 60s, they deserve a Social Security pension that funds, on average, 10-to-15 years of their retirement. Company pensions have all but disappeared and 401k plans are not providing adequate pensions for 10-to-15 years. Therefore, a Social Security pension is absolutely essential for the vast majority of Americans. To handle potential illnesses in their senior years, Americans must also have the affordable health care system that Medicare provides. Few senior citizens can live without prescription drugs because most of them suffer a series of medical problems in their retirement years. Most Americans no longer live with a son or daughter during their retirement; they maintain their own apartment, condo or house. In their 80's, some senior citizens move into retirement homes or life care centers. These institutions are expensive, and would be unaffordable without Social Security and Medicare.

Why Americans Must Support Change To Achieve National Goals

Wars, recessions, depressions, and incompetent leadership within private enterprise corporations and government agencies have caused today's mountain of debt with its record annual deficits and interest. As a result, Americans are more dependent now on government leadership and agencies than at any time since the Great Depression of the 1930s. If Americans have peace, prosperity, and an efficient as well as an affordable government, they will have a foundation to build upon for a higher standard of living. Americans must do their part by performing well in school, obeying the laws of our land, and working hard to earn a living that supports themselves and their families. This is democracy; not socialism, communism or fascism.

Today, our country suffers from a lack of a vision and national goals. To protect our way of life and our standard of living, we Americans must become more involved in seeking the truth about the key issues that are being debated and voted on at all three levels of our government. The ideological statements and slogans of our two political parties are not the national goals. The parties are miles apart in their platform, and their slogans and programs are often merely illusions. Neither political party has communicated an overall plan for an economic recovery from the 2008 meltdown of the housing market, the financial institutions, and the overall economy. The speeding train of spending will continue to drive this country into a deep economic depression if the major changes outlined in this book's upcoming lessons are not implemented. Voters need to ask many questions of the 2012 candidates to learn how their plans and programs will achieve the national goals.

The President who is elected in 2012 must do a better job of connecting with our citizens. This could be accomplished by a two word title for the vision: "Rebuilding America." Yes, very wealthy American may exclaim, "Why do we have to rebuild our country when it is already the finest country in the world?" But the middle class, the working poor, and unemployed who represent 90 percent of our nation truly believe that major changes are required for our country due to problems that have surfaced during the past decade. This is the reason why they voted for change in 2008 and 2010.

Keep in mind that President Clinton achieved the national goals of peace, prosperity, decent retirement, and affordable government in the 1990s. All of these goals are attainable in this decade if an outstanding leader in the White House achieves systemic change in the areas discussed in the next eight lessons of this book.

NOTES FOR LESSON 5

1. *Are You A Leader?* Ken Blanchard, Rancho Bernardo Community Presbyterian Church, San Diego, CA, November 20, 1999, page 2
2. "Nearly Half In U.S. Suffer From Debt Stress," Jeannine Aversa, AP, SAN DIEGO UNION-TRIBUNE, May 31, 2010, page A4

PART II

HOW MEDICARE AND SOCIAL SECURITY CAN BE AFFORDABLE

Every major industrial country provides health care and a pension for their senior citizens. It would be a giant step backwards for the United States to reduce benefits for its seniors. In fact, it would be similar to a major tax increase if seniors who now receive benefits have to pay more for their health care or receive a reduction in their Social Security checks. The next two lessons will explain why Social Security and Medicare are essential for the American standard of living as well as affordable. It is important to establish Social Security and Medicare as two separate self-funding government agencies. Pension checks and Medicare benefit checks should not be paid out of the General Fund. Payroll taxes should not go into the General Fund. The President and Congress can then focus on the excessive spending and mountain of debt existing within the General Fund. This action would also force the health care community to focus on quality and cost containment. The vast majority of Americans do not want their payroll taxes for Social Security and Medicare to be transferred to the General Fund to support excessive spending in other areas of the government. And while they will accept some changes in Social Security, they do not want to means-test their benefits or have their pension checks reduced. Also, Americans do not want Medicare benefits reduced, but they do support more quality measurements and lower costs within the health care system.

LESSON 6

LASER FOCUS ON QUALITY AND COST OF HEALTH CARE

Major Changes In Health Care Systems

Prior to World War II, General Practitioners (GPs), made house calls because many of their patients did not have automobiles. They arrived with a black doctor's bag full of pills, but at the time, there were no antibiotics such as penicillin. Rarely, did a patient have to enter a hospital. A GP physician delivered babies, treated children for childhood diseases, and performed numerous operations such as the removal of tonsils, adenoids, appendix, gallbladder, and ulcers. They also treated all types of broken bones and burns. Some would even serve part-time as the Chief of Staff at a local hospital. They had one great advantage. They really knew their patients and felt totally responsible for healing them. There were few specialists in those years other than surgeons. Most important, health care was affordable and few persons needed health insurance.

Modern-day medicine is completely different. GPs have almost disappeared and have been replaced by internists who do annual physical examinations. Internists prescribe medications and now almost every American is on some medication. An internist does not always visit patients in a hospital because the hospital often assigns its own internist to each case. An internist will quickly turn a patient over to a specialist whenever a medical problem is diagnosed. Specialists can be found in the following fields of medicine:

- Acupuncture
- Allergy
- Bariatrics (weight control)
- Cardiology (heart)

- Colon & Rectal Surgery
- Dermatology (skin)
- Knee and Hip Surgery
- Nephrology (kidneys)
- Neurology (nervous system)
- Nutrition
- Obstetrics and Gynecology (Women's health)
- Occupational Medicine
- Oncology (tumor disease)
- Ophthalmology (eye)
- Orthopedic Surgery (bone, spine & joint)
- Otolaryngology (ear, nose & throat)
- Pain Management
- Pediatrics (infant, child & adolescent)
       (5 sub-specialties within Pediatrics)
- Physical Medicine & Rehabilitation
- Plastic & Reconstructive Surgery
- Proctology (colon & rectum)
- Psychiatry
- Pulmonary Diseases (lung)
- Rheumatology (arthritis)
- Sleep Disorders
- Sports Medicine
- Cardiac Surgery
- Thoracic Surgery (chest)
- Urology (urinary tract)
- Dentistry (teeth and gums)

As American citizens age, it is not uncommon for them to have three-to-ten doctors trying to keep them healthy and free of pain. Modern medicine enables most persons to live much longer and healthier lives. Accordingly, the amount of knowledge required to treat a patient has expanded significantly. The number of medications has grown to the point where many citizens spend far more on prescription drugs than on doctor bills. Health care is now a system of split responsibility where no one doctor coordinates all the medical care for a patient and it consists of many examinations, tests, and duplicate treatments. As a result, the national health care system is now very expensive.

How Costly Is the Modern Medical System?

The vast majority of children are healthy now because vaccines have eradicated most childhood diseases. Young adults and even a majority of middle-age Americans are healthy. As an individual ages into the senior years, often medical problems start to arise. However, if anyone at any age contracts a serious illness, the ensuing medical bills are terribly expensive. A trip to a hospital emergency room can cost between $5,000 and $10,000. Operations can cost anywhere from $25,000 to $150,000. Medications can cost thousands of dollars. After an operation, a patient may spend many days in an expensive rehabilitation center because a patient is only allowed a few days in a hospital. Every year, numerous patients are readmitted to a hospital through an emergency room. According to a 2009 study published in the NEW ENGLAND JOURNAL OF MEDICINE, approximately 20 percent of discharged Medicare patients return to the hospital within 30 days due to infections, inadequate follow-up, or additional medical problems caused by their surgeries. These readmissions cost billions of dollars annually. (1)

Health insurance is now as vital as automobile or fire insurance. No one wants to have a claim, but if one contracts a major illness, one must have health insurance. A small percentage of Americans are so wealthy that they can afford to self-insure against illness, but over 98 percent of citizens must have health insurance from the day they are born to the day they die. People who cannot afford health insurance are dependent on free clinics. Even with the new 2010 Affordable Care Act, nearly 15 million Americans will still have no health insurance. The National Association of Free Clinics operates a network of 1,200 free clinics that are staffed by volunteers. Unfortunately, too many people avoid these clinics and delay medical care, which makes their illnesses even more expensive and life-threatening.(2)

Other industrial nations spend approximately 10 percent of their GDP (total economy) on health care. The United States currently spends an estimated 18 percent, a figure that is predicted to rise to 20 percent or double what other nations spend. Britain's health care system costs 9 percent, which is 50 percent less than the United States. How did our national health care become so expensive? In 1973, President Nixon and a bipartisan Congress passed The Health Maintenance

Organization Act which required employers with health care benefits to offer HMO plans. The HMO was supposed to be the grand plan to control health care cost through private insurance companies.(3) Instead, the HMO system failed to control health care costs except by rationing care with the following practices:

- Refusing to enroll sick individuals or anyone with a serious past illness.
- Dropping coverage to customers with costly illnesses.
- Refusing to pay benefits if there was a pre-existing condition not disclosed by the patient.

As a result, many Americans who need health care the most cannot afford or obtain it.

Some political leaders believe that Americans need to be more aware of medical costs and should negotiate with medical personnel for fewer treatments, less costly treatments, or lower fees. This approach is not realistic. When people are in pain or in fear of dying, they are in no position to negotiate lower costs. They also do not have the knowledge to determine what treatments they require.

The total cost of health care is currently $2.5 trillion per year. Cost increases in 2008 were 4.4%, in 2009 they were 5.7%, and in the years 2011 to 2019, costs are predicted to rise 6.1% annually according to the Office of Management and Budget.(4) Prescription drug bills are now $246 billion and are expected to grow by 6.3% annually. Hospital bills are projected to increase 6.1% annually. All these increases are coming in a period when inflation is projected to be less than 2%.

Under the current employer-funded insurance system for Americans who are younger than 65 years of age, there is plenty of choice, but also lots of complexity. Doctors who study all the various insurance plans have a difficult time determining which plan is appropriate for their patients. Most Americans call their friends to gain insight on what are the best plans. Corporate Human Resource departments often are unable to write clear and concise documents that describe the pros and cons of each plan. Consequently, millions of mistakes are made every year on health insurance plan selections.

Who Has Good Health Insurance?

Americans over 65 years of age have Medicare (funded by a 2.9% payroll tax that is paid 50% by employers) which is a single pay system administered by the federal government that allows senior citizens to see any doctor they want. President George W. Bush added a prescription drug benefit (D coverage) to Medicare and President Obama is going to close the "doughnut" hole of no payment over several years. Government employees, education, and medical personnel also have very good health insurance that typically features a 20 percent co-pay and an annual deductible. Low-income children have a federal insurance plan. Veterans have the VA Hospital System that covers prescription drugs as well. Millions of Americans have good health insurance that includes prescription drug coverage from their employers. However, these plans now have higher co-pays and larger annual deductibles.

Self-employed, unemployed and underemployed Americans who have no company health insurance plan have the greatest exposure to large medical bills. Too often, they have to declare bankruptcy if they suffer a major illness. In California, the number of uninsured citizens rose from one in five in 2007 to one in four in 2009, a 25 percent increase. In 2010 it was close to 20 percent across the nation.

Nine million Americans lost this health care when they lost their jobs due to layoffs, downsizing and outsourcing. People in the 50-65 age bracket are particularly exposed because employers are reluctant to hire workers who may increase their health insurance costs. Once unemployed, a worker becomes responsible for the entire monthly premium of $1,500 or more to keep a family covered. President Obama included a 65 percent subsidy in the 2009 economic stimulus bill which reduced this monthly cost to $525, but Congress let that subsidy expire on May 31, 2010. Under COBRA, laid-off workers generally can stay on their former health plan up to 18 months, but they must pay the full premium which averages about $13,500 per year. This amount is simply unaffordable for families who have no income.(5) The United States has to protect Americans who are between jobs. In every other major industrial country, a citizen never loses his/her health care after being laid off because health care is funded entirely through payroll taxes. A 2008 survey commissioned by the Commonwealth Fund reported that 82 percent of those surveyed thought the U.S. health care system needed to be overhauled. (6) In the future, numerous companies and not-for-profit organizations may cancel health care as a benefit just as they did for retirement pensions.

Summary of 2010 Affordable Care Act

Many of the 2010 Affordable Care Act benefits will be phased in over several years:(7)

- By the fourth quarter of 2010, insurance companies will not be able to cancel a policy due to pre-existing conditions. Insurance plans will be prohibited from placing lifetime limits on how much they pay to an individual policy holder. Patients will receive a one-year $250 rebate to help pay for medications if they have the Medicare policy. Insurance companies will have to provide coverage for dependent children up to the age of 26. A $5 billion temporary reinsurance program will be created for employers to provide health care coverage for retirees over the age of 55 who are not eligible for Medicare. Small businesses with less than 25 employees and average annual wages of $40,000 will receive tax credits to provide insurance for their employees.
- In 2011, funding will increase by $11 billion for community health centers that provide medical care to Americans who have no insurance. Drug companies will be required to provide a 50% discount on brand-name prescription drugs for seniors who face a gap in drug coverage. By 2020, the "doughnut hole" will be closed. Primary care doctors and general surgeons practicing in areas that lack primary care doctors will receive a 10 percent bonus payment under Medicare. Health insurance companies would be required to provide rebates to enrollees if they spend less than 85% of their premium dollars on health care as opposed to administrative costs. A voluntary long-term care program called CLASS will be created. After at least five years of contributions, enrollees will be entitled to a $50-a-day cash benefit to pay for long-term care.

- In 2012 and 2013, the Medicare tax will increase from 1.45% to 2.35% on earnings over $200,000 for individuals and $250,000 for families. There will also be a 3.8% tax on unearned income.
- In 2014, most Americans will be required to buy health insurance or pay a fine of $95 per individual (up to $285 per family) per month or 1% of taxable household income, whichever is greater. Companies with 50 or more employees will pay a fine if any of their full-time workers qualify for federal health care subsidies.
- By 2014, every state is required by the federal law to create a Health Benefit Exchange to provide a system for small businesses and people without employer based insurance to join together to buy health insurance at lower rates, aided by federal subsidies to low and middle income consumers. California is the first state to establish an Exchange which will benefit millions of its citizens who now pay top dollar for health insurance.
- In 2015 and 2016, penalties will increase for individuals who do not have health insurance.
- In 2018, a 40% excise tax will be imposed on health care plans that cost more than $10,200 for individual coverage and $27,500 or family coverage.

The goal of the 2010 Affordable Care Act is to motivate Americans to have health insurance just as they have automobile insurance. The bill brings over 30 million more Americans into insurance plans, and over 50 percent of Americans will be covered by a government health plan. The new health care law keeps Medicare sound for nearly 12 more years until 2029 and reduces the U.S. deficit by an estimated $143 billion.(8) Over 40 percent of citizens covered by private health care insurance companies will be subject to larger deductibles and higher co-pays, cost increases that will surely be hot topics in future elections. The HMOs will probably continue to raise their rates each year with significant increases for individual policies.

Competition To Lower Costs for Health Care

The federal government will be under great pressure to improve the quality of health care and to reduce costs. The government has a distinct advantage because it operates a nationwide organization with low administrative costs, few marketing expenses, no requirement to achieve record profits each quarter, and no need to pay multi-million-dollar wages and bonuses to senior executives. Former President Bill Clinton delivered a key message at the 2011 Fiscal Summit sponsored by the Peter G. Peterson Foundation in May, 2011. He stated the payment and administrative side of Medicare was doing an excellent job and it would be a mistake to destroy the Medicare program. He also claimed that the delivery of medical services requires substantial changes which have been started by the 2010 Affordable Care Act. He urged both political parties to focus on cost containment and quality changes such as the twelve described below.

1. **Development of Online Diagnostic System**—The current bell curve of inaccurate diagnostic decisions results in major cost with millions of expensive errors in the medical system.
2. **Development of Online Pharmaceutical System**—The current bell-curve of writing prescriptions for patients results in tens of thousands of costly errors in the medical system. Off-label drug prescriptions are also a costly problem.
3. **Implementation of Online Patient Health Records**—Duplicate procedures by multiple doctors in the current system add billions of dollars to the overall cost. The cost for every doctor to maintain medical records for each patient is expensive considering that the majority of Americans are seeing three-to-ten doctors to stay healthy as they age.
4. **Implementation of Best Practices for Procedures**—Unnecessary care kills 30,000 Americans every year, according to estimates made by Dr. Elliott Fisher of Dartmouth Medical School. Dr. Brody at the University of Texas Medical Branch estimates at least $500 billion a year goes towards tests and treatments that do not benefit a patient. Too often, a prescribed treatment just happens to be

the care that costs the most money. A $500 million fund is being established by the government called "comprehensive effective research."

5. **Implementation of Best Practices Within Hospitals**—The current bell-curve of management systems with countless errors adds billions of dollars to the cost of medicine.
6. **Greater Supervision of Medical Personnel To Avoid Health Care Mistakes and Malpractice**—Improvements in this area alone could save billions of dollars.
7. **Move More Procedures To Nurses and Physician Assistants**
8. **Encourage Providers and Insurers To Have An Integrated Medical System for Patients**—Examples include Kaiser Permanente, Mayo and Cleveland Clinics, Geisinger in Pennsylvania, Finland, and New Zealand.
9. **Focus on Cost Containment in Research Studies With Significant Rewards That Are Directed To Cures—Rather Than To Doing Mere Research**
10. **Eliminate Fraud in Medicare and Medicaid**—In 2009, there were more than 275,000 cases of medical information theft in the United States. There are tens of thousands of persons trying to steal money from government health care programs. The new law contains important new tools to help crack down on criminals seeking to scam seniors and steal taxpayer dollars.
11. **Use Medicare Buying Power To Lower the Cost of Prescription Drugs for Medicare and Medicaid**
12. **Reform Medical Malpractice Laws and Consider Malpractice Courts To Provide Realistic Judgments**

A person's final illness is another area in which too many tests and procedures are performed as "dramatic last gestures" that prolong death only by a few days or weeks. If an 89-year-old woman has a stroke in the evening and dies within eight hours, it is common to see hospital bills ranging from $4,000 to $10,000 for such a patient. On the other hand, when young or middle age people are struck down with cancer or other life-threatening diseases, they want to live long enough to see a child graduate from high school, to marry or even to have a child remember them. The medical profession must try to extend those lives.

An article in the March 15, 2010 BLOOMBERG BUSINESS WEEK reported the $618,616 death of a husband and father who had fought cancer for seven years. The 4,750-page mountain of paperwork related to this man's illness showed how insurance companies spend so much on administrative costs. In the end, the wife posed the question "How do you put a price on the last 17 months?"(9) Very wealthy Americans are willing to spend unlimited amounts on their final illness because they can pay for the extra costs, but middle-class and poor people can afford only what their health insurance will cover.

Case Study for Improved Quality and Lower Costs

Since 2001, The Geisinger Health System has operated under the leadership of Dr. Glenn Steele in Danville, Pennsylvania. Geisinger is a fully integrated health care system that started in 1915 with the intended vision of becoming a regional medical center modeled after the Mayo Clinic. Today, it is a physician-led system engaged in health care, education, and research that produces $2.1 billion in revenues. The Geisinger system employs 800 physicians, spans 43 counties over 20,000 square miles, serves a population of 2.6 million, and treats up to 500,000 patients annually. Geisinger also has its own health insurance plan which covers 240,000 members, approximately 30 percent of its patients.

Geisinger calculates it has effectively bent the cost curve and lowered projected spending by nearly 7 percent. Dr. Steele is convinced that improved health care quality lowers costs. He has moved the providing of health care from good intentions and best efforts to a management system that focuses on improved quality and reduced costs. He is aiming for implementing best practices and achieving mastery of performance. The center has reengineered and standardized the medical process. Dr. Steele is eliminating the bell-curve of performance and supplying the proposed Centers for Medicare and Medicaid Services with demonstration projects and randomized clinical trials.

A recent RAND Consulting firm study concluded that somewhere between 40 and 45 percent of what hospitals and doctors practice are either not helpful or may be hurtful. Undoubtedly, if a focus is implemented on measuring the time and cost to cure a patient with best practices, the cost of health care can be reduced.

A new effort called Accountable Care Organization (ACO) will be helpful in determining these best practices. Geisinger is working with Intermountain Health Care, Dartmouth-Hitchcock Medical Center, Mayo Clinic, Cleveland Clinic, and Denver Health on ACO studies. Geisinger is also working with Dr. Don Berwick, the current administrator of the Centers for Medicare and Medicaid Services (CMS).

The question now is whether these leading-edge medical centers that have best practices, high-quality procedures, and lower costs can influence the thousands of hospitals and millions of doctors now operating in the nation's fragmented and disorganized medical system. Now financing more than 50 percent of medical bills, the federal government clearly has an opportunity to play a leadership role. Traditional HMO insurance companies need to take a leadership role in future years. They continue to focus on how much money they can charge for each procedure and how they can ration the number of those procedures. Although it lowers the quality of medical care, this approach increases earnings and compensation packages for senior HMO executives and stockholders. This approach may also lead to price controls which could lower health care quality even further.

Geisinger and other leading health care centers are not socialist organizations. They pay their doctors and all key employees above the national average. Geisinger's compensation from specialty to specialty, on average, is significantly above the Association of American Medical Colleges levels. Their primary care physicians earn more than most private practice primary care physicians.

The information for this case study is based on the June, 2010 article of HEALTH AFFAIRS written by Susan Dentzer, who is the editor-in-chief. It is also based on meetings with Dr. Steele and his staff, who are experts in the field of health care.

Peter Orszag, the first Director of Management and Budget for President Obama, promoted the concept of "best practices" based on the Dartmouth Atlas of Health Care Study. This report stated that $700 billion in annual savings could be achieved by eliminating wide disparities in the cost of similar procedures, especially those in which pricier options do not produce better outcomes. Orszag stated,

"Huge efficiencies could be gained if we change the way we practice medicine." Both political parties need to support major changes in raising the quality of health care while simultaneously lowering costs. It is not helpful at all to have one political party fighting against change and supporting the status quo that guarantees large annual increases in medical care costs.

The October 2, 2010 issue of NEWSWEEK featured an article by Claudia Kalb entitled "Do No Harm: Medical Errors Kill Some 100,000 Americans Every Year. How We Can Reverse The Trend." Recent books by Harvard's Dr. Atul Gawande, *The Checklist Manifesto,* and Johns Hopkin's Dr. Peter Pronovost, *Safe Patients, Smart Hospitals,* are calling on doctors and hospitals to institute checklists of best practices to improve safety modeled on the aviation industry. Undoing a culture is hard, especially one steeped in hierarchy and intimidation where doctors tend to reign supreme and nurses, pharmacists, and technicians often do not speak-up when poor procedures are utilized. What underlies it is arrogance, states Dr. Pronovost, the director of Johns Hopkin's Quality and Safety Research Group. He maintains we have learned to tolerate mistakes.(10) Many leaders in the medical profession are ready and willing to implement quality procedures and measurements. It is important the civil war in Congress does not get in the way of this important effort to improve health care.

Existing and Potential Two-Tiered System

In the United States today, Free Clinics are held in major cities once or twice a year that are staffed by thousands of volunteers, nurses, technicians, and doctors. They serve thousands of Americans, but sadly, only on a hit and miss basis. With millions of citizens currently uninsured and millions more who will not be able to afford health insurance even after the Affordable Care Act is implemented, the country needs a two-tiered system.

In the military, if a service person is ill, he/she goes to a dispensary where medicines and first-aid treatment are available at no charge. Medical technicians handle all patients in the dispensary. If there is a serious medical problem, the patient is sent over to a base hospital to be treated by doctors and registered nurses. This two-tiered system significantly reduces the cost of medical care, ensures quick medical care, and ensures that patients who go to emergency rooms have real medical emergencies.

Some Boston neighborhoods have a medically equipped RV that operates like a dispensary on military bases. The medical technicians in these RVs do not charge for checkups, treatments or prescriptions. This service has been operating for 18 years, and is funded through donations and government grants. Most of the patients are treated for obesity, high cholesterol, hypertension, alcohol abuse, and depression. For every dollar invested in RV's operation, an estimated $36 is avoided in emergency room visits. In Boston, this medical van system spared the health care system over $20 million last year while costing the city only $500,000. There are now 2,000 such mobile health clinics across the country.(11) In Massachusetts, a state with a universal health care plan, spending on health care has increased by 52 percent since the state enacted its own health reform system in 2006.(11) Boston has some world famous hospitals, that are also expensive because of the traditional methods of providing health care employed there.

There are now 46.8 million Americans currently enrolled in Medicaid with 3 million joining since last year, and estimates project that figure will increase to 50 million, which is about 15% of all citizens. This spike in persons turning to Medicaid reflects the millions of Americans who have lost jobs and who are underemployed with no health care.(12) The spurt in Medicaid caseloads has had a damaging impact on federal and state budgets. The country needs more creative solutions on how to provide close-to-free medical care for the unemployed, the underemployed, and families below the poverty line who simply cannot afford the elaborate American health care system. The cost of Medicaid at both state and federal levels has exceeded $400 billion, and in a few years will exceed $500 billion. Before a payroll or VAT tax is required, the federal government should investigate less costly systems for citizens using Medicaid. Governors would support a payroll or VAT tax to fund Medicaid which would solve many of their deficit problems.

How Do Other Countries Pay for Their Health Care Systems?

Opponents of health care reform are always telling stories about delayed or low-quality health care in the government financed health care systems within other countries. In his book *Prescription For Real Healthcare Reform,* Dr. Howard Dean stated, "All other industrial European and North American nations already provide health coverage to all their citizens." Dean claims France has the finest overall system: a single pay and simple administrative system overseen by the government that sets reimbursement fees with physicians and establishes premiums. Anyone can see any doctor at any time without a referral, and the system has the highest satisfaction level among all Europeans countries. Countries with other successful health care systems include Switzerland, the Netherlands, Germany, Great Britain, Australia, and Canada.(13)

Citizens of these countries would never trade what they have for the American system that costs far more and you lose your health insurance if your parents or you lose your job. No other country has a health care system featuring a complex maze of insurance companies, with different forms, different rules, different procedures, and a motivation to deny coverage in order to inflate earnings and their stock values. Our expensive health care system provides great care for wealthy citizens and for upper middle class who work in government or successful corporations. In contrast, millions of Americans have an expensive and second-rate health care system. Yes, there are a few wealthy citizens of foreign countries who come to the United States seeking care at our most famous hospitals, but they represent less than one percent of the citizens from their country.

First Steps To Improve Quality and Reduce Costs

In July 2010, President Obama made the "recess appointment" of Dr. Donald Berwick to administrator of the Centers for Medicare and Medicaid Services (CMS). Dr. Berwick's job is to use the large Medicare and Medicaid programs as laboratories to increase health care quality while simultaneously reducing the costs that now exceed a trillion dollars in government funds. A former professor at the Harvard Medical School, Dr. Berwick has done extensive studies on how these two systems can provide better care at lower cost. This CMS post had been unfilled since 2006 because some Senators were stalling the nomination to score political points. That is why the President used a recess appointment. Health care experts such as Denis Cortese, a former chief executive of the Mayo Clinic, and Tony Cosgrove, chief executive of the Cleveland Clinic, believe our country should use existing public medical programs such as Medicare and Medicaid to create models of lower cost, higher quality care that could be spread nationwide. The President has also directed the Department of Justice to start a "full court press" on reducing fraud in the two medical systems.(14)

Parents and Grandparents Are Supporting Health Reform

Many parents and grandparents have had good health insurance for decades because they had steady employment in the military, government jobs, health care system, education industry, or corporations. Today, their children or grandchildren are not so fortunate. Adults in their 30s, 40s or 50s are often unemployed due to companies downsizing or outsourcing jobs overseas. Often their offspring are working in small organizations that offer minimum or no benefits. Therefore, these citizens support health reform because with inadequate or no health insurance, their children or grandchildren look to parents or grandparents to help pay their medical bills. These bills can run into thousands of dollars. They want their children and grandchildren to have medical insurance from the day they are born to the day they die. In the 2008 Great Recession, too many children returned home with no job and no health insurance, and it became a burden on many parents and grandparents.

Different Strategy Between Political Parties

In his March 25, 2010 column entitled "The Democrats Rejoice," David Brooks stated, "Democrats protected the unemployed starting with the New Deal, then the old, then the poor. Now thanks to health care reform, millions of working families will go to bed at night knowing that they are not an illness away from financial ruin. The Democratic Party has, at its best, come to embody that cause of fairness and family security. Over the past century, Democrats have built a welfare system, brick by brick to guard against the injuries of fate. For the past 90 years or so, the Republican Party has, at its best, come to embody the cause of personal freedom and economic dynamism. In the 19th Century, Republicans built the railroad and the land-grant colleges to weave free markets across great distances."(15)

Unfortunately, the Republican Party is also the party that gave Americans the 1930s Great Depression and the 2008 Great Recession. Americans are no longer impressed with the corporations and leaders who have laid off over 15 million Americans and made our economy stagnant. As Lesson 3 showed, the Republican Party has been a major contributor to the national debt that has the federal government on the road to fiscal ruin.

On health care reform, David Brooks wrote, "Members of the Obama-Pelosi team spent a year on a wandering, tortuous quest—enduring the exasperating pettiness of small-minded members, hostile public opinion, just criticism and gross misinformation, a swarm of sockeyed ideas and the erroneous predictions of people in the press, who thought the odds were against them on health reform."(15) Republicans now want to repeal the reform bill and return to all the problems caused by the HMO system that rations healthcare to increase profits and stock values. To date, over 20 states have filed lawsuits against the Affordable Care Act.

By February 2011, two federal judges ruled the health care law unconstitutional and one federal judge on November 30, 2010 upheld the constitutionality of the act. This means the legality of health reform is on the way to our Supreme Court. The major issue is whether the federal government can mandate all citizens to buy health insurance. Some political leaders want each state to have its own health care system like former Governor Romney implemented in Massachusetts. The Republican Party is trying to sell the concept of 50 laboratories of innovation which sounds good, but would drive up the cost of health care by billions of dollars. Every other nation has a national health care system to drive up quality and to reduce costs. Our country would have a hodge-podge system being great in some states, so-so in many others, and very inadequate in many others. For example, the issue of fluoridated drinking water has taken over 60 years to be implemented in most American cities and millions of Americans still do not have a proven way to reduce cavities while fluoride is used by over 60 percent of citizens in our country. The 50 different health care systems is another illusion.

Opting out of health insurance is a decision to throw oneself on other taxpayers and emergency rooms rather than pay one's own fair share for adequate health care. Mandatory coverage is not the first step on a slippery slope to socialized medicine. It will be a great step in reverse if the health care reform law is declared unconstitutional by the Supreme Court. If that happens, one political party will probably try to sell a phased-in program of "Medicare For All" which will pass the courts' constitutional tests as Medicare has already been approved by the courts. Senior executives of corporations would no doubt support "Medicare For All" because it would eliminate the costly health insurance benefits with a more affordable payroll tax. Senior citizens could also vote for "Medicare For All" because all their children and grandchildren would have health insurance from the day they are born to the day they die.

Unfortunately, the Republican Party has too often been on the wrong side of this debate even though it has had numerous opportunities to make health care more affordable. Much of the 2010 reform bill contains ideas from the 1974 Richard Nixon health care initiative, the proposals Senate Majority Leader Bob Dole made in 1994, and the 2006 health care plan Governor Mitt Romney enacted in Massachusetts. Americans want a comprehensive health care system at a reasonable cost, and both parties should work together to achieve that goal. A high-quality and affordable health care system based on a working partnership between government and private hospitals, supported by doctors in private practice, is not socialized medicine. In the minds of most Americans, health care for all is now a civil right.

Republican congressional leaders were convinced they had a mandate to repeal the health care reform law after their stunning victory in the 2010 mid-term elections. In January 2011, the Republican majority in the House of Representatives voted with a handful of Democrats to repeal the entire law. This would mean over 50 million Americans would not have health insurance. Millions of other Americans would hope their insurance was not rescinded due to pre-existing conditions or their health insurance would not be cancelled if they had a serious illness. A recent government survey revealed 129 million Americans under the age of 65 have pre-existing conditions. Young people would be without health insurance after high school or college until they found an employer who provides health benefits. Republicans have also rejected information provided by the Congressional Budget Office which is a nonpartisan agency rarely criticized for biased information.

There was a belief by Republicans that many Democrats would also vote to repeal the job-killing health care bill, but that did not happen. The Senate voted 51-47 against repeal along party lines. The emotional words of job-killing simply are not believable as the new law helps small businesses offer health insurance and exempts many small businesses from having to be involved with health insurance. When 30 million Americans are added, insurance companies will be adding jobs. As more benefits are phased-in, a majority of Americans support each major improvement and do not want the health insurance reform bill repealed. In a CBS News/NEW YORK TIMES survey, 43 percent of Americans claim the top priority of Congress should be job creation and only 18 percent stated it should be health care.

For years, Republicans had the majority in both houses of Congress and a Republican President and they offered no alternative plan for health insurance as millions of Americans suffered with inadequate or no health insurance coverage. After trying to repeal the reform bill, Republicans have no realistic and affordable alternative plan. Therefore at this time, only one political party is capable of achieving the national goal of Adequate and Affordable Health Care For All Citizens.

Looking back at the 20ᵗʰ Century, there is no doubt the current American health system is much improved over the years where almost every doctor was a general practitioner with a few pills in a black bag as they made house calls. Today, specialization by doctors and advances in treatment and medicines that have been developed over the last 80 years has been a giant step forward which is why Americans live longer than they did 100 years ago. It is now time to take another giant step forward by implementing quality measurements to support "best practices" that will greatly improve the health care system as well as lower costs. The HMOs have not been able to accomplish this, so it is up to the federal government with Medicare, Medicaid and VA hospitals to develop the management systems required to achieve the level of performance that exists today in a few leading edge hospitals.

The airline industry at one time had many crashes and accidents due to inadequate design of aircraft, poor maintenance, pilot errors, inadequate communication and navigation systems as well as inaccurate weather forecasting systems. The airline industry realized that this level of performance was totally unacceptable and they concentrated on having almost no accidents and crashes by implementing improvements in every aspect of the commercial airline system. This is exactly what the health care system must do in the 21st Century. Good intentions have been the main motivation in the past. In the future, it must be quality performance with almost no mistakes which has been accomplished in a few hospitals and medical practices. A few islands of success are not acceptable in this century. It is a leadership challenge. Going from an environment of good intentions to mastery of performance requires several years of outstanding leadership and the education of American citizens to support the required changes which was not accomplished in the first phase of health care reform.

Restructuring the American health care system is one of the greatest challenges facing our political leaders. The Affordable Care Act should be viewed as Phase One. It is trying to build a foundation for Phase Two. In Phase Two, the focus on quality must be expanded to more hospitals and doctors and the government should offer a public option for Americans from age 50 to the Medicare age because these citizens must have health insurance. Unfortunately for this age group, many are laid off due to their higher wage rates and the increase cost of benefits. It is difficult for them to get a job as good as the one they had in their 20s, 30s and 40s. Often the new job offers little or no benefits. The rolls of all unemployed white professional men have more than doubled to a million (not including sales jobs, which add another 300,000). When other categories of unemployed and women are added to this number, there are millions of Americans in this age group without adequate health care. One solution for these people is to become independent contractors and consultants, which means buying very expensive personal health care policies.

Eventually, there probably will be Phase Three of health care reform which will be a well-thought-out single payer universal health care system that will achieve a real breakthrough in cost containment. All of this will require a massive education program by our political leaders because the Kaiser Family Foundation/Harvard School of Public Health survey in January, 2011 found that 20 percent of Americans want to repeal Phase One (Affordable Care Act) and 23 percent want to repeal it and replace it. So only 57 percent want to move forward with common-sense solutions including cutting administrative and bureaucratic costs, giving basic health insurance to the uninsured, closing the doughnut hole for seniors, accepting pre-existing conditions, reforming malpractice laws and using electronic records as well as monitoring doctors and hospitals for quality performance. While there will always be some percentage of citizens who rail against the government being involved in health care, eventually Americans will want our country to be both first in quality care with an affordable system.

No matter who is elected President in 2012, that person and the Secretary of Health and Human Services must continue down the road to improving the cost and quality of the American health care system. This issue will be a major one for many elections to come. It has taken bold leadership by several American Presidents and leaders of Congress to move the United States into the 21st Century for health care, but there still is more work to be done. Medical funding should be separated from Social Security and the General Fund budgets. The Medicare program would be a self-funding government agency which would force both political parties to focus on improving health care quality as well as reducing overall cost.

Paul Ryan Plan for Medicare Is Not Popular

First of all, it is not an accurate statement to claim Medicare will go bankrupt. The only way Medicare goes bankrupt is when one political party refuses to properly fund the health care system for senior citizens, which could happen if voters elect candidates who want to destroy Medicare. But every voter eventually becomes a senior citizen and they will be shocked if they do away with one of the most important programs that enable Americans to have a decent retirement which should be one of our national goals.

The Paul Ryan plan offers a voucher of several thousand dollars to each senior citizen. Then each person must go on the open insurance market and buy an individual health care insurance policy which could cost anywhere from $5,000 to $10,000 more than the voucher depending on age. And with pre-existing conditions that policy for seniors over age 75 could consume the entire income from Social Security, assuming Social Security still exists. Keep in mind, political leaders who will eliminate Medicare as it exists today would not hesitate to eliminate Social Security checks.

The House Republican budget would leave up to 44 million low-income citizens uninsured as the federal government cuts states' Medicaid funding by about one-third over the next ten years, according to a report by nonpartisan groups. Almost one-third of all Americans would have no health insurance.(16) The major change in funding Medicare does not take place for 10 years, which means record deficits during those years.

Pundits and political leaders supporting the Paul Ryan plan always talk about the cost of Medicare (26.5 percent of the unified federal budget), but they never tell how the payroll taxes are a major part of the revenues in the federal budget. Americans have paid into the Medicare insurance system for over 45 years. If the surplus funds had been reserved in a real trust fund, there would not be a problem. Rather than improve the quality of medical treatments which would lower the costs, Paul Ryan wants to destroy the Medicare System. American voters are not stupid and they are not buying his voucher system which could double their costs based on the projections of the Congressional Budget Office. The medical profession, including doctors and hospital administrators, are turning against the Paul Ryan plan which could cost the Republican Party many votes in 2012. It is always easier to inflict severe financial pain on Americans rather than fix a system, but voters want to see Medicare improved—not destroyed.

The belief that market competition can solve all the growth in health care costs is another illusion. There are over 1,000 companies issuing health care insurance and the annual increases have been twice the inflation rate for years. In health care, the consumer has little impact on the price. Patients cannot have a competitive bidding process with dozens of doctors or five hospitals. The Ryan plan solves the cost of health care for the government, but it could bring financial ruin to senior citizens and it is doubtful that any political party will support this in the 2012 general election. Republicans in the House made a grand strategic mistake by approving the Ryan plan and Senators voted down the Ryan plan by 57 to 40 with five Republican Senators voting no.

Americans are beginning to see the cost of health care moving in the right direction. Effective July 1, 2011, the Department of Health and Human Services is reducing premiums by up to 40 percent for citizens in the federally administered Pre-Existing Condition Insurance Plan that is found in 17 states. This plan helps Americans with pre-existing conditions that have medical problems such as arthritis, diabetes, and cancer.

Reducing or eliminating Social Security benefits will add to the economic downturn and it is not politically possible to pull the rug out from under senior citizens. Lesson 7 will explain how to solve the revenue problems of Social Security.

NOTES FOR LESSON 6

1. "Farewell, and Don't Come Back," Ann Carrns, U.S.NEWS & WORLD REPORT, August 2010, pages 20 to 23

2. "The Nation's Biggest Free Clinic," Joel Brenner, PARADE MAGAZINE, SAN DIEGO UNION-TRIBUNE, May 9, 2010, page 6

3. "Health Reform Derailed 36 Years Ago," Alex Tallarida, SAN DIEGO UNION-TRIBUNE, March 5, 2010, B7

4. "Continuing The Fight," A Barry Rand, AARP BULLETIN, March 2010, page 32

5. "Congress Lets Health Care Aid For The Unemployed Expire," Ricardo Alonso-Zaldivar, ASSOCIATED PRESS, SAN DIEGO UNION TRIBUNE, June 13th, 2010, page A5

6. *Killer Politics*, Ed Schultz, Hyperion, 2010, page 67

7. "Health Care: What You Could See," Julie Snider, USA TODAY, March 23, 2010, page 6A

8. "A New Beginning," A Barry Rand, AARP BULLETIN, April 2010, page 26

9. "Lessons Of A $618,616 Death," Charles Babcock, BLOOMBERG BUSINESSWEEK, March 15, 2010, pages 32 to 40

10. "Do No Harm," Claudia Kalb, NEWSWEEK, October 4,m 2010, pages 48 & 49

11. "A Little Van With A Big Impact," Mary Carmichael, NEWSWEEK, July 12, 2010, pages 52 and 55

12. "Medicaid Case Loads Soar In Every State," THE WASHINGTON POST, February 19, 2010, page A3

13. *Prescription For Real Healthcare Reform,* Dr. Howard Dean, Chelsea Green Publishing Company, 2009, pages 99 to 108

14. "Health Care's Change Agent," David Ignatius, THE WASHINGTON POST, SAN DIEGO UNION-TRIBUNE, July 10, 2010, page B6

15. "The Democrats Rejoice," David Brooks, THE NEW YORK TIMES, SAN DIEGO UNION-TRIBUNE, March 25, 2010, page B6

16. "Report Says GOP Budget Plan Would Uninsure Millions," SAN DIEGO UNION-TRIBUNE, May 11, k2011, page A1

LESSON 7

COMMON SENSE ADJUSTMENTS TO SAVE SOCIAL SECURITY

History of the Social Security System

David Gergen, the former White House Communications Director for both political parties, wrote an article in the May 9, 2010 issue of PARADE magazine entitled "How Much Government?" "Seventy-five years ago, President Franklin D. Roosevelt was eager to weave a safety net under millions of impoverished Americans who were retired and had no savings. Republicans argued that it would bankrupt the country and undermine people's habits of thrift and self-reliance. Sound familiar?"

"FDR, ever the master, came up with an ingenious solution: create a program in which Americans would be asked to contribute to a social savings account that government would manage on their behalf and would be there for their retirement. Instead of a big government handout, it would be a partnership that would encourage individual thrift and responsibility." Employers would pay 50 percent of the payroll tax and workers would pay 50 percent.

In August 1935, the most popular and the most simple administratively social program in the country's history was born in the heart of the Great Depression. With a vote of 77 to 6 on final passage, a majority of Republicans finally joined Democrats in the Senate because they did not want to be on the wrong side of history with senior citizens.(1) For the first time in the history of our country, sons and daughters did not have to house and financially support their parents in their retirement years. The "poor" farms and houses began to close across the country.

The original Social Security program provided retirement income to eligible participants (early retirement at 62 years and a full retirement check at 65 years) and to their spouse after they passed away. The program also has a disability income component for participants who lose their ability to work prior to reaching early retirement age. Widows or widowers who lose a working spouse before age 62 years are also eligible to receive a benefit check if they are caring for a child or if they have a disabled child. Benefits were to be tax free. Social Security checks were never intended to be the sole source of a person's retirement income. Checks now average 40% of the income for Social Security participants. Citizens were expected to have personal savings (house, stocks, bonds, bank accounts, etc.) and, until recently, a company pension.

Loss of Company Pensions and New 401k Plans

Many company pensions have been eliminated over the years and replaced with a 401k plan to which some companies contribute. A number of these company matching plans were reduced or eliminated during this current severe recession. As a result, personal savings has become essential for retirement, and Social Security checks are crucial for the millions of Americans who do not earn enough money to setup personal retirement accounts. Current estimates indicate that 35 percent of retirees rely on Social Security for 90 percent of their income. That rate will increase significantly in the future with the loss of company retirement plans because 48 percent of workers over 55 years of age will have total savings and investments of less than $50,000. (2) The average 401k account balance dropped 30 percent in 2008 to just below $46,000, but back to $71,500 which is a fraction of what company pensions used to provide. On average, contributions to 401k plans are 7.3 percent of payroll and that is slightly more than the Social Security tax of 6.7 percent. The projection of an average account with 40 years of contribution is $216,875 which could buy an annuity of $12,000 per year. This is far less than a company pension of $25,000. After nearly three decades of 401k contributions, the average account balance for people nearing retirement age is about $60,000 which is only 10-to-20 percent of a company pension or a Social Security check if an annuity was purchased. (3) All the tax-free contributions going into 401ks, Keoghs, and other retirement schemes reduce federal tax receipts by $193 billion a year. Nearly 80% of the tax breaks for retirement plans go to the top 20 percent of taxpayers which tells us that a small group of citizens have several hundred thousand dollars in their 401k accounts.

The Social Security Administration reports the average U.S. wage for 2009 was $40,712, which is a decrease from 2008. Median household income for the U.S. was $50,221. If a median household made $50,000 per year for 45 years that would amount to $2,250,000. If they set aside 10 percent of each year into a 401k account, it would only amount to $225,000 plus interest. Being able to save that amount from a paycheck at this salary with the cost of living being what it is, is probably unrealistic. For minorities such as African Americans, one-third expect Social Security to be their major source of retirement income.

Current Status of Social Security

Currently, 53 million Americans receive monthly Social Security benefits averaging $1,067 per participant. Social Security is projected to run out of funds by 2037 by using the IOUs in the Social Security Trust Fund.(3)

Social Security is financed largely on a pay-as-you-go basis with the payroll taxes of current workers paying for the Social Security checks of retired workers. Some opponents of Social Security call this system a Ponzi scheme. With the exception of life insurance, all insurance would be considered a Ponzi scheme because some people collect more benefits than others. For example, when an American buys fire insurance, he or she hopes not to need the benefit, but knows the benefit payment may far exceed the annual premiums if there is a fire. If a single person dies at 62 years of age, he or she will never collect a dollar of Social Security benefits. People who live pass ninety, on the other hand, collect much more than they paid in payroll taxes.

Many conservative Republicans were against Social Security, including Ronald Reagan when he was a spokesperson for the American Medical Association in the 1950s. They were afraid Social Security would be expanded to cover health care for retirees. President Eisenhower, much to the great disappointment of conservatives, expanded Social Security to include disabled Americans. President Nixon encouraged Congress to pass an automatic cost-of-living plan in the 1970s. Some political leaders call Social Security a form of welfare. When Americans pay thousands of dollars each year over a 45-to-50-year period, it is not a welfare check—it is a pension check.

No Cash in the Social Security Trust Fund

In 1982, the Social Security fund was about to pay out more than it collected in payroll taxes. President Reagan reacted by convincing Congress to tax Social Security benefits for the middle class, reducing payment by 10-to-20 percent. He also created a bipartisan commission headed by Alan Greenspan to solve the Social Security revenue problems after his budget director David Stockman's proposal for a large reduction in benefits was rejected by the Senate with a 96 to 0 vote. This commission agreed to increase the payroll tax to 6.2 percent per worker with a matching 6.2 percent by an employer and to shift the retirement age gradually from 65 years to 67 years of age over a 12-year period. These increases would keep the Social Security fund solvent until 2060 in order to provide full benefits to the "baby-boomer" generation.

In the 1960s, President Johnson unified the federal government budget in order to combine the General Fund, the Social Security Trust Fund, and the Medicare Trust Fund. This revised budget enabled him to use the surplus from the Social Security and Medicare Trust Funds to reduce the size of the annual deficit caused by the Vietnam War. The surplus was not all that large in those days, but after the payroll tax for both Social Security and Medicare rose to 15.3 percent, $2.4 trillion of surplus had accumulated for the large "baby-boomer" generation's benefits. By law, this surplus was supposed to be invested in Treasury special-issue securities in order to earn the going rate of interest. These securities are government IOUs much like Treasury Bonds. The United States should not default on Social Security bonds any more than they would default on Treasury bonds that are owned by foreign governments, financial institutions and American citizens. Since President Johnson, every White House continued to take the surplus cash generated by the payroll taxes from the Trust Funds and spend it on General Fund expenses such as interest, defense, and health care. The exception was Vice President Gore and President Clinton who wanted to put real bonds into a "lock box" to ensure Social Security benefits could be paid well into the 21ˢᵗ Century. This plan was abandoned soon after the Supreme Court decided George W. Bush had won the presidential election in 2000. President Bush's ensuing tax cuts, military build-up, pre-emptive wars, nation-building projects, and occupations of Iraq and Afghanistan created record deficits from 2002 to 2008, so there is no cash in the Social Security Trust Fund. However few Americans realized how these payroll tax increases represented a second income tax on employees and employers rather than cash for pensions.

Practical Solutions for Social Security

Amazing enough, the Social Security revenue shortage can be resolved with a combination of changes. The $2.4 trillion in special-issue U.S. government securities are currently not listed as liabilities on the government financial statements. New and higher tax revenues will be needed to payoff these securities in the future. Here are some suggested recommendations from which to choose:

1. Reduce the cost-of-living adjustments by half a percent and implement a "cap" on the annual indexing.
2. Raise the early and normal retirement age from 62 to 65 years and raise the normal retirement to 70 from 67 years over a 20-year period. Today nearly half of Social Security recipients choose to begin getting benefits at age 62. If the retirement age is 70, there must be an extra effort to end age discrimination for employees 55 years and older. Today, companies do not want to hire older employees because a number will have major illnesses from 55 to 70 years old. This problem does not exist in nations with government single pay health care systems, but it is a problem for American companies because of the higher premiums that insurance companies charge for older employees. No other country has a retirement age over 67 years. Only Norway and Denmark have 67 years as a retirement age. The majority of countries have 65 years as the age to retire.
3. Gradually increase the cap on taxable wages from $106,800 in 2009 to approximately $150,000. Some political leaders

believe the cap should be raised to $250,000 or eliminated altogether.

4. Increase payroll taxes to 6.5 or 7.3 percent.
5. Some conservatives want to "means test" Social Security payments which would result in reduced benefits for wealthy and middle-class retirees. This approach is fundamentally wrong because workers paid into this system under the pledge that they would receive a monthly check in their senior years. With few company pensions and with the 401k Plans looking more like 201k Plans, Americans need their Social Security checks. Less than two percent of the population would not have their standard of living impacted if their checks were "means tested." Wealthy Americans who do not need their Social Security checks could donate the money to their favorite charity or just not sign up to receive Social Security benefits.

President Bush tried to solve the Social Security problem in 2005, but Congress did not buy his strategy for several reasons. To enable workers to invest their Social Security money in the stock market would have increased the national debt by one trillion dollars. This money would have been needed to replace the payroll tax revenues in the existing pay-as-you-go system that funded the benefits of retirees who were receiving monthly checks. President Bush never achieved bipartisan support for this "ownership society" concept because Americans want a secure pension check rather than a hope that the stock market will increase their benefits every year. If President Bush's plan had been adopted, middle-age workers would have experienced two shocks to their investments in 2008: their 401k plans decreasing by 50 percent and their Social Security individual accounts also losing 50 percent of value. It would have been a disaster. In 2010, when the market dropped 998 points in just one day, Americans would have felt yet another shock. This approach to the Social Security revenue shortage should not be promoted by either political party at this time as it is an illusion.

At the end of January 2010, new congressional projections disclosed that Social Security will post nearly $600 billion in this decade in deficits over revenue from the Social Security payroll taxes which supported an article by Charles Krauthammer, "Still An Empty Lockbox." In 2011, the projection is $45 billion which means money will have to be borrowed as there is no cash in the Social Security Trust Fund. Much of this revenue problem is due to the Great Recession of 2008 and the weak economy that has existed from 2007 to 2011 which could last additional years.(4) In addition, the number of early retirements has increased because many Americans who are in their 60s were laid off and cannot find new jobs. This situation shows the President and Congress they must make some adjustments in Social Security benefits to increase revenues by an average of $60 billion per year during the next ten years.

Political Solution To the Social Security Problem

The bipartisan Committee On Fiscal Responsibility and Reform believes that Social Security is one of the most important problems for our county to solve. Now that the federal bipartisan Deficit Reduction Commission has issued its report after the midterm election in 2010, the President and Congress will need to address the recommendations so this issue can be resolved long before the general election in 2012. The majority of Americans do not want a reduction in their Social Security checks.

Unfortunately, there is so much inaccurate information about the availability of Social Security checks for future generations of Americans, that young and middle-age voters are often convinced they will never receive a Social Security check. This is another illusion. If the age for receiving a full Social Security check is increased to 68, this means Americans will work for 45-to-50 years before they retire. The average American will only enjoy ten years of retirement. Therefore, the myth that only two workers will be supporting a retiree in 2040 is a false statement. Our country continues to have more births and immigrants than deaths which states there will be about four workers supporting each retiree just as it is today. Our country has had growth in population throughout its entire history. In 1940 there were 132 million citizens, in 1980 there were 226 million, in 2010 the number was 309 million with a 9.7 percent growth since 2000. The Millennium generation, those born between 1979 and 1997, are roughly 80 million which is five million more than the baby boomers who were born between 1946 and 1964. The average annual income from Social Security based on a cost-of-living adjustment will grow from $12,804 today to $15,000 in the future which will be funded by the four-or-five Americans working for every retiree collecting a Social Security check. Under no circumstances should Americans be asked to put 6.2 percent of their wages for 45 or more years into a government pension and then be told there is no pension when they become 65 years old. Most employees are not that productive after 68 years of age, so there is a limit to how high the retirement age should be raised.

Like the Medicare program, Social Security should be established as a separate government agency that is self-funding to protect its surplus funds from being used by the General Fund. Hopefully, the final legislation will include a feasible plan to keep Social Security Trust Fund surpluses in real government bonds or AAA corporate bonds, rather than in IOUs, so there will be cash surpluses for years to come.

A consensus appears to be building to slowly move the retirement age from 67 years to 68 by one month every two years after it reaches 67 years under the current law. The cost-of-living adjustment would be lower due to a new calculation on CPI. Newly hired state and local government employees would be included in Social Security after 2020. The taxable maximum amount would be increased to capture 90 percent of wages by 2050. The age for early retirement would be moved from 62 years to 64 years which would help workers who have physically demanding jobs to still retire early.

This issue may show our nation how well the Democratic and Republican parties can work together in the new Congress after the midterm elections of 2010. Their civil war needs to give way to a greater effort of bipartisanship that will solve national problems. Social Security adjustments in 2011 would not damage either political party for the 2012 election if it is done with a large positive vote by both parties. It will also take great leadership by the President of the United States to solve the Social Security revenue crisis. Social Security benefits should not be funded from the General Fund. The President should appoint a bipartisan commission in 2011 to solve Social Security revenue requirements.

One dark cloud hanging over the Social Security System is the tax compromise agreement President Obama made with congressional leaders of the Republican Party in late 2010. Payroll taxes for Social

Security in 2011 are reduced from 6.2 percent to 4.2 percent which means the country has to borrow nearly $300 billion in 2011 to adequately fund Social Security benefits. This is truly a second economic stimulus package projected to create 1.3 million jobs. Whether Congress will restore the Social Security tax to 6.2 percent in 2012 or 2013 is truly the question.

In October 2010, Barry Rand, CEO of AARP, published a survey that showed the 50 year old plus voter has the following concerns:

90% are concerned about jobs
89% are concerned about the stability of Social Security
88% are concerned about the cost of health care
85% are concerned about annual budget deficits
80% are concerned about wars in Iraq and Afghanistan
78% are concerned about energy costs

This group has had the highest percentage of voters in past elections. Barry Rand also stated that they feel vulnerable and many believe their security is under attack. They feel the problems facing our country are too great for the intense partisanship in politics today.(5) And they believe a political party that would eliminate Medicare would eventually eliminate Social Security.

Now that we have examined the Social Security revenue problem, it is time to read about a much more challenging financial concern for our nation: the affordable size of the military budget.

NOTES FOR LESSON 7

1. "How Much Government," David Gergen, PARADE MAGAZINE, May 9, 2010, page 15
2. "Facing Up To A Pension Crisis," George F. Will, THE WASHINGTON POST, SAN DIEGO UNION-TRIBUNE, May 18, 2010, page B6
3. "I'll Say It Again: Dump the 401(k)," Teresa Ghilarducci, BLOOMBERG BUSINESSWEEK, July 25, 2010, page 56
4. "Huge U.S. Social Security Deficit Looms," Stephen Ohlemacher, ASSOCIATED PRESS, SAN DIEGO UNION-TRIBUNE, January 28, 2011, page A4
5. "A Chance To Make A Difference," A Barry Rand, AARP BULLETIN, October 2010, page 32

PART III

REDUCING THE SIZE AND COST OF GOVERNMENT

The General Fund includes all revenues and expenses, except those of Social Security and Medicare, and will soon have a $16 trillion debt projected to be approximately $20 trillion by 2016. Leaders of Defense/Intelligence/Homeland Security/Veterans' Benefits, Education, and Health Care have not focused on cost containment, and their areas of the General Fund have long ago left the boundaries of being affordable. These government departments have had large annual increases for over ten years when revenues only grew by seven percent. "Tinkering-around-the-edges" to control costs is not sufficient leadership. Leaders must develop and implement systemic change to eliminate this crisis in management which has resulted in the current financial crisis. There must be five separate Presidential Commissions, including one to recharge the private enterprise system, focusing on these four excessive spending areas. The fifth commission must focus on economic growth and job creation. This section of the book provides a blueprint for reducing both the size and cost of government over a four-to-eight-year period.

LESSON 8

REDUCTION IN THE COST OF MILITARY AND VETERANS BENEFITS

Escalating Costs for Preemptive Wars

When President Truman entered the Korean Civil War and when President Johnson escalated the United States' involvement in the Vietnam Civil War, they both believed our superior American military forces would achieve a quick victory and their approval ratings would rise. When the Chinese entered the Korean War, it turned into a no-win situation lasting until President Eisenhower approved an armistice three years later. The Korean War cost our taxpayers billions of dollars and 157,530 casualties, including 38,000 soldiers killed in action. Millions of Koreans were killed or wounded and 90 percent of their country was damaged or destroyed. The Vietnam Civil War involved American troops for eight years with 58,000 servicemen killed in action and several hundred thousand wounded. Millions of Vietnamese were also killed or wounded. The cost was several hundred billion dollars. Was all this blood and money worth the sacrifices? That debate still rages on today.

In both of these wars, Presidents Truman and Johnson with the help of Congress passed a surtax on income tax to help pay for the wars, which reduced the impact on the national debt. By the end of both wars, American voters were upset over the cost of these wars as well as the number of casualties. Voters also believed the country had gained little or nothing from these wars, so they ended the political careers of both Truman and Johnson.

When President Bush (43), Vice President Cheney, and Secretary of Defense Rumsfeld sold Americans on the preemptive invasion of Iraq and the participation in a civil war in Afghanistan, they decided to borrow trillions of dollars for their War on Terror rather than add a surtax to the income tax. Their 2001 tax cuts and the War on Terror doubled the national debt to $10 trillion. The decision to staff the war with a volunteer military service which included the National Guard and Reserves added billions of dollars due to a series of pay raises and bonuses needed to maintain adequate reenlistments under the very stressful conditions in Iraq and Afghanistan. In addition, hundreds of thousands of contract personnel were hired to staff the war effort. For example, there were 100,000 U. S. military personnel and over 50,000 contract personnel in Afghanistan by the end of 2010. To maintain this War on Terror and to spread freedom to many Middle Eastern, Asian, and African countries, a 25 percent surtax or VAT tax would need to be passed in 2012. Political experts do not believe any Congress could sell such an increase in taxes, so the War on Terror needs to be phased down. President Bush (43) signed an agreement to end the Iraq occupation by 2011, and President Obama has indicated American forces will start leaving Afghanistan in 2011 with a potential end date of 2014. With the War on Terror lasting from 2002 to 2014, it has cost our country an estimated $5 trillion in borrowed money.

Only recently has the Secretary of Defense started sending signals to our military services leadership that the "open checkbook" for the War on Terror is coming to an end. He has told the Pentagon to reduce administrative costs by more than $100 billion.(1) The major military contractors are now concerned because they have enjoyed record profits ever since military spending soared after the 9/11 terrorist attacks. If the $100 billion is spread over 10 years, that will amount to only a 1 percent reduction. If it is spread over 5 years, it will be a 2 percent reduction. The $100 billion figure sounds impressive, but it is really a small reduction when one considers the total defense budget plus veterans' benefits, medical costs (active duty and retired), intelligence agencies, homeland security, and interest on borrowed money which now exceeds one trillion dollars.

Our military services continue to spend as if the War on Terror will go on for decades. They built a half-billion-dollar prison camp at Guantanamo Bay(2), and are in the process of building a $100 million Special Operations headquarters in Afghanistan. The Special Operations forces are now operating in approximately 73 countries with expansion planned for Asia, Middle East, Africa, and South America, funded by a multi-billion-dollar budget.(3) A secret directive signed in September, 2009 by General Petraeus authorized sending U.S. Special Operations troops to both friendly and hostile nations to gather intelligence and build ties with local military forces. Its goals are to build networks that can penetrate, disrupt, defeat or destroy al-Qaeda and other militant groups, as well as to prepare the environment for future attacks by U.S. or local military forces.(4)

Accordingly, other nations believe our military wants to be the policemen of the world, and wants to expand its regime change strategy. This approach led to the Iran Contra scandal that rocked President Reagan's administration, the two preemptive wars, and the terrorists' bombings in Uganda, Somali, Yemen, and Saudi Arabia that killed and/or wounded hundreds of people.

Required Change in Foreign Policy

For decades during the Cold War, the United States and its allies maintained a foreign policy which avoided wars and contained the threat of Communism. Eventually, the Soviet Union collapsed, the Warsaw Pact countries of Eastern Europe, China, and even Vietnam adopted a more capitalistic economy, and the war threat decreased. Cuba was also contained even though it still has a socialistic economy. In addition, over the past two decades, nine former Soviet Union states have joined the NATO alliance.

Our country's foreign policy changed after September 11, 2001 when President Bush (43) and Vice President Cheney announced their War on Terror. Like Presidents Truman and Johnson, they expected quick victories and a spike in their approval ratings. A declassified Army plan from 2002 stated the U.S. government expected to have only 5,000 soldiers in a peaceful and well-run Iraq by 2008. Instead, it became embroiled in an unaffordable nine-year war. President Obama is now transitioning back to a foreign policy strategy that has the United States trying to contain terrorism rather than obliterate it through costly preemptive wars, years of occupying hostile countries, and multi-billion-dollar nation-building projects. Terrorists can operate out of at least 50 different countries in the Middle East, Africa, Asia, and the Pacific Islands, so it is not feasible to have preemptive wars, regime changes, and occupations in that many countries. History has also proven no other nation can successfully occupy an Islamic country.

President Obama and Secretary of State Hillary Clinton are determined to change our foreign policy. In May, 2010, President Obama told West Point graduates, "The burdens of this century cannot fall on our soldiers alone. It also cannot fall on American shoulders alone. Diplomacy and muscle must work together with a renewed engagement from diplomats, along with development experts, intelligence, and law enforcement agencies, and first responders."(5)

Political opponents believe President Obama is too soft. They want him to behave like President Bush and Vice President Cheney, even though their aggressive style turned off our allies, cost us trillions of borrowed dollars, and cost thousands of Americans their lives. Queen Elizabeth II recently stated, "It has perhaps always been the case that the waging of peace is the hardest form of leadership of all."(6)

While some American politicians want to view Russia and China as future enemies to justify a massive military organization, it makes no financial sense to create enemies for such a purpose. The United States has to have friendly relations with as many nations as possible. There will always be some nations causing trouble in the world. For example, North Korea has been a troublemaker for decades, but has been contained by China, Russia, Japan, and South Korea as well as the United States. Even if North Korea has a nuclear bomb, it cannot use it without destroying itself. Americans must accept the fact that some parts of the world will always be messy and it is not our responsibility to fix every problem. Iran is another troublemaker that is building nuclear power plants. If the United States puts a defense umbrella over the Middle East, Iran will not be able to use any super bomb or missile without destroying its country.

President Obama and his Secretaries of State and Defense are working hard to reduce the number of nuclear bombs in the world. President Obama and President Medvedev of Russia have signed a treaty to slash their nuclear arsenals to the lowest levels in half a century. These initiatives are supported by former Secretaries of State George Schultz, Henry Kissinger, Colin Powell, former Secretary of Defense Bill Perry, a former Chairman of the Armed Forces Committee, Sam Nunn, and

other political leaders. The Senate ratified these new agreements with the required 67 votes.

One major advantage of the global economy is the fact it is in the interest of all industrial countries to avoid wars because wars can trigger recessions and depressions in the participating countries and can bankrupt them after the war. After World War II, Thomas J. Watson, CEO and founder of IBM, adopted a slogan of "World Peace Through World Trade." His vision could become a reality in the 21st Century.

Adequate Defense Organization in the 21st Century

In 2000, the United States had a defense budget of $304 billion which was funded by income tax revenues in the General Fund. This funding covered eleven aircraft carriers and over 50 submarines that were part of the largest and most powerful Navy (283 ships) in the world. Our Air Force was vastly superior to any other country's Air Force with 50 squadrons of aircraft. Our Marine Corps, Army, Navy, and Air Force totaled nearly 1.5 million service personnel.(7) We also had thousands of tanks and other combat vehicles. This military might was sufficient enough to invade Iraq and fully occupy the country within weeks, and it also destroyed the al-Qaeda terrorists' bases within weeks in Afghanistan.

Wartime Defense Budget

In 2008, the United States defense budget was $711 billion (actual spending was $767 billion) while the total worldwide defense budget of all nations was $1,475 trillion. The U.S. defense budget was 48 percent of the worldwide budget, but spending exceeded 50 percent. The following chart lists the expenditures in other areas of the world:

Country	Defense Budget	% of Total Budget
Europe (All countries)	$289 billion	20%
China	$122 billion	8%
East Asia & Australia	$120 billion	8%
Central & South Asia	$30 billion	2%
Russia	$70 billion	5%

Middle East/No. Africa	$82 billion	5%
Sub-Saharan Africa	$10 billion	1%
Latin America	$35 billion	3%

The British Navy has been reduced to 56 ships and 39,000 personnel with a further reduction slated in the coming years. Many countries are reducing their military budgets due to the deficits created by the Great Recession.

The U.S. military had 1,840,002 personnel in 2005 and, with contractor personnel, the number soared to over two million. There were also 473,306 Defense Department civil service employees and 203,328 local hires. The U.S. military owns 737 bases in 63 foreign countries on 687,347 acres of land. In the United States, there are hundreds of military bases on over 29 million acres of land.(8) Another study in 2008 claimed the United States defense spending exceeds the next largest 14 budgets combined from other countries. Not one of these 14 nations is an enemy of our country. In 2010, defense expenses expanded to $889 billion according to the 2010 Financial Report of the United States Government that included accrual for pensions.

Five years after the United States invaded Iraq, Nobel Laureate and former World Bank chief economist Joseph Stiglitz co-authored *The Three Trillion Dollar War: The True Cost Of The Iraq Conflict* with Harvard professor Laura Bilmes. According to this book, one of the largest defense costs will be future health care and disability costs for veterans. After factoring in the cost of weapons and operations, health care, interest on debt, and future borrowing, these authors believe that the Iraq and Afghanistan wars will actually cost America $5 to $7 trillion.(9) This is all borrowed money which is one major reason why the national debt has soared from five trillion to $15 trillion. Tax cuts, the 2008 Great Recession, and unemployment during the war years also contributed to this mountain of debt.

The United States cannot be the policemen of the world and cannot spend trillions of dollars to spread freedom throughout the world. Citizens of the Soviet Union finally realized that it was costing trillions of dollars to try to spread Communism throughout the world. They revolted and the Soviet Union collapsed. Their military services were significantly reduced and their senior citizens, who had survived World War II, suffered major reductions in their pensions. Today, Russia is doing nation-building within its own country and its citizens are supporting these strategic directions by 72 percent. In order to prevent a revolt by American taxpayers who want to rebuild their national infrastructure, the Defense Department must develop a strategic plan to downsize to around $500 billion (66 percent increase over 2000 budget) which would maintain a vastly superior defense organization which existed in 2000 at $300 billion.

What Has Been Gained By the Iraq War?

The first justification for entering into the preemptive invasion of Iraq was the intelligence reports claiming Iraq had or would soon have weapons of mass destruction. This claim proved to be false information. The second justification was that Iraq was serving as an al-Qaeda training ground for planning terrorist attacks, but there were no al-Qaeda groups in Iraq before the invasion. Americans were then told Iraq would emerge as a model of democracy that would spread throughout the Middle East. In reality, after the United States spent trillions of dollars to invade Iraq, to occupy it for nearly eight years under hostile conditions, and to invest billions of dollars in nation-building projects, Iraq is now anything but a model of democracy.

President Bush was pressured by Iraq's leaders to sign an agreement promising that all U.S. military troops would be withdrawn from Iraq by the end of 2011. At the peak of the war, there were 160,000 military personnel and close to 90,000 contract workers (250,000 Americans) involved in the occupation. Nearly 4,400 Americans were killed, 38,000 were seriously wounded, and many thousands more were treated for mental problems and minor injuries at military and veterans' hospitals. The cost of the war has been understated by our military and political leaders, and is now in the trillions of dollars. All this effort and money has failed to prevent al-Qaeda from carrying out bomb attacks on Iraqis who work with Americans or the Iraqi government. A majority of Americans believe the war was not worth our efforts and almost everyone wants to see it end. Some conservative political leaders and a few journalists state the war was a success because Saddam Hussein was killed, but these people represent a shrinking minority view of the war.

The vast majority of Iraqis do not accept the American invasion as a positive event. Unemployment reached 35 percent in Iraq and nearly every government agency was destroyed. Citizens lost billions of dollars in investments, real estate, and pensions. Two million Iraqi citizens were forced to leave their homes. Thousands of homes and businesses were destroyed as were mosques and religious buildings. Public utilities, roads, bridges, transportation systems, government buildings, museums, and parks were also destroyed. Worse yet, hundreds of thousands of men, women and children were killed or wounded during the civil war and occupation. Electricity is spotty, and with temperatures exceeding 100 degrees on many days, living conditions are intolerable. A food shortage has persisted throughout the country. Thousands of Iraqis were imprisoned in detention centers and jails under deplorable conditions. Sunni Arabs, Shiites, and Kurds needed months to decide who should be the Prime Minister of Iraq. Their government barely functions and bombings are a daily event. There is no sign of a great Iraqi democracy arising from the ashes of war. Iran has been elevated to a leadership role in the Middle East, and Israel is in much greater danger today than it was before the Iraq invasion. The departing General claimed it would take three-to-five years to determine if the war was worth our efforts. In Vietnam, it took only two years.

One justification for the Iraq War that President Bush (43) offered was to spread freedom throughout the Middle East. One major part was to be freedom of religion which Islamic countries are determined not to tolerate. Christians in Iraq are being persecuted, their churches are attacked, and their clergy have been killed or run out of the country. With Iran gaining more influence in the Middle East, freedom of religion is just another illusion that has failed in the War on Terror.

In 2010, the United States maintained 94 military bases in Iraq with 50,000 non-combat troops. After our military forces leave, the State Department will be responsible for working with the Iraqi government through the largest embassy in the world employing 2,400 Americans in Baghdad and through two $100 million outposts to head off potential confrontations between the Iraqi army and Kurdish peshmerga forces. There will also be 7,000 security contractors to form a "quick reaction force" to rescue Americans in trouble plus thousands of vehicles, planes, and helicopters to support our personnel.(10) Simply put, Iraq will be the largest and most expensive State Department location in the world at over $5 billion annually.

The State Department's influence will be directly dependent upon how many billions of American taxpayer dollars are available to influence Iraqi decisions. If Congress reduces these funds as it did in Vietnam, the Iraqis could tell Americans to go home. Our military leaders are trying to sell Prime Minister Al-Maliki on a long-term strategic partnership in which the United States would combine training Iraq's military and police forces plus other security assistance. This training will cost billions of additional dollars. So far, the Prime Minister states no American troops should be in Iraq after 2011 and there were riots in Baghdad at the thought of troops remaining.

What Could Be Gained From the Afghanistan War?

Our war in Afghanistan started in 2002. President Obama has stated we will start withdrawing our troops after July, 2011. A majority of Americans would like the war to be concluded by the end of 2012. President Kurzai has entered into an agreement with the U.S. and international partners to support the training of Afghan forces up to 2014, which is the end of his term in office. President Obama has an exit plan, but he has not signed any agreement as President Bush (43) did to phase down the Iraq War by 2011. It is always difficult to withdraw from a civil war. General Petraeus made it possible to phase down the Iraq War and hopes to do the same in Afghanistan. Over 150,000 Americans as well as billions of dollars in equipment need to be shipped home from Afghanistan which has no seaport. President Bush never provided sufficient resources to achieve a positive ending to our involvement in Afghanistan. Therefore, President Obama had to develop a plan which he did with General Petraeus.

President Obama was realistic to the point where he established a limited goal, "to disrupt, dismantle, and defeat al-Qaeda." That strategy does not include winning a civil war against the Taliban. It does include training the Afghan army and police so U.S. troops can start the costly phase-down in July, 2011 and so the Karzai government can continue its civil war with the Taliban or seek a peace treaty. This ending of the war could have been achieved in 2002 or 2003. If the Taliban did not live up to its agreement, the United States could have attacked with bombers, drones, and Special Forces. CIA Director Leon Panetta estimated in 2010 that the number of al-Qaeda in Afghanistan to be "60-to-100, maybe less."(11) There is no way to justify the tens of billions of dollars, over 150,000 Americans, and thousands of American casualties for this limited threat. The time has come to phase down and leave Afghanistan as quickly and honorably as possible especially now that Osama bin Laden is dead.

The United States had every right to send in the CIA and Special Forces in late 2001 to try to eliminate the al-Qaeda forces in Afghanistan who executed the 9/11 attack on the United States. That approach proved to be a successful strategy and those Americans should have been pulled out after their victories. It was a tragic mistake to take on the Taliban in a ten-year civil war. National Security Advisor General Jim Jones, in an interview with David Ignatius at the White House, stated, "The Taliban generally as a group has never signed on to the global jihad business and doesn't seem to have ambitions beyond its regions."(12) The United States has spent billions of dollars over several years in training Afghan National Police and they simply are not effective. Many desert after their training.(13) The United States trains our troops in less than six months before sending them into battle, but training Iraq and Afghanistan soldiers and police takes years for some unknown reason. In 2010, 134,000 Afghan National Army troops and 109,000 police officers were on the U.S. payroll.

Donald Rumsfeld, a former Secretary of Defense, vowed to fight a different kind of war. In days following the 9/11 attack, Rumsfeld spoke about how American's success in Afghanistan depended on the U.S. military being seen as liberators, not infidel invaders. Secretary Rumsfeld sent in citizen soldiers, with day jobs as judges, lawyers, carpenters and clerks into the Afghanistan countryside to restore electricity, build roads, and spread good-will. "While we may engage militarily against foreign governments that sponsor terrorism, we may seek to make allies of the people these governments suppress," Rumsfeld stated in a speech on September 27, 2001. Days later, he proclaimed on Fox News, "We want to make sure that we can do everything we can to help the misery of the Afghan people, which has been imposed on them by Al Qaeda and by the Taliban leadership.(14) But as Rumsfeld's new memoir, *Known And Unknown,* makes clear, his heart was never really in that fight. "I did not think resolving other countries' internal political disputes, paving roads, erecting power lines, policing streets, building stock markets, and organizing democratic governmental bodies were missions for our men and women in uniform . . . The risk was that those nations could become wards of the United States," Rumsfeld stated.(14)

The war in Afghanistan is similar to the final phase of the Vietnam War. Only a minority of Americans and members of Congress believe there will be a great victory. Our country will not support hundreds of billions of dollars for a nation-building program in Afghanistan like the ones that failed in Vietnam and Iraq. It is an illusion to think that the United States can invade Islamic nations, occupy them for years, and produce a model of democracy. Our political and military leaders need to stop selling this illusion.

Information Provided in Bob Woodward's Book

Bob Woodward's October 2010 book, *Obama's Wars*, is a great title for selling books, but clearly President Obama has no intention of claiming title to either war any more than Eisenhower did with the Korean War or Nixon wanted to claim title to the Vietnam War. The Korean War was President Truman's war, and the Vietnam War belonged to President Johnson even though Nixon took four years to end it.

At the back of Bob Woodward's book are six pages (385-390) that contain President Obama's Final Orders For Afghanistan/Pakistan Strategy or Term Sheet, dated November 29, 2009. In summary, these orders state, "The United States' goal in Afghanistan is to deny safe haven to al Qaeda and to deny the Taliban the ability to overthrow the Afghanistan government. The strategic concept for the United States, along with our international partners and the Afghans, is to degrade the Taliban insurgency while building sufficient Afghan capacity to secure and govern their country, creating conditions for the United States to begin reducing its forces by July 2011. In each area secured by U.S. forces, the agreed concept and goal are to accelerate transition to Afghan authorities in 18-to-24 months from July 2009, then to adjust the mission and thin out U.S. forces in that area." Woodward's book is clear: the goal is to achieve a decent exit from the Afghanistan War just as we are doing in Iraq.

On June 22, 2011, President Obama announced that 10,000 soldiers would leave Afghanistan by the end of 2011 and 23,000 more would be out by the end of the summer of 2012. His plan is to completely phase out of the Afghanistan War by 2014 which is three and a half more years. Of course, this withdrawal could be accelerated at the NATO meeting in August 2012 if public opinion begins to move much higher than the 56 percent of Americans who now want the war to end as soon as possible. Congress will, no doubt, have a great influence if they decided to reduce funding for the war and support of Afghanistan as they did in 1975 for Vietnam. When Americans and Congress realize the War on Terror actually has cost substantially more than a $1 trillion, there could be great pressure to end the war by 2013. This war will go down in history as less than a success story, and it should be used as a case study at the War College on the disadvantages of invading and occupying Islamic countries for long term periods.

How Much Has the War on Terror Cost Taxpayers?

It is difficult to obtain an accurate cost figure for the War on Terror and there are many estimates given in hundreds of reports and articles. Using the federal government financial statements and starting with year 2001 as the last year of peace and 2014 as the predicted end of the Iraq and Afghanistan wars, the statements tell us the cost of this War on Terror is approximately $5 trillion.

Some other estimates have ranged from $3 to $7 trillion. There will be additional costs in the future for replacing equipment destroyed or left behind. Medical costs for wounded and disability pensions will go on for decades. Americans should never forget that at the end of 2010, 4,420 U.S. service members had been killed in the Iraq War and 1,341 killed in the Afghanistan War for a total of 5,761. With the future predictions of casualties in 2011 to 2014 in Afghanistan, more than twice as many Americans will have been killed in the War on Terror than in the 9/11 attacks by al Qaeda. Hopefully, the final exit in these two civil wars will not be as calamitous as it was in 1975 in Vietnam.

Is It Possible To Phase Down the Intelligence Budgets?

In July, 2010, THE WASHINGTON POST published the results of a two-year investigation called their "Top Secret America" article. In its first installment of a series of articles, the POST stated there are now over 1,200 government organizations and more than 1,900 private companies working on counterterrorism, homeland security and intelligence in some 10,000 locations across the United States. Some 854,000 persons have top-secret security clearance. These analysts produce so much information that many are routinely ignored.(15) In Washington, D.C. and surrounding areas, 33 building complexes for top-secret intelligence work are under construction or have been built since September, 2001. Together they occupy the equivalent of nearly three Pentagons or 22 U.S. Capitol buildings, which is 17 million square feet of space.(16)

A former top CIA counterterrorism officer who currently runs a consulting company, Harry Crumpton stated, "You need to cut back in dramatic ways and empower people in the field. We have just been throwing money at the problems, producing a breathtaking lack of coordination."(17) The new Director of National Intelligence must not only do a great job of providing meaningful and accurate intelligence, but he must also reduce this agency's costs.

Strategies To Phase Down Cost of Military and Intelligence

In 1991, our military performed a successful operation in the Gulf War. With financial help from our allies, the United States military forces quickly ran the Iraqi army out of Kuwait. The first President Bush made the right decision not to occupy Iraq and our troops came home with a clear victory. The reputation of American military forces was at an all-time high since WW II. In Bosnia and Kosovo, President Clinton refused to enter the civil war until there was a cease fire. He effectively used air power to force the cease fire. Clinton then sent in our troops with other allied troops as a peacekeeping mission. The United States had almost no casualties and achieved another successful military operation.

The military budgets of other nations indicate no nation has a military organization capable of attacking the United States. More important, if one studies the massive amount of ships, landing craft, air power, and troops required to invade the islands in the South Pacific or the coast of France on D Day in 1944, one concludes that no nation could invade the United States.

In February 2011, Defense Secretary Robert Gates bluntly told an audience of West Point cadets, "In my opinion, any future Defense Secretary who advises the President to again send a big American land army into Asia, or into the Middle East or Africa, should have his head examined, as General MacArthur so delicately put it."(18) Gates implied that in the future any potential conflicts should be fought with air and sea power rather than conventional ground forces. This means the Army and Marine Corps will be increasingly challenged to justify the number, size, and costs of large standing armies. This speech may go down in history like the remarks of President Eisenhower who warned us to beware of the cost of your military forces.

Unless the United States plans to enter more long-term and no-win civil wars with no end in sight, there simply is no need for the United States to maintain hundreds of thousands of troops stationed at military bases in the United States training for a potential World War III. Hopefully, future Presidents will have the common sense not to end their political careers by committing the military to another expensive civil war.

There has never been a better time to reduce the Defense budget to a practical and affordable amount. Americans used to be concerned about our country getting involved in European wars. Today, both European and Asian countries do not want to get involved in future American wars. Yes, there are always some Americans who wish our country would become involved in another war, but they are a small minority. Americans do not want to give up their health care or Social Security pensions, or pay for a major tax increase, to maintain a massive military organization.

The United States has 300,000 military personnel deployed overseas in Korea, Japan, Germany, as well as in Iraq and Afghanistan. A strategic plan to bring a majority of these troops back to United States bases should be developed. Many contract positions should also be eliminated by the end of the wars in Iraq and Afghanistan.

A future military strategy should be considered to reduce a threatening nation to poverty with our air and naval power by destroying their government buildings, military bases, airports, bridges, roads, railroads, seaports, manufacturing plants, power plants, and computer systems. Our fleet of over 50 nuclear submarines is capable of blockading almost any country, including Iran, Pakistan, North Korea and many Middle Eastern countries. Special Forces troops could be used for commando raids, if necessary. Troops on the ground should be avoided, according to Senator Jim Webb of Virginia. We should also avoid nation-building programs and long-term occupations of hostile nations.(19)

According to Department of Defense documents, the average annual cost of enlisted personnel is now $53,000 and that of officers is above $100,000. These costs are simply unaffordable for a peacetime defense organization. The lifetime career voluntary Army and Marine Corps could be changed to a force that would serve two years and then be discharged with a robust G.I. Bill that exists today to attend colleges or trade schools. The cost of 200,000 new scholarships each year would be a fraction of the cost now incurred for 20-to-30-year military career personnel whose families are supported with housing allowances, health care and a lifetime pension.

The health care costs for over five million Americans who are on active duty, in the reserves, or retired and their families is now around $100 billion. In 2010, the expense for Veterans' Affairs was $235 billion. The Constitution of the United States mandates our country should maintain a Navy (now an Air Force and Navy) in peacetime and raise an Army in wartime. To reduce these costs and still fulfill this Constitutional mandate, thousands of career officers and non-commissioned officers would comprise 25 percent of the total Army and Marine Corp. Many of these officers would be ROTC who would serve three years. Those officers and service personnel who only are on active duty for two or three years would have a four-year active reserve obligation. In case of a long-term war, reserves could quickly increase the size of our military force to over two million service personnel.

In September 2010, Lawrence J. Korb, a Senior Fellow, and Laura Conley, a Research Assistant, at the Center for American Progress organization published a white paper entitled "Strong and Sustainable: How to Reduce Military Spending While Keeping Our Nation

Safe."(20) This document explains how the Defense and Veterans' benefits were affordable in 2000, but became unsustainable ten years later. The paper outlines potential reductions of about $100 billion per year, and concludes the current defense budget can be scaled back to help reduce the General Fund's annual deficit with minimal risk to our national security.

The Defense Department should be directed to develop a phase-down budget over a four-year period (2013-2016) by the President elected in 2012 with the existing or new Secretary of Defense. President Nixon did this in 1969 when he requested a phase-down plan of the Vietnam War from his new Secretary of Defense, Mel Laird. The following questions could become the framework for this budget:

1. What expenditures are required for the defense of our 50 states?
2. What expenditures are required for a short war (months) that reduces a hostile nation to years of poverty without an invasion, occupation, and no nation-building projects?
3. What expenditures are required for a short war (months) that requires troops on the ground as the Gulf War did in the early 1990s, but avoids occupation and nation-building projects?
4. What expenditures are required for a long-term war that requires troops on the ground, occupation of a hostile nation, and nation-building projects? This approach would include a scale-up of the following personnel:
   – First phase: Active duty personnel
   – Second phase: Active Reserve personnel
   – Third phase: Military Draft personnel

A phase-down budget would include moving large numbers of overseas troops back to the United States, closing bases, mothballing some ships and planes, reducing orders for future weapon systems, and converting some future military personnel from 20-to-30-year careers to short 2-year term volunteer enlistments with a robust GI Bill.

In November 2010 and in June 2011, Afghanistan's President Karzai called for the United States to reduce its military operations in his country. He made this statement prior to a major NATO meeting that will plan the transition of NATO operations to Afghan forces over the next 18-to-24 months with the goal of ending NATO and U.S. combat operations by 2014. Karzai's statement followed his push to disband private security companies protecting foreign assistance projects and puts at risk billions of dollars in development aid and nation-building projects. Karzai stated he wants U.S. troops to be less intrusive in the lives of Afghans, and they should strive to stay on their bases and conduct only the "necessary activities" along the Pakistan border. These statements are in contrast to the overall strategies that General Petraeus planned to implement and President Obama approved.(21) Every month, there are situations where Afghanistan soldiers, police and even pilots kill United States and NATO troops. This situation is just another indication that the Afghanistan War should be phased down as quickly as possible because there will be no significant victory to this civil war. It is clear Pakistan wants the United States to phase out of Afghanistan. In spite of their hiding al-Qaeda leaders, including Osama bin Laden, the U.S. must maintain relations with Pakistan so we can exit from Afghanistan.

President Karzai is accepting large sums of money from both the United States and Iran. Like Iraq, the U.S. influence in the future will depend on how many billions of dollars we give them in future years and if the funds are not approved by Congress, the United States will have little influence in either country.

ESQUIRE magazine's November 2010 issue had an article reporting on the meeting that Lawrence O'Donnell of MSNBC held with four retired Senators (two Republicans and two Democrats) that convened for three days. These gentlemen met with Barry Andersen, a former deputy director of the Congressional Budget Office, to outline a plan to balance the federal budget by 2020. This session was called The Esquire Commission to Balance the Federal Budget. This commission came to the following conclusions for the Defense Budget:(22)

Projected savings of $126 billion due to the end of the combat operations in Afghanistan and Iraq.

Projected savings of $169 billion by restructuring the military along strategic lines from nation-state wars to unconventional wars.

Projected savings of $10 billion by reversing the 2011 growth in the Army.

Projected savings of $4 billion with weapon systems reductions. The Center for American Progress study projected a savings of nearly $20 billion in this category.

There is no doubt that the Defense and Intelligence budgets can be reduced by several hundred billion dollars with a change in our foreign and defense strategies to focus on containment rather than waging preemptive wars, occupations, and nation-building.

On December 2, 2010, USA TODAY published an editorial entitled, "Don't Spare The Pentagon From The Budgetary Ax." This article covered many facts that are documented in this lesson. The final sentence stated, "If Congress ever gets serious about curbing runaway spending and borrowing, the Pentagon is a particularly target—rich environment." The rebuttal was entitled, "Defense Cuts A Non-Starter," by the Republican Congressman who is the Chairman of the House Armed Services Committee in the 2011-12 Congress. He based his argument on polls. "Gallup poll recently found that Americans are more likely now to say the United States national defense is not strong enough. And, the Hill's 2010 Midterm Election Poll in battleground districts clearly states that six in 10 Republicans and 53% of independents said they could not accept cuts to defense and homeland security spending." The question a poll should ask is: Would you support a 25 percent surtax on your income tax to continue the War on Terror or do you want to phase down two civil wars? The vote would be a small minority of Americans because you get different answers when the cost is revealed.

In the April 24, 2011 issue of TIME magazine, there was an article by Mark Thompson on pages 24-29 entitled, "How To Save A Trillion Dollars." This article stated to stop building aircraft carriers and order fewer planes to save $500 billion. Another $287 billion could be saved by reducing U.S. troop strength in Asia (including Okinawa), Europe, and the Middle East. The article also recommended a reduction of $112 billion within intelligence agencies as well as $60 billion less for missile defense. The author agreed that Gates should reduce the 952 generals and admirals by 102. The article concluded that the reductions would leave the U.S. military as the most powerful in the world by any measurement. Using a recent NEW YORK TIMES/CBS poll, it was found if Americans had to choose, 55 percent were willing to reduce the defense budget while only 21 percent would accept a reduction in

Medicare benefits and only 13 percent would accept a reduction in Social Security benefits. The article concluded by stating U.S. taxpayers should demand that their government only spend what is needed to defend our country—not a penny more.

Enhanced Programs To Prevent Terrorist Attacks on U.S.

Increased resources may be needed for the Coast Guard, U.S. Customs and Border Protection, FBI, Intelligence Services, Interpol, and local police departments in selected cities to prevent future terrorist attacks. 240,000 people in various Homeland Security Departments are currently the first line of defense for stopping certain external and internal terrorists from conducting successful operations within the United States.

The State Department may also need additional resources to recruit allied nations to do more to reduce terrorism. Large countries such as Russia, China, Japan, Korea, India, Pakistan, and the European nations all have the funds and capabilities to help control terrorism. It is in their best self interests to be proactive on containing terrorism. The United States does not have to be the policemen of the world, but we should remain a leader in the fight against terrorism.

Dealing With Rogue Nations in Future Years

When the United States is dealing with a country threatening our allies in another area of the world such as Europe, Asia, South America or the Middle East, engaging our military must be the last option. To ensure it is the last option, Congress must be forced to approve the following three decisions after they are proposed by a U.S. President:

1. Declaration of war on a country.
2. Implementation of a large surtax on income tax to pay for the war.
3. If a large number of "troops on the ground" strategy is to be utilized, both young men and women must be drafted into service.

These three decisions will make the President and Congress rethink their strategies before they commit trillions of dollars and thousands of families to "gold star" status in another civil war with no end in sight. When a large majority of citizens must contribute to the war effort, Congress and the President will do all they can to avoid involving the United States in a long-term and costly war that would create another financial crisis, and no doubt end the political career of the President.

Required Leadership By Congressional and Presidential Candidates

Some politicians are calling for an increase in defense spending which will, of course, increase the national debt and lead to a financial meltdown of the federal government. No Presidential or Congressional candidate can be serious about reducing the size and cost of government, the growing size of the national debt, or the exploding cost of interest on debt unless they are willing to bring both the Iraq and Afghanistan wars to a conclusion as Presidents Eisenhower and Nixon did with the Korean and Vietnam wars. In addition, candidates must support a multi-year plan to reduce our defense, intelligence, and veterans affairs budgets to affordable levels while maintaining a vastly superior military organization. Downsizing should be accomplished in a thoughtful and careful manner that considers the sacrifices service personnel made during the two wars, which is why it will take four years to complete the downsizing. At the completion of World War II, the United States conducted a major phase-down of military spending that transitioned over 14 million military personnel back into civilian life in less than four years. After every war, there has been a major reduction in the defense budget. It is feasible to reduce the defense budget over a four-year period to $500 billion without jeopardizing the defense of our nation. The Secretaries of State, Defense, and Homeland Security should be charged with the responsibility to create new strategies that significantly reduce costs, but still protect our country from both terrorists and rogue nations. This strategy must provide superior defense and intelligence systems that are affordable and require no borrowed funds in the future. The President who is elected in 2012 must focus on streamlining the overall defense and homeland security strategies and budgets to prevent a meltdown of the federal financial system in this decade. With Congressman Ron Paul leading a group of conservatives who want to end the wars and downsize the military along with a majority of Democratic Congressional members wishing to achieve the same objectives, this could be accomplished in the 2012 to 2014 time frame. More articles and reports are now being written supporting a downsizing of the defense budget in future years. It is a leadership challenge.

With Leon Panetta as Secretary of Defense and General David Petraeus in charge of the CIA, there is an experienced team of leaders to work with President Obama to reduce the various budgets to an affordable level. When history books are written about the al-Qaeda organization and Osama bin Laden, there will be stories about the terrible terrorists attacks all around the world in Indonesia, Pakistan, Yemen, Tanzania, Nairobi, Kenya, Iraq, London, Spain, and of course, the United States. Equally important will be the story on how the United States spent over $5 trillion on the War on Terror against a group of rebels who had no air force, navy, army, or even a real headquarters. The War on Terror was a major contributor to the unbelievable mountain of debt that accumulated during the years the United States tried to wipe out al-Qaeda. An entire industry wants to fight on with an endless war, but unless voters will approve a major surtax on their income tax, it is time to design a more affordable and realistic program to contain terrorism.

If President Obama is reelected in 2012, his administration will achieve a major accomplishment if they end the Iraq and Afghanistan wars, reduce the defense budget to $500 billion, which is a 66 percent increase over the $300 billion adequate defense budget in 2000. The tax revenues for the General Fund grew by $171,582 billion in 2010 compared to 2001. All of the growth is given to the Defense Department to expand their budget from $300 to $500 billion. To reach $500 billion, the Defense Department must implement a cost-effective method of using young men and women for two or three years rather than 20-to-30-year career people for basic military jobs. President Obama and his administration would be viewed as fiscal conservatives and our federal government would be back on the road to a balanced budget. A Republican Presidential candidate could also endorse such a strategy in the 2012 campaign. This approach would help reverse the Republican Party's record of uncontrolled spending for the military that Bush and Cheney as well as Reagan built during their administrations.

The second largest financial problem facing our country is recharging our private enterprise system to return the country to prosperity and high employment levels. To address this problem, we need to understand why some corporations and institutions have become "too big to fail." Lesson 9 deals with this subject.

NOTES FOR LESSON 8

1. "Pentagon Push To Cut Costs Will Target Firms," Christopher Drew, NEW YORK TIMES NEWS SERVICE, SAN DIEGO UNION-TRIBUNE, June 8, 2010, page A6

2. "The Half-Billion-Dollar Camp," Scott Higham and Peter Finn, WASHINGTON POST, THE DALLAS MORNING NEWS, June 20, 2010, page A12

3. "Army Pouring $100 Million Into Special Operations Headquarters In Afghanistan" ASSOCIATED PRESS, June 5, A6

4. "Petraeus Expands Covert Operations," Mark Mazzetti, NEW YORK TIMES NEWS SERVICE, SAN DIEGO UNION-TRIBUNE, May 25, 2010, page A3

5. "Obama Stresses Need For Diplomacy," Darlene Superville, ASSOCIATED PRESS, SAN DIEGO UNION-TRIBUNE, May 25, 2010, Page A3

6. "The World According To Elizabeth II," Jon Meacham, NEWSWEEK, July 19, 2010, page 4

7. *No Apology,* Mitt Romney, St. Martin's Press, 2009, pages 83-94

8. *Seeing The Elephant,* Peter Marber John Wiley and Sons, 2009, pages 153 to 158

9. *Seeing The Elephant,* Peter Marber, John Wiley and Sons, 2009, pages 150 to 155

10. "As Final Combat Troops Leave Iraq, A New Era Begins," NYT NEWS SERVICE and ASSOCIATED PRESS, August 9, 2010, pages A1 and A9

11. "We're Not Winning. It's Not Worth It. Here's How To Draw Down In Afghanistan," Richard N. Haass, NEWSWEEK, July 26, 2010, pages 30-35

12. "What To Do About Pakistan," David Ignatius, THE WASHINGTON POST, SAN DIEGO UNION-TRIBUNE, July 29, 2010, page B6

13. "The Gang That Couldn't Shoot Straight," by T. Christian Miller, Mark Horsenball, and Ron Moreau, NEWSWEEK, March 29, 2010, pages 25-31

14. "Rumsfeld Memoir," Mark Benjamin and Barbara Slavin, NEWSWEEK, February 14, 2011, page 31

15. "Intelligence Gathering Is Unwieldy, Report Says," ASSOCIATED PRESS, SAN DIEGO UNION-TRIBUNE, July 20, 2010, page A7

16. "Open Secrets," Hendrik Hertzberg, THE NEW YORKER, August 2, 2010, pages 17 and 18

17. "No Secret: Leaner Is Meaner," David Ignatius, THE WASHINGTON POST, July 22, 2010, page B6

18. "Gates Cautions Against Future Wars Like Iraq, Afghanistan," Tom Shanker, NEW YORK NEWS SERVICE, SAN DIEGO UNION-TRIBUNE, February 26, 2011, page A 4

19. *A Time To Fight*, Jim Webb, Broadway Publishers, 2008, pages 142 to 164

20. "How To Reduce Military Spending While Keeping Our Nation Safe," Lawrence J. Korb and Laura Conley, Center For American Progress, September, 2010, pages 1 to 22

21. "Afghans Warned About War Criticism," Joshua Partlow, THE WASHINGTON POST, SAN DIEGO UNION-TRIBUNE, November 15, 2010, pages A1 and A6

22. "Balance Five Men, One Room, and A National Crisis," Richard Dorment and Mark Warren, ESQUIRE Magazine, November, 2010, pages 156 to 164

LESSON 9

REGULATION OF "TOO BIG TO FAIL" INSTITUTIONS

The Decline of Small Businesses as an Employer

Almost every political leader and candidate discusses the importance of small businesses for our economic recovery. Of course, owners of small businesses make significant campaign contributions to candidates during an election. But truth be told, small businesses have been in decline for decades.

After World War II, nearly every neighborhood had a small cluster of stores which people could walk to because the vast majority of families had either no automobiles or just one automobile. These days, small family-owned grocery stores have nearly all disappeared and been replaced by large food store chains such as Albertsons, Ralphs, Vons, Stop and Shop, Trader Joes, and Jewel.

Local bakeries have mostly disappeared because the large grocery stores have an extensive bakery goods department. Family-owned meat markets and delicatessens have been replaced by large grocery stores as well. Even small card shops have left towns due to the cards available in Hallmark stores, large pharmacies and large grocery stores. Family-owned drugstores rarely exist nowadays. Small local stationery stores have given way to Staples and Office Depot. Neighborhood hardware stores have been replaced by Home Depot, Lowes and ACE hardware. Family-owned restaurants have been significantly impacted by national chains such as McDonald's, Burger King, International House of Pancakes, Jack In The Box, KFC, Marie Callender's, Olive Garden, Pizza Hut, Macaroni Grill, Soup Plantation, Subway, Taco Bell, and Wendy's.

When one visits a small town, the downtown area often resembles a "ghost town" with many empty stores and a few "second-hand" shops.

As you drive out of a community, quite often there is a beautiful new Super Wal-Mart Center that has become the new downtown. Wal-Mart has everything that used to be on Main Street, including a dentist, eye doctor, bank, florist, toys, clothes, appliances, sports equipment, and food.

Family-owned department stores are almost all out of business. Modern shopping centers can have anywhere from 25-to-200 different stores and restaurants. In most malls, not one of the stores is a local family-owned business.

Most small manufacturing companies have gone out of business or been purchased by a large corporation. Marketing and sales expenses often overwhelm a small business before it is successfully sold to a large corporation. Over an extended period of time, only 18 percent of small businesses are successful.

Yes, there are still millions of small businesses across our country, but they do not represent a major growth area. During the Great Recession, small businesses hired a few employees, while large corporations laid off hundreds or thousands of employees. Most of the jobs in small businesses are low wage positions with few or no benefits. The owners are usually the only workers who have high incomes. Some statistical indicators suggest 60 percent of all new hires are being made in small businesses. These statistics just highlight how few people are being hired by large corporations. Some political leaders believe small businesses will provide the employee growth necessary to end the Great Recession. This viewpoint is an illusion.

On July 14, 2010, David Brooks wrote in the NEW YORK TIMES, "Small businesses are dead in the water and are not growing. They are not hiring. They are struggling to stay alive."(1) Millions of small businesses went bankrupt in the 2008 Great Recession.

Advantages of Big Organizations

With their superior computer and communication technologies, large corporations have substantial economic advantages. In a well-managed company, certain major tasks need to be performed at headquarters instead of at local operating units. For example, at a company like Wal-Mart, the following tasks and departments would be managed at headquarters:

- Determine new areas for expansion and for buying real estate
- Design of operating facilities
- Supervision of building new operating facilities
- Central buying of merchandise for large discounts
- Management of shipping and distribution
- Allocation of merchandise to stores
- Central finance and accounting systems
- Central computerized merchandising system
- Central human resources department and services
- Central public relations department
- Central legal department
- Central information systems department
- Central planning and budgeting department
- Central purchasing department
- Provide standard operating procedures for operating units

Many operating units would perform the following tasks:

- Develop and manage a local competitive workforce
- Receive and store merchandise
- Stock shelves and display merchandise
- Provide outstanding customer service
- Record sales and bag merchandise
- Keep a store and parking lot clean
- Participate in local community activities

At both locations, employees and managers have embraceable responsibilities. Using this two-level organizational structure, a company saves millions or billions of dollars in overhead and benefits further from more specialized performance at each location. These advantages make it nearly impossible for a local family-owned business to compete. For this reason, many small companies are purchased and merged into large corporations.

Industries and Companies That Are "Too Big To Fail"

Years ago, the airline industry was deregulated. Many airlines, including Pan American, Eastern, Peoples, Northwest, Ozark, Mohawk, and Capitol went out of business. Except for Southwest and American, the remaining major airlines (Delta and United) all went through bankruptcy. Thousands of employees were laid off and the remaining employees' incomes were reduced. Billions of dollars in additional fees have been imposed on passengers. Today, customer service is at an all-time low and so is customer satisfaction. Hundreds of small cities have insufficient or no air transportation. Mergers and less competition have steadily increased airfares and, with fewer flights, more planes are full. Bargain fares are disappearing. The positive benefits of deregulation have mostly disappeared.

Some people believe the airline industry needs to be regulated in order to improve performance and customer service. There is little competition in many cities. United Airlines will have 10 hubs servicing 370 destinations in 59 countries when its merger with Continental is completed. The four large airlines could do serious damage to the overall American economy if their senior executives make the wrong decisions.

The "Big Oil" industry consists of Shell, BP (British Petroleum), Exxon, Mobil, Texaco, and OPEC in the Middle East. In the 1970s, these companies created a gasoline shortage that did extensive damage to our national economy. A few years ago, the price of gasoline soared to over $4 per gallon. The price hike damaged the U.S. automobile industry which had been successfully selling SUVs and trucks to Americans who wanted to drive these types of vehicles. The United States imports only 9 percent of its oil from Middle Eastern countries. But the turmoil in the area was used once again in 2011 to raise prices and, of course, profits before any higher priced oil arrived in our country. Once again, Big Oil had a negative impact on the American standard of living and our economy with over $4 per gallon. Who will ever forget the oil spills in Santa Barbara, Alaska, and the Gulf of Mexico. The oil industry needs to be regulated to protect the American economy and our standard of living.

The defense industry has been whittled down to a few corporations that manufacture our military vehicles, weapon systems, aircraft, and

Navy ships. The Pentagon is already in charge of supervising the performance of these defense contractors. Still this area of regulation needs to improve in order to eliminate waste, missed schedules, cost overruns, and ineffective performance.

The pharmaceutical industry is already regulated by the government to ensure medicines are properly manufactured, research projects are properly managed, and drugs are administered correctly. With Medicare and Medicaid, the government will play an even greater regulatory role in improving quality and reducing costs of the American health care system.

The American automobile industry has been reduced to two companies—Ford and General Motors. They almost disappeared in 2009 with the simultaneous bankruptcies of General Motors and Chrysler. If Chrysler and GM had failed, many suppliers who sold to Ford would have been destroyed as well. Ford would probably have ceased to exist had it not been for the bailouts granted to GM and Chrysler that were not supported by the Republican Party. Republicans want the American Autoworkers Union to go bankrupt even if it means tens of thousands of additional Americans being unemployed. Here again, the federal government's regulation and oversight has saved jobs and an industry critical to our country's security. A restructured General Motors is now starting to succeed.

The insurance industry has been regulated by the 50 State Commissioners of Insurance, a system that worked in the 20th Century. However, in the Great Recession of 2008, A.I.G. and other large insurance companies, including those that insured municipal bonds, were technically bankrupt after the meltdown of the real estate market, the stock market, and some large financial institutions. In some cases, these "too big to fail" companies were selling insurance, but they had insufficient capital to pay benefits. They now operate on a national and international scale so state regulation is inadequate. Consumers and corporations need to be protected from inadequate management by large insurance companies.

In Lesson 11, we will learn that local school boards, district superintendents and Chief State School Officers have failed during the past 27 years to contain costs and to solve the student learning crisis within the American public schools. University administrators have also failed to contain costs at institutions of higher education. Therefore, state and local departments of education need to be regulated by the federal government before it provides them with billions of dollars in bailout funds.

The food industry is a great success story. According to the U.S. Department of Agriculture statistics in 1929, 23 percent of a family's income went to purchase food. In 2008 that figure had dropped to 9.6 percent. However, small family-owned farms are disappearing and are being replaced with mega farms. Tyson and Pilgrim's Pride produce about half the chickens in our country today. In 2005, Smithfield, Tyson, Swift & Company, and Cargill owned nearly 64 percent of the hog market. Tyson, Cargill, and National Beef Packing slaughtered 84 percent of the cattle in the United States.(2) These companies are also "too big to fail."

Government Responsibilities To Regulate "Too Big To Fail" Companies

Some political leaders constantly look for the quick-fix and sound-good action programs that will appeal to uneducated voters. For example, some members of Congress believe we should put millions of illegal immigrants on buses and planes and send them back to their native countries. This policy would involve expelling millions of immigrant children who were born in the United States and who are American citizens. Our country could not even evacuate thousands of people in New Orleans before Hurricane Katrina, and all these Americans just wanted a ride out of town.

These same political leaders want to break up the big banks on Wall Street. They also want to break up all organizations that are "too big to fail." If they would study the major antitrust cases of the past century, they would learn it takes years, sometimes decades, and billions of dollars to break up large corporations such as Standard Oil, AT&T, IBM, and Microsoft. In most antitrust lawsuits, the government loses the case and/or settles the case through a consent degree that does not break up the large corporation.

Frankly, the United States needs large and successful corporations to compete in the intensely competitive world economy. Once the government approves a merger, it is nearly impossible to break up that merger through antitrust lawsuits. During the past 30 years, there have been thousands of mergers and acquisitions that have created well over a hundred corporations and banks that are now considered "too big to fail." Therefore, what we need now is effective government regulations of the "too big to fail" corporations to ensure that their customers are treated fairly, that they have good human resource programs for employees, that they have stability in their workforces, that they have expansion plans to provide additional employment, that they contribute to and support their communities, that they compete fairly in the marketplace, and that they have goals and strategies to achieve industry leadership.

Some people will claim all this oversight is the responsibility of these companies' Board of Directors. Unfortunately, Board of Directors now have stock options just like the senior executive team and too often greed takes over as their number-one priority rather than doing what is best for their customers, their employees, their country, and their stockholders.

Government regulations come in several forms. There is the adversarial approach where the government is viewed as a troublemaker that merely causes problems for an industry. This approach rarely works so it must be avoided. The second approach is the opposite tactic: government regulators being too close as allies with the industry they are overseeing. The "Big Oil" companies were so close to regulators that safety was not monitored and the result was a record oil spill in the Gulf of Mexico. Enron was permitted by its government regulators to perform criminal acts including large rate increases on states and customers that gave their company record revenues, earnings, and inflation of their stock.

The Department of Agriculture has taken a third approach which is a balanced performance. The Farm Bill provides $44 billion for food stamps, school lunches, and other nutritional programs. The Agriculture Department also provides subsides to large and profitable corporations, a practice it needs to curtail if not halted altogether. One major problem with government regulation is its inherent temptation that allows politicians to buy votes with billions of dollars in government funds.

Most senior executives want complete freedom to manage their organizations with no influence from government, unions, customer associations, business press, or state governments. Unfortunately, in this environment, the greed for earnings and inflated stock values have turned too many successful companies into workplaces with millions of unhappy customers, a declining market share in the world economy, thousands of laid-off employees, and damaged communities that were once their base of operations. New government regulations must be established to achieve balanced performance from our large corporations and financial institutions.

Regulation of Financial Institutions

There is no better example of how much damage deregulated corporations can do than the meltdown of the large American financial institutions in 2008. As a result of this event, millions of employees were laid off. Thousands of businesses had to close their doors due to the credit shortage. Trillions of dollars were lost in the stock market and hedge funds. Trillions of dollars were also lost in the value of homes which triggered millions of foreclosures.

In March, 2008, the government arranged a merger between Bear Stearns and J.P. Morgan with $29 billion of government financing provided for the troubled assets of Bear Stearns. With leveraged strategies of thirty dollars of debt for every dollar of tangible capital, Bear Stearns nearly collapsed even though it reported record profits in 2007. The giant insurance conglomerate A.I.G. was also facing a liquidity crisis because it had insured billions of dollars in mortgage assets, but had insufficient cash to pay clients as the credit-default swaps started to fail. The Federal Reserve had to loan A.I.G. $85 billion to keep it alive. Fannie Mae and Freddie Mac had to be bailed out with massive government loans. Merrill Lynch had become one of the largest underwriters of mortgage-backed securities, a disastrous position to be in when the housing bubble burst. For this reason, Bank of America had to take over Merrill Lynch.

The failure of Lehman Brothers resulted in the oldest money-market fund (Primary Fund) going out of business. The stock market dropped 504 points (4.4 percent) on September 15, 2008 after Lehman Brothers failed. Over 1,900 hedge funds also went out of business. The Secretary of the Treasury and Chairman of the Federal Reserve received the support of President Bush and Vice President Cheney to ask Congressional leaders for a $700 billion "troubled-asset relief program" (TARP) that ultimately passed by a bipartisan vote in the Congress. Wells Fargo had to take over the failed investment bank of Wachovia Securities.(3) Hundreds of local banks failed over the next two years as well. The Federal Deposit Insurance Corporation from the 1930s saved billions of dollars in bank accounts.

The United States now has six very large financial institutions that are considered "too big to fail":

Bank of America
Wells Fargo
J.P. Morgan/Chase
Citigroup
Morgan Stanley
Goldman Sachs

Financial Meltdown Was Avoidable

The 2008 financial crisis was an "avoidable" disaster caused by widespread failures in government regulation, corporate mismanagement, and needless risk-taking by Wall Street, according to the conclusions of a federal inquiry. The government commission that investigated the financial crisis casts a wide net of blame, faulting two administrations, the Federal Reserve, and other regulators for permitting a calamitous concoction: shoddy mortgage lending, the excessive packaging and sale of loans to investors, and risky bets on securities backed by the loans. The greatest tragedy would be to accept the refrain: no one could have seen this coming and thus nothing could have been done.(4) Unfortunately, one political party would not endorse the 633-page report even though 12 of the country's 13 most prominent financial institutions, including Goldman Sachs, had been on the verge of collapse within a week or two in 2008.

New Regulations for Financial Institutions

After two years of discussion, some Congressional leaders are adamantly against any new regulations of American financial institutions because they believe new regulations will tighten credit, slow job creation, stop the expansion of the economy, and reduce creativity in the financial industry. Fortunately, most House and Senate members voted for an overhaul of regulations to prevent future financial institution meltdowns. The highlights of the new regulations are:(5)

A new ten-member council of regulators led by the Treasury Secretary will monitor threats to the financial system.

A Consumer Financial Protection Bureau will write and enforce rules covering mortgages, credit cards, and other financial products. American consumers need to be protected from financial institutions that gamble their deposits in extremely high risk investments.

The legislation gives the government new powers to seize and shut down large, troubled financial companies such as the failed investment bank of Lehman Brothers. Under the new rules, the vast market for financial instruments called derivatives will be subject to government oversight. Shareholders will gain more say in how corporate executives are paid.

Regulators must utilize simpler mortgage disclosure forms and lenders will have to ensure borrowers will be able to repay their loans. Enablers like Moody's, Standard & Poor's, and Fitch that rated high risk bonds as Triple A and gave recklessly bad advice could be legally liable for investor losses. The practice of bond rating companies being paid by organizations that issue bonds led to improper ratings.

The intent of the new regulations is to rebuild trust and confidence in what is now a badly battered financial system. If Americans have any doubt about the need for more regulation for financial institutions, they should see the Oscar-winning movie *Inside Job* or the HBO *Too Big To Fail*. These films argue that the financial earthquake was very predictable given the steady erosion of oversight in the financial markets.

Stabilizing Wall Street

In April, 2010, Treasury Secretary Timothy Geithner told Congress that the administration believes the final cost of the government's heavily criticized financial bailout effort could be as low as $87 billion. In

August the Congressional Budget Office estimated it to be $66 billion. This figure is almost unbelievable considering trillions of dollars were made available by the Federal Reserve, Treasury, FHA, and FDIC to protect assets. It appears that TARP will be one of the least costly forms of saving our financial institutions and no congressional member from either political party should lose an election over their vote. However, this figure does not include large liabilities on the Federal Reserve's balance sheet which covered the losses of the Federal Home Loan Association, Fannie Mae and Freddie Mac. The biggest offset to those losses will be $115 billion in earnings that the Federal Reserve will realize from the extraordinary assistance it gave to inject liquidity into the financial system.(6)

In March, 2011, Robert J. Samuelson wrote a most interesting article in NEWSWEEK, "TARP: The Rescuer Everyone Loves To Hate." Samuelson stated, "One lesson of the financial crisis is this: When the entire financial system succumbs to panic, only the government is powerful enough to prevent a complete collapse." Douglas Elliott of the Brookings Institute stated, "TARP is the best large federal program to be despised by the public. Most Americans believe that taxpayers spent $700 billion and got nothing in return." A new Treasury Department calculation claims there will be a $24 billion profit from the Wall Street rescue. And most Americans never realized that the alternative was to nationalize major banks which would have cost unbelievable sums of federal dollars.(7)

NEWSWEEK columnist Robert J. Samuelson also wrote an article, "The Bailout That Might Have Prevented Panic," that questioned the decisions by the Secretary of the Treasury Paulson and Federal Reserve Chairman Bernanke for allowing Lehman Brothers to fail in 2008. Once Lehman went out of business, the economy went into a frenzied freefall. Credit tightened, interest rates on corporate bonds increased, stocks tanked, consumer spending and business investments fell, employment collapsed, other financial institutions failed, and companies hoarded cash. Only the U. S. government could save Lehman, but the decision was made to let it fail because the government didn't want to put taxpayer money into saving Lehman Brothers.(8) This stance is exactly what conservatives and Tea Party supporters advocate: let big organizations go out of business if they fail. However, panic was so rampant after the failure of Lehman Brothers that a $700 billion

TARP government loan guarantee was needed to save other financial institutions on Wall Street and to avoid an economic depression.

The number-one problem with TARP is Congressional members' inability to explain to potential voters that without TARP the entire American financial system would have collapsed. There would have been massive losses of investments and thousands more employees would have been laid off across the nation.

Financial planners and investment sales personnel are once again selling Americans the notion that the only way to build a fund for college, an emergency, or retirement is to put as much money as possible in common stocks. With all the turmoil in the world, the weakness of the euro, and the civil war between the two major political parties, stock market investments have lots of inherent risks due to external events. Furthermore, senior executive management teams are not performing very well in the global economy. Firms that sell stocks try to act like experts, but they almost all failed in 2008 when the stock market experienced a major meltdown. Millions of Americans want to get rich in the stock market, but few people achieve that goal. TV's 60 MINUTES had a program in September 2010, "Flash Trading" which explained how 70 percent of stocks are traded by a few hundred people with large computer systems who are only interested in a quick profit. For those profits, they will sacrifice thousands of jobs or even companies. The stock market will create great winners and losers in the future. On May 6, 2010, 19 billion shares were bought and sold (3 billion shares is a more normal trading day) and the DOW momentarily fell 9.2 percent. The U.S. stock market is actually a network of 50 different markets connected by computers. There was a 20-minute loss of $862 billion in stocks on May 6. For example, one well-known consulting firm watched their stock go from $40 to eleven cents in minutes. SEC reviewed up to 10 terabytes of market data to figure out what happened. Twelve days later, the agency conceded it had no firm answer.(9) Americans need to heed the warning May 6 gave them: beware of how much you invest in the stock market.

U.S. banks now have more capital as a percentage of assets than in any year since 1935. The stock market has rebounded from its 60 percent drop in 2008/2009, but few people are getting rich in the stock market. Bonds are safe, but paying little interest. The economy is growing again. Companies are hiring more than they are firing. Home values have stabilized. Some time ago, everyone including President Obama was talking about shutting down Fannie Mae and Freddie Mac. This pleased Republican members of Congress, as they continue to try to shrink the size of government. But mortgage bankers, homebuilders, and real estate agents were all claiming this would rattle the housing industry and perhaps our entire economy. Without the government guarantee of mortgages, the cost of mortgages would rise a significant amount and millions of homes would be less affordable. Some members of Congress claim it would devastate the housing market. Under President Bush, the government was forced to take over Fannie Mae and Freddie Mac in September, 2008 when the housing market crumbled. At present, there is no consensus to shut them down. The recovery has started, but it is not in full gear and millions of Americans are still looking for a job.

Expanded Responsibility for the Federal Government

In a perfect world, senior executives should be able to manage major corporations and financial institutions without oversight from a government agency. Recently, though, too many senior executives have failed to manage their organizations for the benefit of their customers, their employees, their country and their stockholders. Accordingly, the government must now take on additional oversight responsibilities to protect all stakeholders. If it does not take on these responsibilities, this country will have more multi-billion-dollar debacles like British Petroleum caused with the great oil spill in the Gulf of Mexico and the one caused by the Wright County Egg business in Iowa in 2010. In the latter case, nearly 1,470 Americans became ill from salmonella bacteria poisoning, resulting in a recall of 550 million eggs from two farms. Low-cost vaccines that are used in many other countries and farms could have prevented this major health problem.

Before Sarbanes-Oxley, accountants and auditors were guided primarily by standards established by industry associations and the profession was largely self-regulated. That self-regulated procedure proved costly in the wake of corporate scandals—Enron, Adelphia Communications, and a number of other companies. With the economy in a downturn and the stock market experiencing dizzying gyrations, the public and politicians demanded stricter financial oversight of U.S. companies. Sarbanes-Oxley was the result.

Sabanes-Oxley is intended to protect shareholders and the general public from accounting errors and fraudulent practices. The Public Company Accounting Oversight Board (PCAOB) sets standards for auditing of public companies, and includes provisions designed to ensure auditor independence and promote financial disclosures. The new regulations increased penalties for fraud, and made the failure to certify corporate financial reports a criminal offense.(10)

During the discussion on new regulations for Wall Street, the famous Volcker rule was debated. The former Chairman of the Federal Reserve had a strong belief that commercial banks should be separated from investment banks as they were before the meltdown of nearly every major bank in 2008. Wall Street executives did not want the separation so they could manage all the assets in their drive to once again maximize earnings.

Every industry regulation is based on a serious crisis of performance or massive loss of taxpayer funds in previous years. For example, the Savings and Loan scandals in the 1980s cost taxpayers several hundred billion dollars, including interest on debt because, once again, senior executives took excessive risks to inflate their incomes with the belief the federal government and taxpayers would bail them out if their investments failed. Exactly what happened. Our country cannot afford to let this occur in future years.

In 2011, BLOOMBERG GOVERNMENT INSIDER published an article, "The Regulator: Why Business Loves Rules." In their poll of December 2010, 70 percent stated government regulation is needed "in most cases to protect the public interest" vs just 25 percent who claimed it was not required. Fifty-three percent of respondents agreed that "most American businesses" cannot be trusted to act in the public interest vs 41 percent who disagreed.(11) The Obama administration is adding more regulations in certain areas such as food safety, financial institutions, healthcare, and manufacturing, but they have pledged to rein in the red tape regulations that are a burden to small businesses.

After all the problems of 2008, Americans are willing to accept this expanded role of government. To say that our federal government should not be involved in the regulations of financial institutions or "too big to fail" corporations is a stance that could lead our country into a great depression like the one President Hoover allowed to occur in the 1930s.

While there are some political leaders who believe the United States cannot afford to provide Social Security and Medicare benefits to senior citizens who paid into these two government programs for 40-to-50 years, they will find out that these two programs are also "too big to fail." The vast majority of Americans will only vote for candidates who will protect their Social Security and Medicare benefits. If Wall Street's big banks, large corporations, and major insurance companies can be protected with federal government funds, so can the two most popular government programs that ensure our senior citizens will have a decent retirement, which should be one of our national goals.

The next lesson will address another major challenge facing the President and Congress who are elected in 2012. The 2008 Great Recession can be compared to the Great Depression of the 1930s in the sheer number of unemployed and underemployed workers. However, solving the employment problems caused by the 2008 Great Recession will require entirely new strategies and tactics discussed in Lesson 10.

NOTES FOR LESSON 9

1. "An Economy of Grinds," David Brooks, THE NEW YORK TIMES, SAN DIEGO UNION-TRIBUNE, July 14, 2010, page B6
2. *Killer Politics,* Ed Schultz, Hyperion, New York City, 2010, pages 50 to 53
3. "Eight Days: The Battle To Save The American Financial System," James B. Steward, THE NEW YORKER, September 21, 2009, pages 58 to 81
4. "Financial Meltdown Was Avoidable, Federal Inquiry Says," Sewell Chan, NEW YORK TIMES NEWS SERVICE, SAN DIEGO UNION-TRIBUNE, January 26, 2011, page C5
5. "Congress OKs Financial Overhaul," Brady Dennis, WASHINGTON POST, SAN DIEGO UNION-TRIBUNE, July 16, 2010, page A3
6. "Geithner Lowers Financial Bailout Estimate To As Low As $87 Billion," Martin Crutsinger, SAN DIEGO UNION-TRIBUNE, April 24, 2010, page C1
7. "TARP: The Rescuer Everyone Loves To Hate," Robert J. Samuelson, NEWSWEEK, SAN DIEGO UNION-TRIBUNE, March 28, 2011, page B5
8. "The Bailout That Might Have Prevented Panic," Robert J. Samuelson, NEWSWEEK, SAN DIEGO UNION-TRIBUNE, September 16, 2010, Page B7
9. "The Machines That Ate The Market," Jeff Kekarns, Whitney Kisling, Peter Coy, BLOOMBERG BUSINESSWEEK, May 30, 2010, pages 49 to 55
10. Leading The Charge," Ira Solomon and Mark Peecher, PERSPECTIVES, College of Business at the University of Illinois, Fall 2010, pages 8, 9 and 11
11. "The Regulator: Why Business Loves Rules," David Lynch, BLOOMBERG GOVERNMENT INSIDER, Winter 2011, pages 51 to 53

LESSON 10

RECHARGING THE PRIVATE ENTERPRISE SYSTEM FOR EMPLOYMENT

In his book *No Apology: The Case For American Greatness,* Mitt Romney stated, "As every American discovered beginning in the fall of 2008, a strong economy is the foundation of our citizen's prosperity."(1) Many political leaders and senior business executives want to sell the illusion that the American business community is as strong as ever. This is simply not the case. If one looks at the 150 successful American multi-national corporations that led their industries in the 1950s, 1960s and 1970s, one will be shocked at where these companies are today. Many have lost billions of dollars in market share to foreign companies in the global economy over the past 30 years. They have also eliminated millions of jobs through outsourcing and downsizing. Some of these famous American companies have even gone out of business. And some have billions of dollars in losses instead of the record earnings they used to post routinely. In 2008, 80 percent of corporate earnings disappeared and the U.S. stock market declined by over 50 percent. How did all this happen?

Characteristics of a Successful Private Enterprise System

In the early 20th Century, the United States emerged from being an agricultural country to becoming a great industrial powerhouse that led the world with breakthroughs in productivity and innovation. Romney wrote, "Raising the productivity of a nation and the prosperity of its citizens depends on two types of innovation—one that improves existing goods and services, and another one that invents new ones."(2)

In the past, the productivity of most great American corporations was based on new products and services. In addition to superior products, companies developed innovative manufacturing methods for mass production and innovative marketing programs. Senior executives were typically the founders of a company. Most of them did not have a college degree in business administration and almost none of them had a Master of Business Administration (MBA) degree. They used common sense and leadership skills to grow their business, and guided operations through the following fundamental goals:

- Products and services must be superior with competitive prices.
- Marketing and sales must create and expand the business with highly satisfied customers. Creating demand was essential for growth.
- There must be a commitment to leadership in markets that the company selects to serve.
- There must be a competitive workforce with high morale that knows more and does more with excellence in execution.
- Stock market value must increase for shareholders.
- The company will be a good citizen and support the communities in which it operates, including a goal to provide employment.
- Ethics of all personnel must be impeccable.

Influenced tremendously by the founders, the second generation of senior executives continued to grow these profitable businesses. Unions grew in numbers and influence in the 1930s and 1940s because President Roosevelt wanted to create a strong and large middle class that could afford the products produced by the United States' great industrial base. Roosevelt's opponents were always against the union movement, but history has shown that unions improved working conditions, wages, benefits, and respect for employee rights within successful corporations and government agencies. The United States achieved a level of prosperity that was the envy of the world with good management and unions.

Greed Takes Over the Private Enterprise System

Many economists believe government intervention and regulation generally damage the free enterprise system. They also professed that corporations should not be concerned about community service or charities. In their opinion, the sole goal of a company should be to make profits. They opposed Lyndon Johnson's Great Society program and predicted that its social engineering goals would never be achieved. With the election of President Reagan in 1980, the American government moved away from Roosevelt's achievements to a new vision that stressed deregulation, lower taxes, increased productivity, and reduced influence by unions. The rich would become even wealthier with this new vision.

Accordingly, the goal of being a successful senior executive is completely different today. With intense pressure from investment managers of money market funds, pension funds, and foundations, the one goal that supersedes all other goals is to increase shareholder value by record earnings in each quarter. Many corporations have spent billions of dollars from their earnings to buy back their own common stock, believing this action will increase the value of their stock. For example, General Motors spent nearly $35 billion to buy back their stock rather than invest in new car models, better engines, and new technologies such as hybrids. General Motors stock was practically worthless when the company was technically bankrupt, which is why it needed a multi-billion-dollar federal government bailout. Since 2002, IBM has invested $68 billion in buybacks of their stock. Microsoft has spent more than $103 billion.

In the name of increased productivity, many companies have eliminated research, reduced their investment in new products and services, outsourced manufacturing, reduced customer service, minimized employee training, and eliminated or downsized sales organizations and marketing budgets. These strategic moves have resulted in a loss of market share, reduced revenues, less profits, and a decline in overall brand reputations.

Today, American companies rarely have breakthroughs in new products and services. Companies such as Apple are an exception. Customer service is a minus rather than a plus, and few companies are leaders within their industries.

Jim Collins, a professor who wrote the bestsellers *Good To Great* and *Built To Last,* has now written a book entitled *How The Mighty Fall.* He has developed the following five-stage framework for the path to failure that many corporations have traveled in recent years:(3)

Stage 1: Arrogance of Success

Stage 2: Undisciplined Pursuit of More
>   (We are so great, we can do anything)

Stage 3: Denial of Risk and Peril
> (Internal signs begin to mount, yet external results remain strong enough to "explain away" disturbing data or to state "nothing is fundamentally wrong." Often they blame external factors.)

Stage 4: Gasping For Salvation
> (Implementing quick-fixes such as untested strategies, a hoped-for-blockbuster product, a game-changing acquisition or a charismatic visionary leader. Layoffs are usually frequent and large in Stage 4.)

Stage 5: Capitulation to Irrelevance or Failure

Professor Collins uses Zenith as an example of a once successful company that took three decades to move through all five stages. Rubbermaid traveled the path to failure in just five years. Bear Stearns and Lehman Brothers traveled it in only a few months. Other companies that have failed in recent years include Ames department store, Circuit City, Great Atlantic & Pacific Tea Company (A & P), three dime store chains, Zayre department stores, Montgomery Ward, General Motors, Chrysler, Kodak, Arthur Andersen and Co., Eastern, Pan American, Peoples Express Airline, many famous magazines and newspapers, over a dozen computer companies, many banks and investment firms, Bethlehem Steel, U.S. Steel, Addressograph, and McDonnell Douglas. The list grows with new failures annually. In defense of these senior executives, pressure from Wall Street for record earnings every quarter has significantly damaged many corporations. Wall Street not only ruined some of our large companies but also bankrupted most of its own investment banks.

Some companies make it all the way to Stage 4, but through great leadership by a new executive team, rebound to becoming a successful company again. Nordstrom, Disney, and IBM are examples of such rebounds. Motorola is currently in Stage 4, so only time will tell which way it will go in this decade. General Motors and Ford may rebound.

Requirement for a Successful and Larger Private Enterprise System

The United States has to regain leadership within the major industries for our country to remain a global leader, to have a tax base that affords a strong defense organization, restores full employment, and soaks up the surplus workforce that the downsizing of our military services and three levels of government will create. This monumental task may be the greatest challenge for the President and Congress who are elected in 2012.

American corporations have in the past ten years created millions of jobs in Asia, Europe, South and Central America. By outsourcing millions of jobs to foreign countries, there is a $500 billion contribution to the annual deficit which added trillions of dollars to the rising mountain of debt during the past decade. This situation cannot continue if the federal government's budget is to be balanced in the second decade of the 21st Century. The sad truth is neither political party is focused on correcting this situation. Too many political leaders and members of the press are telling voters it is Social Security and Medicare that are causing the deficits when it is the unemployment problem, unfunded wars, and the runaway costs of health care causing the problem.

The loss of income and other taxes in the 2008 Great Recession for the federal government due to unemployment was estimated to be $268 billion in 2009 and the cost of supporting unemployed and underemployed Americans has grown to $224 billion, a total of nearly a half trillion dollars of borrowed money added to the deficit annually. (4) Our country simply cannot afford to have millions of unemployed Americans wading through years of stagnation during a long-term recession. The federal government must step in and partner with

American corporations to expand the economy and increase job growth. The Business Roundtable (the nation's largest 200 corporations), the Chamber of Commerce, and trade associations must develop a positive working partnership with the President and Congress in order to recharge the private enterprise system.

Tax cuts will not solve the country's economic problems, according to three Federal Reserve Chairmen who all have been appointed by a Republican President. Tax cuts create a bounce in the economy, but create a much larger federal debt with growing interest expense every year. Telling voters that small businesses will create most future jobs is another illusion, as stated in Lesson 9. Small companies sell to large corporations so the country needs successful large corporations that lead their industries with new innovation in products and services.

What motivated senior executives to make so many erroneous decisions during the past 30 years that ultimately damaged their companies and resulted in millions of lost jobs? Executive compensation that includes stock options is a major motivator. The fastest road to improved earnings for executives under this compensation plan is to lay off thousands of employees and/or reduce their benefits. Wall Street cheers whenever layoffs are announced and rewards that company with an increase in its stock value. Closing a manufacturing plant becomes a positive story on page one of the financial news, but brings a great deal of pain and suffering to a local community.

Chief Executive Officers and other senior executives in the Standard & Poor's 500 companies are now earning more than in 2007 which was the last year of prosperity. They did suffer two years of declining earnings in 2008 and 2009. This is because profits readily improved in 2010 and 2011. On average, these large corporations had a 41 percent increase in profits. This increase plus a rising stock market has produced a great year for executive compensation. CEOs now earn between $20 million and $84 million in one year. Stock options for future years are presently worth $2.2 billion. Therefore, it is difficult to convince senior management they need a new set of performance measurements and compensation plans to achieve a more balanced performance, including growth that creates millions of jobs. But, that is exactly what must be accomplished. The President, along with the Secretaries of Commerce and Labor, needs to focus more on job creation with a new highly visible recognition program. In addition, the public sector must create jobs as it did in the 1930s until the private sector can help return our country to full employment.

How Does The United States Develop A Competitive Workforce

Ever since the landmark "A Nation At Risk" report was published in 1983 describing the deplorable conditions within the American public school system, almost everyone has concluded that the number-one education crisis in our country is the student learning problems in public schools. However, from an economic viewpoint, that honor belongs to employee-training programs. Nearly every corporation, not-for-profit organization, and government agency has inadequate training and support systems. Not only are they underfunded, but too often, the existing courses have almost no impact on overall organizational performance. Moreover, program results are so poorly measured that many organizations do not even realize they have a problem. Millions of American employees, including managers and executives, go to work every day untrained or partially trained to do their jobs. This situation led Dr. W. Edwards Deming to state, "The greatest waste in America is failure to use the abilities of people."(5)

Despite major technological investments, downsizing, restructuring, and reengineering to cut costs and improve competitive advantages, the vast majority of organizations are missing the greatest opportunity to gain more productivity through the performance of their employees. Organizations that are constantly downsizing, laying off workers, losing market share, discontinuing product lines, and even going out of business have often failed to invest in the performance and productivity of their workforce. Recent studies tell us that innovation, not how cheap or expensive labor costs are, determines whether a country will succeed in manufacturing. Manufacturing makes up only 11 percent of our economy while the service sector represents about 70 percent. Most nations, including the U.S, are calling for the return of producing real goods.(6) As the cost of labor in countries such as China increases, the difference between Chinese and American wages is now only 30 percent. More American companies should plan to return manufacturing to the United States.

The government has two choices. Sit back and hope that our corporations decide to do more manufacturing in the United States, which has been the policy for the past 10 years. Or, the government has to establish programs providing incentives for corporations to do more manufacturing in our country. Americans do earn premium wages, but wages are often a small part of manufacturing. American workers must become more productive. When jobs have been outsourced to other countries, American factories have usually become dated with old methods, ineffective training, outdated tools, etc. Once again, it is a leadership challenge that must be solved. China now has 960,000 millionaires because they and other Asian business leaders are focused on having superior manufacturing facilities, methods, and well-trained employees.

Fortunately, some American organizations do an outstanding job of training and supporting their employees to achieve maximum performance at the lowest cost. They have a competitive workforce that knows more and does more to increase market share, improve financial performance, focus on customer satisfaction, and expand operations which creates new job opportunities. They have management systems within their training and management development departments that enable their employees to adjust quickly to new business opportunities, objectives, and strategic directions. These organizations know a well-trained workforce produces more, has a lower error rate, and requires less supervision than a workforce with little or no training. These organizations have demonstrated American companies and organizations can still have workforces that are the envy of the world.

In the 1990s, the American Society for Training and Development sponsored the ASTD Chief Training Officer Workshop with the creative assistance of the Accenture Education Department. Out of that effort, a new management system was developed: the Systems Approach for Workforce Performance, as shown on the next page.(7) This new management system integrates the best practices of organizations that have achieved strategic advantages through the performance of a competitive workforce, resulting in:

-Increased productivity of the workforce
-Lower operating expenses
-Increased revenues and market share
-Elimination of the need for massive downsizing
-Creation of new job opportunities

SYSTEMS APPROACH FOR WORKFORCE PEFORMANCE

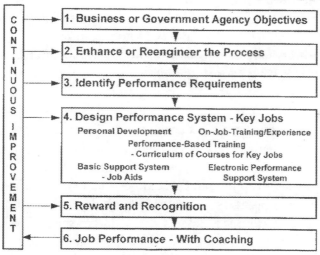

SYSTEMS APPROACH FOR WORKFORCE PERFORMANCE

The Secretaries of Labor and Education should work with leaders of trade associations to identify the key jobs within their industries. Trade associations should then develop training and performance systems within their industry for every key job. Development costs could be recovered through tuition and through selling course materials to training departments within an industry. Once again, it is not a financial problem to fix this lack of real job training. The performance problems of employees, managers, and executives are usually caused by a lack of leadership within the senior management team. Germany has recovered from the Great Recession faster than most major industrial countries. Germany's unemployment has declined from 8.6 percent in 2007 to 6.9 percent in 2010 with the aid of farsighted government reforms. German companies have poured money into research and development projects enhancing existing products and creating new ones. Union leaders have cooperated with management to make it easier for companies to hire and fire employees as well as to achieve real productivity gains. Management is focused on selling itself out of the recession with superior products and services. In Germany there is a formal system for identifying key jobs within an industry and then providing skills based-training. Some predict if the U.S. did this the unemployment would drop by one percent. Germany also has a great apprentice system to support a superior workforce that is well paid and German companies continue to expand their market share. The U.S. Department of Labor identified the key jobs within each industry years ago. This highly visible action program would not add to the federal deficit, national debt or cost of interest.

The President of the United States should urge the Secretaries of Labor and Commerce to identify organizations that have invested in the development of workforces in order to provide the United States with a competitive advantage in the global economy. A new recognition program could bring this issue up to a level that would accelerate an economic recovery. Leaders of large labor unions could do much more to ensure their members are properly trained and supported to become a competitive workforce. Senior Vice Presidents of Human Resources should also be recruited for this effort. In too many organizations, the Human Resources Department is treated as a minor support group rather than as an important department that can significantly impact an organization's financial and operating results.

Is Full Employment a Realistic Goal?

Years ago, a few outstanding American companies had a full employment policy. Companies would grow year after year, even in the 1930s Great Depression and World War II years, so their employees knew they had secure jobs as long as they remained productive, ethical, and loyal workers. As the company expanded, employees had plenty of opportunities for promotions, job enrichments, merit increases, promotional increases, and good working conditions. Morale was constantly measured and maintained at high levels. Strategic changes, new products, and greater services enabled a large corporation to move swiftly into new opportunities. If a job became obsolete, an employee was given another job without any decrease in salary or job level with the added assurance that he or she would be fully trained and coached to succeed in the new job. IBM doubled its business every five years with this laser focus on growth, job opportunity, superior performance, and employee morale from the early 1920s to the early 1990s.

Unfortunately, Wall Street, several business professors, the business press, and some consultants started to tell senior executives at these successful companies that they could achieve more earnings and inflate their stock value by giving up the full employment policy. After all, it is easier to lay off employees than to put in the work required to grow a business or retrain employees. In too many situations, our corporate leaders and Wall Street have accepted poor performance and loss of market share due to inferior products caused by inferior engineering in American corporations over the past 30 years. A new attitude must be developed to win back markets with superior products and services that have been lost over the years.

These same so-called "experts" ridiculed large and successful Japanese corporations that had built their businesses from the ashes of World War II to become industry leaders over a forty-year period. As Japan hit the economic wall due to an inflated stock market, unrealistic real estate values, and mismanagement by their financial institutions, these experts wrote off full employment simply as an outdated business strategy. As the successful Japanese corporations gave up full employment, they suffered the same results as successful American corporations: slower growth, reduction in market share, and lower financial performance.

Only people fortunate enough to work in organizations that have full employment know how this fundamental strategy creates a superior organization. Government agencies once had a difficult time attracting outstanding candidates for employment, but today, they are now able to hire many of the top graduates because they have evolved to provide job security, good salaries, superior training programs, great benefits, and outstanding work conditions. American corporations and senior executives need to re-examine the potential advantages of a full employment policy.

Implement Programs That Create Demand

Too many organizations are waiting for the 2008 Great Recession to end with the hope, and it is only a hope, that demand levels of the 1990s will return to their business. Chief Executive Officers will have to demand creative new marketing and sales programs in order to return their companies to prosperity. With all the cash ($1.8 trillion) on their balance sheets, companies need to invest in new marketing programs. The United States, at one time, had great sales organizations that created new markets. Many of those sales organizations have been downsized or eliminated during years of prosperity. Rather than buy back their stock, companies need to hire more sales personnel and train them better. Advertising and direct mail marketing are often insufficient in recession years.

Will State Capitalism Overtake Free Market Capitalism?

Since 1980, one party's political leaders have claimed that government is the problem. These pundits believe American businesses must avoid regulations and interference from any level of government so they can have the freedom to pursue maximum profit and shareholder value. This grand strategy helped lead the United States into an economic depression in the 1930s and into a recession during the fourth quarter of 2008. Numerous European countries followed this same strategy, and they too entered into an economic depression.

Mr. Jan Bremmer, President of the world's leading global political risk research and consulting firm Eurasia Group, wrote *The End Of The Free Market: Who Wins The War Between States And Corporations.*

Bremmer's book discusses the emergence of state capitalism and how it will compete against free market societies such as the United States and how it will shape the global economy's future. Major economies that currently practice state capitalism include China, Russia, and the Arab monarchies of the Persian Gulf. A number of developing world countries are moving in the direction of state capitalism and avoiding free market capitalism.(8)

In state capitalism, governments use various kinds of state-owned and private companies to manage the exploitation of resources that they consider a state's crown jewels in order to create and maintain large numbers of jobs. They also select privately owned companies to dominate certain economic sectors. Their goal is to maximize the best of both public and private resources to achieve full employment, market leadership, prosperity for their citizens, and sustain political power for decades based on high approval ratings.

How did this new economic system emerge? Most people believe that the end of the Cold War provided the final victory for free-market capitalism. At the end of 1991, the Soviet Union essentially went out of business because Mikhail Gorbachev and his government decided to quit trying to spread communism throughout the world with the massive military organization that had relegated Soviet citizens to decades of poverty. This action was not a reaction to the size of the United States military. Gorbachev told President Reagan that he was going to do a terrible thing to the United States: he was going to withdraw the Soviet Union from the Cold War. Former Warsaw Pact nations started to move towards membership in NATO and the European Union. Even Fidel Castro decided to try some capitalist experiments. Leaders in China decided they did not want to suffer a meltdown like the Soviet Union, so they conducted pilot tests of innovation and free market projects. As these nations moved away from the command economy of communism to a free-market capitalistic system, they realized it was a long row to hoe. They decided to develop the state capitalist system rather than go all the way to a free-market capitalist system, a move that enabled them to avoid many problems in the economic depression of 2008.

Japan also had a state capitalist system with its country-wide industrial policy developed by the Ministry of International Trade and Industry (MITI), an institution created in 1946. It orchestrated strategic industrial cartels, research, development, mergers, and investment decisions. This system shielded Japanese companies from foreign competition. Until the 1980s, this economic and political organization produced most of Japan's prime ministers. MITI guided the development of new technologies and, as a result, many Japanese corporations became industry leaders in automobiles, steel, appliances, electronic, and even musical instruments.

The state capitalistic system has also been practiced in the Scandinavian countries of Sweden, Norway, Finland and Denmark. Political and economic systems in these countries have raised the standard of living to among the highest in the world and narrowed the gap between rich and poor. There are few nationalized companies in these countries, but there is a strong partnership between government and private companies.

France has struggled since World War II to adopt a workable partnership between its government and private companies. However, France has had some successes such as a large network of nuclear power stations, TGV high-speed trains, and the production of jet airliners by the Air Bus Corporation.

State capitalism is not socialism. Vladimir Putin of Russia has stated, "Any Russian who doesn't support the disintegration of the Soviet Union has no heart, but one who wants to revive it has no head."(8) The current governments of China and Russia have no intention of pushing their countries backwards toward communism. They want to control their economies so they can raise the standard of living for their citizens and provide full employment.

Ian Bremmer claimed in his book that the economic meltdown of 2008 made clear the need for better government, not less government, because it reminded us that investors and commercial strategists too often play for short-term gains and ignore longer-term risks. That's one reason why we should not expect markets to regulate themselves and why intelligent and limited government intervention can help prevent market failures from generating shock waves throughout entire societies and countries. (8)

The financial crisis and global economic recession has ensured that state capitalism will be with us for at least a couple of decades. China has become the symbol of state capitalism, and it will determine how long this trend survives. China's leaders and its citizens believe state capitalism is a better system than free market capitalism. Look at the record: China has enjoyed thirty years of double-digit growth. They now have $2.3 trillion in foreign currency reserves compared to the United States' debt of $15 trillion that is moving towards $20 trillion. China rebounded quickly from the recession because it could implement a multi-billion-dollar nation-building stimulus program. China's goal is to create 10-to-12 million new jobs each year while having an economic growth rate of at least 9.5 percent every year.(8)

Free market countries such as the United States believe that the only reliable long-term engine of sustainable growth is their economic system. Without strong and effective action programs to compete against state capitalism countries, the United States will sink into Phase Three of decline. Again, the illusion that small businesses will solve all our economic challenges will not be a successful strategy in future years. Complaining about China manipulating the value of its currency is also not a breakthrough strategy because the Chinese can point to our government and its manipulation of the low interest rates to manage our mountain of debt.(8)

Regaining Our Manufacturing Industry

Our nation rose from the ashes of the ten-year Great Depression to having the world's most productive manufacturing sector during the five-year period from July 1, 1940 to July 31, 1945. The TIME-LIFE BOOK OF THE 20TH CENTURY dedicated to the 1940's, the "Decade of Triumph," showed the following manufacturing statistics for that five-year period:

296,429	Aircraft
71,062	Naval Ships
5,425	Cargo Ships
372,431	Artillery Pieces
20,086,061	Small Arms
41,585,000,000	Rounds of Ammunition
5,822,000	Tons of Aircraft Bombs
102,351	Tanks and Self-Propelled Guns
2,455,964	Truck and Jeeps

After 15 years of depression and war, the resulting pent-up demand for automobiles, houses, appliances, radios, furniture, and clothes enabled our manufacturing sector to transition successfully from wartime to peacetime production.

With "free trade" agreements, much of our manufacturing sector has been outsourced to Europe and Asia over the past 30 years. If the United States still had a robust manufacturing sector, it would have full employment rather than millions of unemployed workers. One Asian organization employs over 900,000 Chinese workers who are building high-tech products for American stores. The federal government needs to renegotiate the "free trade" agreements so that the American manufacturing sector can be expanded in future years. After all, it is Americans who buy the finished products. For example, once a foreign automobile company has achieved a certain volume of sales within the United States, it could be told to build an automobile manufacturing plant in our country. With proper training, American workers can be at least as productive as foreign workers. Today, our automobile companies have competitive wages and benefits compared to their counterparts in Korea, Japan, and Germany. In time, wages and benefits will be comparable to other countries as well. We need more products that have: "Made In America" stamped on them and incentives to make it happen in this decade.

Nation Building Within the United States

Infrastructure within the United States is becoming second and third class compared to other major industrial countries. The Secretaries of Commerce, Transportation, and Labor should work with the Business Roundtable, Chamber of Commerce, and trade associations to develop expansion strategies and hiring plans over the next six years. If the private enterprise system is not going to expand and create a few hundred thousand new jobs each month, the federal government should implement a second major stimulus that is focused entirely on lowering the unemployment rate by 40-to-50 percent. Projects that would help employ some of the 26 million Americans unable to find full-time work include:

- Interstate highway improvement (including building bridges)
- Nationwide, cost-effective energy network
- New instructional system for public schools
- New government buildings
- Upgrade airports and rail systems
- Seed grants for new markets/technologies

Recently, a study headed by two former Secretaries of Transportation concluded that an additional $134 billion to $262 billion must be invested per year through 2035 to build and improve the nation's roads, rail systems, and air transportation to properly serve the United States in the 21ˢᵗ Century. If the investment is not made, it would undermine the ability of our country to compete in a global economy. This investment could be funded with an increase in the 18.4 cents per gallon gas tax that has not been increased for nearly 20 years. Once again, many political leaders refuse to support any increase in any taxes which is causing the decline of the United States to be a second-class country in the new global economy.

Some political leaders claim that only the private sector can create real jobs. This is not true. The public sector has millions of real jobs and, frankly, the unemployed do not care whether they have a private or public sector job. Too many public policy people believe the government should send money to state or local governments with the hope it will create some new jobs or put more money in American paychecks by lowering taxes, with again, the hope that increased spending will create jobs. So far these programs have only made a small contribution to creating new jobs even after trillions of borrowed dollars have been allocated to well-intentioned programs. Hopefully in 2012 and the next administration, government will create real jobs both in the private and public sectors based on rebuilding America.

In the Great Depression, the unemployment problem remained unresolved for 10 years, and it took that long to reach the goal of prosperity. From 1940 with the build-up to World War II until 1945 when the war ended, the United States was a classic example of state capitalism. The private sector had a bipartisan working relationship with the government to produce ships, guns, planes, trucks, tanks, weapons, clothes, and food for the war effort. Our country certainly does not want to repeat history by having World War III solve our economic problems. When the recession is ended, the cost of unemployment services will be reduced by $250 billion and tax revenues increased by $250 billion. Thus, funds for a large nation-building program will be available for the United States rather than for Iraq, Afghanistan or any other country that harbors terrorists.

Leadership Required in Private and Public Sectors for Employment

Unemployment is at a depression level. By the summer of 2010, the number of Americans who were without a job for 27 weeks or more was close to 7 million, approximately 45 percent of the unemployed population. The United States has few policies in place to deal with the long-term jobless, who become less employable the longer they lack a regular job. Over eight million jobs have been lost in this severe recession. A home that has no income is a depressing environment, and the unemployed do not care whether the country is operating under a free-market capitalist system or a state capitalist system. Laura Tyson, the former chairperson of the Council of Economic Advisers and of the National Economic Council, and her supporters advocate a second stimulus to reduce unemployment significantly. Other economists are against a second stimulus, but they are not running for office. Ms. Tyson reminds everyone that President Roosevelt made putting people to work his number-one objective; not just viewing the depression as a budget problem.

In a severe recession that borders on becoming an economic depression, one stimulus program is not sufficient. The first stimulus program in 2009-2010 helped save the country from a depression. The second stimulus must reduce unemployment. A third stimulus may even be needed to return our economy to prosperity, one of the six national goals. While Republicans rail against the use of stimulus programs, they should keep in mind that three of their Presidents used stimulus programs throughout the past 30 years to end other recessions. Doing nothing, as President Hoover did in 1930, is not a successful strategy and should not be repeated by either political party.

Remember, in state capitalism, the goal is to achieve a rising standard of living for citizens and to achieve full employment based on annual growth with increased market share. Executives are paid well, but they do not become billionaires. Communities expect companies to contribute to their citizens' well-being and standard of living. In free market capitalism, the primary goal is for senior executives and stockholders to get rich. Customer satisfaction, market share, job security, and community relations are all optional objectives.

Fortunately, in the spring of 2010, hiring increased and there were more new jobs, but not a sufficient number to achieve a breakthrough in the unemployment rate. Our country has been waiting for 12 years hoping the free enterprise system would create millions of jobs. It has not happened, so new jobs creating programs are necessary. Our government should consider more jobs for rebuilding our infrastructure. Robert Nardelli, CEO of Cerberus Operations and Advisory Company, wrote an article in the April 5, 2010 issue of BUSINESS WEEK entitled "Job Creation: Enlist the Experts." He suggested putting together a team of former CEOs who are patriots first and have no political agenda. People such as Jack Welch, Lou Gerstner, Andy Grove, Anne Mulcahy, A.G. Lafley, Larry Bossidy and other CEOs who have created millions of jobs could form such a team. Andy Grove wrote an article for BLOOMBERG BUSINESSWEEK in which he stated, "Our country has a misplaced faith in the power of startups to create jobs. It is important for the startups to scale up by building factories and hiring thousands of Americans to make products. The U.S. must not lose the engineering and manufacturing jobs."(9) The President needs to consider such bold ideas. At the same time, credit must be freed up for small businesses. Bank lending has dropped to a frightening level. The current administration has to put more pressure on financial institutions to support businesses with loans.

The working world has changed from lifetime job security with a pension supporting both worker and spouse to changing jobs five or ten times during a 50-year career. Therefore, it may be necessary now for a "grace period" for paying mortgages, student loans, car loans, and health insurance premiums when an American is out of work for a number of months. Interest would continue to accrue, but an unemployed person would not lose everything as such people do now. This proposal may seem like a radical idea, but the pain and suffering incurred several times during one's life due to unemployment needs to be reduced.

The President and his administration also need to focus on the education of new managers and new executives. Thousands of graduate business schools have curriculums that are strong on financial subjects, lessons on how to start a company, and strategic planning. However, these schools are weak in how to develop a competitive workforce, how to create and manage change, how to become competitive in a global economy, and how to expand a business with new products and services. Courses on leadership and on how to create management systems also need fundamental change. The Secretaries of Commerce and Education should meet with the Deans at Graduate Schools of Business to modify their curriculums so American companies can become more competitive in the global economy.

Invalid Excuses for Not Expanding Their Companies

Numerous senior executives and trade associations are offering the following excuses to justify their strategy to hoard cash while downsizing and outsourcing jobs to foreign countries:

1. They claim to be afraid of major tax increases resulting from the country's mountain of debt. *Corporate income taxes fell 58 percent from 2007 to 2009. Taxes are at record lows due to exemptions, the recession, and lobbying for deductions.*
2. They claim to be afraid of more government regulations. *The only regulations that will pass in Congress are those that will prevent a meltdown of the American financial system or the economy, which should provide confidence to expand.*
3. They claim to be afraid of new taxes for health care reform. *This health care bill was passed without placing major tax increases on corporations. For years, corporations have had to accept major increases in health care insurance policies. The reform act is designed to lower health care costs for both employees and employers.*
4. They claim to be afraid of new taxes to provide more energy and a clean environment. *The proposed energy bill is not calling for increased taxes on employers.*

5. They claim the Democratic Party may pass laws that strengthen labor unions. *Only 7.2 percent of the private sector companies are now unionized.*

6. They claim that proposed reinstated tax increases are hurting them. *They were motivated to expand employment during prosperity in the 1990s before the tax cuts were enacted in 2001 and now the tax cuts have been extended.*

It is time to put all these excuses aside and make some bold decisions to grow businesses which will increase the number of new jobs. Executives are being paid more than at any time in the history of American business. Our country needs their leadership and risk taking.

The recession has directly hit more than half of the nation's working adults, pushing them into unemployment, pay cuts, reduced working hours, part-time jobs, and a loss of their overall net worth according to a new Pew Research Center study.(10) The American workforce needs great leadership by senior executives to regain the consumer confidence. The civil war between the two political parties, which has resulted in Congress having an approval rating of 11 percent, does not give confidence to business executives or consumers. There must be a clear plan for creating jobs which will include nothing short of a large scale nation-building program.(11) The Federal Reserve recently reported that America's 500 largest non-financial companies have accumulated an astonishing $1.8 trillion of cash on their balance sheets. Profits are at an all-time high. And yet, most corporations are not spending this money on new plants, equipment, or new workers. In his July, 2010 NEWSWEEK column, Fareed Zakaria stated, "President Obama now needs to outline a growth and competitiveness agenda that will seem compelling to the American business community."(12) We need CEOs to start spending their money in the near term and stop buying back their stock

There is a crisis of leadership within the private sector of our economy. When the loss of market share by American corporations over the past 30 years is reviewed, it is clear there are four types of senior business executives. Some are incompetent and need to be removed by their board of directors before they do damage to a corporation. Many are just capable of maintaining the status quo while their overseas competitors are designing better products and services. The third category of leadership reveals executives who merely improve the value of the stock by cutting budgets with massive layoffs that eventually reduce the viability of a corporation. With better engineering, manufacturing, and marketing, foreign competitors are gaining market share while our status quo executives blame their problems on unions and government regulations. American corporations need more visionary senior executives who are the fourth category and who can gain market share with new or better products and services.

Partnership of Private and Public Organizations Are Essential

Numerous books have been written in recent years that heap praise on how great the American free enterprise system is and how important it is that there be no government regulation or involvement in the economy. *The Battle: How The Fight Between Free Enterprise And Big Government Will Shape America's Future* by Arthur C. Brooks, President of the American Enterprise Institute, is one such book. In this book and in the foreword by Newt Gingrich, these gentlemen leap to the wrong conclusion that any help from government is a giant step forward to socialism, a grand overstatement to say the least. They view Presidents Roosevelt, Clinton, and Obama as leaders who promote socialism, which could not be further from the truth. They live in the past about the glories of free enterprise which had its heyday in the 1940s, 50s, 60s, and 70s. But in recent years, free enterprise has produced endless scandals, inaccurate financial statements, downsizing, outsourcing, millions of layoffs, stock market declines, bankruptcies, low customer service, and a loss of market leadership. Of course, Brooks and Gingrich are against businesses paying any taxes and they never recognize that the excessive spending by certain Presidents caused tax increases. The free enterprise system of the 21st Century is simply not the free enterprise system of the post war years in the 20th Century. Our free enterprise system needs to partner with our government to end the 2008 Great Recession. Companies cannot repeat the mistakes of the 1930s when too many business executives refused to join President Roosevelt in his efforts to end the Great Depression.

The Federal Government Must Protect the Middle Class

Until 1980, corporate senior executives agreed with President Roosevelt that a large and financially healthy middle-class was essential to American economic growth. Today, most senior executives feel little or no responsibility to provide employment or a living wage and benefits to their fellow Americans. If this trend continues, the United States will become a second-class country with the following attributes:

Small, but very wealthy society of rich citizens

Small middle-class (many with two incomes)

Large class of working poor Americans (60 million Americans are now in low-wage service jobs)

Large class of underemployed or unemployed (45 million Americans live in poverty including millions of homeless citizens)

If the free enterprise system is not going to protect the middle-class and with unions nearly out of business, then only the government can step in to insist on living wages, benefits, decent working conditions, and professional respect for employees.

As more Americans move from middle-class jobs to the working-poor jobs, they require more government support and they pay little or no income taxes which contribute to the annual deficits and growing mountain of debt. In San Diego, of the 50 job categories that are projected to have the most hiring opportunities through 2018, 23 pay a median salary of $25,000 or less, including retail clerks, cashiers, waiters, waitresses, maids, and security guards. Nine others pay less than $35,000, including medical aides, office clerks, teachers' assistants, and receptionists. Only 11 pay above the country's median income of $47,700.(13) In one of our most successful cities, the trend year after year is seeing more growth in lower paying occupations which will reduce the size of the middle class. This situation is taking place in nearly every American city.

Proactive Programs Are Required To Regain Prosperity

If the next President and his administration believe the private sector will re-emerge into a world of growth and prosperity without government assistance, they will lead the country into an eight-to-ten year stagnation period. Business executives are often scarred by deep recessions or economic depressions, so they simply do not risk any investment in growth strategies or in new products and services. Once a country sinks into a depression or a severe recession such as the 2008—2011 one, it takes creative new government support programs in order for businesses to return to prosperity.

The Obama administration has been described as anti-business because the President had to re-regulate the financial industry, threatened to raise taxes on senior executives, and complained about the excessive compensation for some executives who were outsourcing American jobs and downsizing their companies. In truth, President Obama has done everything he could to promote American business in world trade and save many major companies in the manufacturing sector. He also provided tax cuts for small businesses. He has taken a country that was on the verge of a long-term economic depression in 2008 and restored it to growth. Contrary to the belief of some people, Obama is nowhere near being a socialist. But, he has not solved the long-term unemployment problems facing our country.

In 2011, Obama made several strategic moves to enhance his partnership with the business community. He met with the leaders of the U.S. Chamber of Commerce. At that meeting, Obama prodded business leaders to "ask yourself what you can do for America, not just what is good for your earnings." He stated he wanted to encourage executives to get in the game. By that statement he meant innovate with new products and services, hire more workers, increase their market share, aim for industry leadership and invest their earnings in expansion rather than buying back their stock. In return, he promised business executives he would go after unnecessary and outdated regulations. He also talked about lowering the rate on corporate taxes, but claimed it would require giving up some deductions and loopholes in the current tax regulations. After all, now only one-third of American corporations pay taxes to the federal government. Obama ended by stating, "I want to be clear: Even as we make America the best place on earth to do business, businesses also have a responsibility to America."(14) The President also wants business leaders to support his plans to rebuild infrastructure within our country.

Obama's new Chief of Staff, William Daley, was once Secretary of Commerce which is another strategic move to build a strong partnership with the business community. Daley, of course, comes with great knowledge of politics as well as business.

Overall, Obama is stressing the United States must be more competitive in the global economy and wants business leaders to be more successful so the United States can greatly reduce the unemployment problem. The President also wants Americans to believe, once again, that government is a force for prosperity and high employment. Obama is also working with CEOs at the Business Roundtable to recharge the American economy. He has created a new President's Council On Jobs and Competitiveness with Jeffrey Immelt, as chairman of the council. The President is meeting with leaders of various industries. For example, he met with Silicon Valley Chief Executive Officers to discuss innovation and jobs. Obama has also been stressing the role of entrepreneurship that has created many success stories in the technology sector. Finally, his tax deal with Republican congressional leaders left in place lower rates on personal income, capital gains, and dividends.

With all this activity, our nation still needs some innovative strategic plans to create millions of new jobs. Tinkering around the edges in 2008 to 2010 did not solve the unemployment crisis. President Roosevelt in the Great Depression sponsored major programs to create new jobs, and it appears that the 2008 Great Recession is going to require new programs for job creation. The country must not accept eight-to-ten percent unemployment as the new norm.

The Republican Party must demonstrate more leadership to solve our unemployment crisis. The illusion that small businesses and small government will solve all problems is not realistic. Republicans need to work with President Obama on developing major employment programs in 2011 and 2012 if they hope to maintain their recent gains in Congress and a victory for the White House. Doing nothing and saying no to every proposal is not a good platform for the 2012 election.

The unemployment rate is decreasing and more jobs are being created than being lost, which is a real accomplishment, but our country must create 11 million new jobs in order to return to the pre-recession unemployment rate of 5 percent. The political party that has realistic plans for employment will probably win the 2012 election. Keep in mind if unemployment remains at the nine-to-ten percent level, several hundred billion dollars has to be borrowed every year due to the loss of income and payroll taxes as well as to pay for all the support to unemployed citizens. Therefore, it is worthwhile to invest in programs that create jobs.

It is time to get realistic. Economists and public policy personnel have not been able to create millions of jobs within the private sector during the past four years (2008 to 2011) with various stimulus programs costing well over a trillion dollars. Sending money to the states with just a hope, and it is only a hope, they will create jobs is not working. Fareed Zakaria on his Sunday morning TV broadcast on June 12, 2011 stated the number-one strategy that is required to lower the annual trillion-dollar deficit is to put Americans back to work. He urged Congress and the President to establish an Infrastructure Bank that issues bonds at very low interest rates to fund projects to repair the U.S. infrastructure that is now a statement in deferred maintenance and projects. This would send money into the private sector to hire millions of construction workers who are unemployed due to the collapse of the housing market. In addition, there must be creative new programs to rebuild the American manufacturing sector. The average unemployed worker has been out of work for nearly 40 weeks. Expecting bank executives who helped destroy the economy in 2008 and corporate executives who have caused the unemployment crisis to provide millions of new jobs without any new government programs is just not realistic. The President and Congress who are elected in 2012 must have new ideas and new programs to solve the unemployment crisis.

Achieving prosperity is also dependent on having a first-class public school system and top-performing institutions of higher education, which are the subjects of Lesson 11.

NOTES FOR LESSON 10

1. *No Apology*, Mitt Romney, St. Martin's Press, 2010, page 101
2. *No Apology*, page 104
3. *How The Mighty Fall*, Jim Collins, Harper Collins, 2009, pages 13 to 26
4. "The Budget For Fiscal Year 2011, Historical Tables," U.S. Treasury Department 2010, pages 30-31, 54-55
5. *Revolutionizing Workforce Performance*, Jack Bowsher, 1998, Jossey-Bass, page 9—Introduction
6. "How To Build Again," Rana Foroohar, NEWSWEEK, July 19, 2010, page 15
7. *Revolutionizing Workforce Performance*, Jack Bowsher, 1998, Jossey-Bass, page 97
8. *The End Of The Free Market*, Jan Bremmer, Portfolio/Penguin, 2010, pages 43 to 84
9. "How To Make An American Job," Andy Grove, BLOOMBERG BUSINESSWEEK, July 11, 2010, pages 48 to 55
10. "Most Americans Seeing Austerity As A Way Of Life," Michael A. Fletcher, THE WASHINGTON POST, SAN DIEGO UNION-TRIBUNE, July 1, 2010, pages A1 and A6
11. "Wrong Track Distress," Bob Herbert, THE NEW YORK TIMES, SAN DIEGO UNION-TRIBUNE, July 1, 2010, page B6
12. "Obama's CEO Problem," Fareed Zakaria, NEWSWEEK, July 12, 2010, page 20
13. "Working for Peanuts," Dean Calbreath, SAN DIEGO UNION-TRIBUNE, April 3, 2011, pages C1 and C3
14. "Obama to Business: Get In The Game," Jime Kuhnhenn, ASSOCIATED PRESS, SAN DIEGO UNION-TRIBUNE, February 8, 2011, page A4

LESSON 11

IMPROVING QUALITY AND REDUCING COST OF EDUCATION

The overall cost of education and training programs within the United States is approaching a trillion dollars per year. Most educators believe there is no saturation point in education, and they assume there is no saturation point in how much money should be spent on education. Since 1983 when "A Nation At Risk" report was published, the operating budgets for the K-12 grades in elementary, middle and senior high school have grown from $130 billion to over $500 billion during a period of low inflation. Costs of a 4-year college or university education have exploded to $100,000 at top-tier state universities and $250,000 at top-tier private universities. Fifty years ago, a college education cost between $5,000 and $10,000. Billions more are being spent on job training and life-long learning courses. One by-product of this severe recession may be our country finally realizing that education must be managed like any other major area of our society. Education cannot be granted annual five-to-ten percent increases in budgets.

The United States Was an Education Leader for Decades

Like other nations, schools in the early years of the United States were not free or public. Many schools were affiliated with churches. In 1852, Horace Mann, the secretary of the Massachusetts board of education, helped pass the first compulsory-attendance law in our nation for children of elementary school age.(1) He advocated standardized lessons, tax supported education, and teachers colleges. By 1885, 16 states had compulsory attendance laws. By the end of the 19th Century, there were school districts, regional schools, and high schools where girls were receiving the same education as boys. Sometimes there were

40-to-60 students in a classroom. Twenty-two million immigrants learned English in these public schools. By 1920, every state had a public school system,*(2)* but only 17 percent of students graduated from high school.

As the public school system expanded, so did institutions of higher education. Today, there are more than 4,000 universities and colleges. In 1940, less than 5 percent of the U.S. population over age 25 had completed four years of college. After World War II, the G.I. Bill expanded higher education through state universities and community colleges. Presently, over 25 percent of the population holds bachelor's degrees.*(3)*

Without a doubt, our country was the leader in education for most of the 20th Century, which contributed significantly to the elevation of the United States as a world leader.

A Nation At Risk Report Rings the Alarm Bell

When Ronald Reagan was elected President, he promised to reduce the size and cost of government. He stated he would eliminate the federal departments of Education and Energy. The new Secretary of Education, Dr. T.H. Bell, created the National Commission on Excellence in Education on August 26, 1981. He directed this commission to examine the quality of public school education within the United States and to present a report to the nation which it did in April, 1983. The famous words from this report (page 5) were, "If an unfriendly foreign power had attempted to impose on America the mediocre educational performance that exists today, we might well have viewed it as an act of war. As it stands, we have allowed this to happen to ourselves."

Today, the kindergarten through high school (K-12) system produces 45 percent successful students based on state tests or 33 percent successful students based on the federal National Assessment of Educational Progress (NAEP) tests.*(5)* In round numbers, 25 percent of students drop out in high school and another 25 percent go to work with only a high school diploma. The third quartile students attend some form of college but do not obtain a degree, and the top quartile graduate from college. In contrast, over 80 percent of students in Asian countries are successful learners and a large majority of European students are also successful students. The United States public school system is now third-class and must be restored to first-class status.

The United States institutions of higher education still have an excellent reputation, but other countries are developing outstanding new universities that are focused on succeeding within the new global economy. In 2005, just 6.4 percent of advanced degrees awarded by American universities were in engineering, while in Japan and South Korea, the percentages were 38.5 percent and 32.3 percent respectively. In that same year, advanced degrees in science accounted for 13.7 percent of the total degrees within the United States, 38.5 percent in Japan, and 45.6 percent in South Korea. The lead we once held in science and engineering has long since vanished, and the consequences for an economy driven by innovation are sobering.*(6)*

European universities continue to stress a 19th Century type of education rather than one focused on business, engineering, science, computer science, and bio-medical, so they are in third place behind Asian countries. It is essential for the United States to maintain a first-place education rating against both Asian and European countries in order to remain the leader of world affairs and to succeed within the global economy.

Four Phases of K-12 School Reform

In Phase One in the 1980s, people believed all the education problems stemmed from societal influences such as too many students that did not speak or understand English, broken-home families, lack of parental involvement, families moving too often, children watching too much TV, or too many homes below the poverty line. In the 1960s, James Coleman at John Hopkins University wrote a report that stated no matter how hard teachers worked, if they had a classroom full of minority children or students who lived below the poverty line, the teachers would have slow learners. The number-one excuse for poor performance became insufficient operating budgets. Many inner-city and rural schools became child care centers because there were virtually no learning standards. This deplorable state-of-affairs influenced President Johnson to commit billions of dollars to a war on poverty as a solution for improving schools.

In Phase Two in the 1990s, Presidents Bush (41) and Clinton established eight national education goals and started to insist on learning standards for each grade level or subject. Over 75 quick-fix and sound-good patches were made to the bell curve/social promotion paradigm that existed in nearly every school. Often with state and local tax increases that were endorsed by the business community, billions of incremental dollars were added to the school operating budgets. Choice was introduced as one of the quick-fix and sound-good solutions to solve our student learning crisis. Choice included vouchers, magnet schools, and charter schools. The only program that achieved over 90 percent successful students was home schooling which grew from a few hundred thousand students to almost two percent of all students. By the end of the 1990s, unlike the space program in the 1960s, not one of the eight national goals had been achieved. One governor at the FORTUNE Magazine Summit in 1993 stated, "We have become masters at measuring poor performance and spending money with little or no improvement in student learning."

In Phase Three which took place during the first decade of the 21st Century, President Bush (43), working with Senator Ted Kennedy, passed the bipartisan No Child Left Behind Act in 2002. The law clearly stated that all schools would have mandatory learning standards and assessments in reading, mathematics, and science subjects. By 2014, over 90 percent of students should be successful learners (A and B grades) in every grade or course with almost no high school dropouts. Billions of additional dollars were added to the operating budgets at the local, state, and federal levels. In addition, corporations, foundations, and universities poured in billions of incremental dollars for more quick-fix and sound-good improvement programs. One benefit of the No Child Left Behind Act was a change in focus. Before this legislation, teachers and administrators believed they were in the business of teaching. They now realize they are in the business of student learning.

At this point, many school reformers concluded there was a massive performance problem within the ranks of teachers, administrators, and somewhat due to resistance to change by teacher unions. However, it is not a personnel problem. The real problem is no new instructional and learning paradigm to replace the 100-year-old bell curve/social promotion paradigm. Simply put, there was no implementation program in the No Child Left Behind vision and law. Both federal and state departments of education tried to rank and shame school districts, administrators, and teachers into better performance. This approach failed and, as a result, the NCLB program will most likely be classified as a failure before 2014. Many NCLB resisters will probably resort to the usual excuses of another federal mandate with insufficient funds and the cry that NCLB had unrealistic goals.

What Is the Root Cause of the Student Learning Crisis?

One reason why there has been 28 years of failure with hundreds of education reform programs is the fact educators cannot agree on the root cause of the crisis. Today, it is clear the root cause is *inconsistent instruction and learning methods* within schools as well as the lack of a state-wide management system for achieving the NCLB vision.

One can come to this conclusion by studying the Korean public school system that rose from almost last place to first place based on a new instructional and learning system designed by Florida State University professors. This system is based on the instructional design methods developed for the U.S. military services. Proof of concept was also provided by the restructuring of corporate training programs and the success of some other Asian school systems using similar instructional design methods. For a number of years, a school district in Mississippi achieved similar results to the ones attained in Korean schools. The success of home schooling, where there are no professional teachers or schools involved, also supports this conclusion.

Numerous education research personnel have also concluded that the quality of instruction within a classroom is the number-one reason for high student performance. In 2009, McKinsey & Company carried out an exhaustive global study of education systems and concluded that the main driver of variation in student learning is teacher performance. A similar study by Bain & Company in the Boston schools reached the same conclusion.*(7)*

Unfortunately, many researchers and education reformers leaped to the wrong solution. They believe existing teachers and administrators had to be replaced by highly qualified teachers and administrators, an approach many education reformers have been professing for over 20 years. Schools hire a million new teachers every decade, so by now, new teachers should be achieving breakthroughs in student learning, but this has not happened. The Florida State University professors and the author of this book believe that as long as schools use a century old bell curve/social promotion paradigm for instruction and learning and as long as there is no state-wide management system for learning, replacing teachers and administrators will never be a successful strategy.

What Causes Inconsistent Instruction and Learning

Except for a few states, there were no state-wide learning standards and the vast majority of school districts did not have learning standards until the late 1990s. There must be state-wide or national learning standards for 75 percent of the curriculum to have consistent instruction. In June, 2010, a Common Core State Standards was published. Alaska, Texas, Kentucky, Hawaii, Maryland, West Virginia, and Wisconsin have agreed to implement these new learning standards. Another 40 states and Washington, D.C. have agreed to adopt these standards in the near future.

Few schools have common course assessments at the completion of each lesson that are aligned with the learning standards, an essential component for consistent instruction and improvement of instruction. Without learning standards or common course assessments, each teacher is expected to develop his/her own lesson plans which has resulted in a bell curve of instruction that guarantees a bell curve of learning. Teachers are also expected to develop their own teaching methods which have added to the bell curves of instruction and learning. New, inexperienced and low-performing teachers receive minimal coaching from well-qualified coaches for improving instruction which also leads to inconsistent instruction. The time to learn a lesson is often fixed and does not allow for slower learners. There is also a lack of coordination between elementary, middle, and senior high schools. Few students live in the same school district for 13 years, so on average, students attend five schools during their 13 years, another contributing factor to inconsistent instruction and learning. Performance of teachers and administrators plays only a minor role in the root problem. The two bell curves of instruction and learning must be eliminated within every school, and must be replaced by a new 21st Century instructional and learning system as well as a state-wide management system in order to achieve the No Child Left Behind law and vision.

Systems Approach for Academic Performance

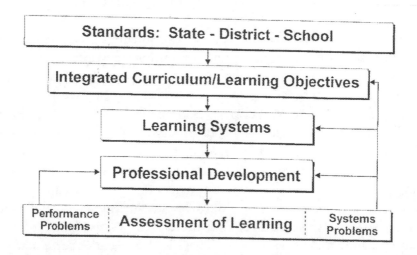

SYSTEMS APPROACH FOR ACADEMIC PERFORMANCE

Learning standards must be world-class and established at the national or state level for 75 percent of the curriculum. This approach will enable a local school district to add learning standards for local history, laws, and traditions of a community. There must be a core curriculum for each state and, perhaps, for the nation.

The curriculum must then be broken down into learning objectives within lessons. These learning objectives will serve as the blueprints for developing the research-based and validated learning systems that will enable over 90 percent of students to become successful learners (grades A and B) in every course at every grade level. Learning systems include all course materials, tutoring systems on personal computers for slower learners, enrichment lessons for faster learners, and audio/video materials to enhance the learning process.

Teachers will be provided with detailed teaching guides as well as in-depth professional development sessions on how to use course materials and tutoring systems to achieve over 90 percent successful learners. All students will be at grade level. Students will not fall behind, get lost, and give up like they do today.

Common course assessments will be on a computerized system to ensure that there is no teaching to the test and to ensure students will not be able to cheat on a test. Assessment systems will constantly improve the effectiveness of instructional and learning systems.

Almost every school must have a Vice Principal of Instruction who will monitor classroom performance throughout the school year and at the end of each module of lessons. No classroom will fall behind. This Vice Principal will be responsible for the professional development of the entire teaching staff and will serve as a coach for new, inexperienced and poor-performing teachers. The school principal will serve as the school's chief operating officer. The new state-wide management system will monitor the progress of schools throughout the year rather than just after the year-end achievement tests.

Who will develop all the elements for this Systems Approach for Academic Performance? Publishers and course development companies will develop the entire system based on state or national requirement contacts. Within these companies, a team of professionals will work full-time on these projects. A team for each grade or course will consist of the following people:

Project Manager

Instructional Designers (Masters in Education)
Subject Matter Experts (Masters or PhDs in Education)
Master Teachers (Superior Teaching Methods)
Assessments Specialists (Masters in Education)
Media Specialists
Computer Specialists
Professional Writers

There will be a multi-million-dollar budget for each learning system, which will require one-to-two years of development time.

Learning systems will use the latest technology to motivate students to learn. There will be no boring lessons. Students will enjoy their lessons and will want to attend school every day because they will achieve success. Success drives up self esteem. The excuses of too few teachers and poor student-teacher ratios will disappear. From 1970 to 2008, the student population increased 8 percent while the number of teachers rose 61 percent. Student-teacher ratios have fallen by 45 percent from 1955 to 2007.(8) Smaller classes and smaller schools have not achieved a major breakthrough in student learning.

The cost to develop a nationwide successful instructional and learning system will be less money than what was spent in Los Angeles ($578 million) for the new Robert F. Kennedy Community complex of schools. The cost could be spread over five years resulting in an average annual expense of $100 million at the federal Department of Education.

Advantages of the New Instructional and Learning Paradigm

This new paradigm will produce the following results:

— Achieve the NCLB vision (21st Century civil right)
— Over 90% of students at grade level
— Major reductions in: high school dropouts and functionally illiterates
— Significantly reduce remediation and operating costs
— Increases in the number of lessons taught each year
— Reduce welfare/Medicaid/prison expenses
— Ensure adequate operating budgets
— Enhance teacher/administrator professionalism

- Provide better working conditions for teachers
- Ensure embraceable workloads for teachers and administrators
- Eliminate the bell curve of teaching performance
- Lower attrition rates for teachers and administrators

Most important, this system will enable the American public school system to move from third place behind European and Asian countries back into first place. All of these dramatic results can be achieved with the existing organization, administrators, teachers, students, and facilities. This system will require no increases in taxes, deficits, or the national debt. With all teachers succeeding, there will be no need to change the current seniority system. However, the teaching profession could be enhanced with a career path for teachers who want to assume greater responsibility.

What Is Required for Implementation?

The Secretary of Education, Governors, Chief State School Officers, and Superintendents must lead the implementation of this new system. They cannot rely on over 100,000 schools to restructure their instructional systems on a hit-and-miss basis. While each state could develop its own Systems Approach for Academic Performance, it would be faster and more economical to have the federal Department of Education develop one system for the entire nation. An organization like NASA would be hired or created to be the general contractor and system integrator. Two states and two cities would serve as the pilot tests to ensure proof of concept before expanding the system to all 50 states. The federal Department of Education would pay for all the design and development costs as well as for the pilot tests. The 50 state governors have the constitutional responsibility for managing a successful state-wide education system. Each state department of education would pay for all course materials, communications lines, audio/video equipment, computer systems, and personnel training. Each local school district would pay for all other operating expenses. After proof of concept, implementation would be phased in over a five-year period to achieve the NCLB vision by 2020 which would be 37 years after the alarm bell of performance was rung.

Missing a Golden Opportunity for Systemic Change

One of the very few areas of agreement between the Republican and Democratic members of Congress is the "Race To The Top" strategy to improve student learning in the American public schools. This strategy has been influenced significantly by the money and leadership of the Gates Foundation and by the changes that Secretary of Education Duncan implemented in the Chicago public school system. These changes are a step in the right direction, but unfortunately, they represent only a small step. They will not pull American schools out of third place.

President and Mrs. Obama could make history if they would take a giant step forward for real systemic change and demonstrate bold leadership to solve the student learning crisis. Only 47 percent of African American males currently graduate from high school. There could be a nearly 100 percent improvement in this statistic which would greatly reduce the number of African American males who enter our prison system, live below the poverty line, and often desert their families.

Our country took a giant step forward over a hundred years ago when it started the phase out of one-room school houses. The new paradigm was a regional or consolidated school where each grade or course had a dedicated teacher rather than one teacher trying to teach a mixture of students in one room that consisted of several grade levels. This was possible due to the inventions of automobiles, school buses and city transportation systems. In the 21st Century, there are communication, computers, and multi-media systems enabling our nation to take another giant leap forward to accomplish the vision where over 90 percent of all students can be successful learners with new instructional and management systems. Once again, it requires leadership. As in health care, our education systems must evolve from the hundred-year-old system of good intentions to a 21st Century system that is mastery of performance. Again, this will require several years of great leadership and must include a comprehensive education of citizens of why this change is essential.

With our cities and states beginning to accept national education standards but lacking the funds to develop a new instructional and learning paradigm, it is the perfect time for the President to instruct the Secretary of Education to develop a strategic plan that will achieve the No Child Left Behind vision and law. After 28 years of small steps and tinkering around the edges with the 19th Century instructional system, the time has come to take a major leap forward.

The solution of "choice" has been a failure over the past 20 years. It is true that successful magnet and charter schools help those fortunate students who are selected to attend these schools, but they represent only a small minority of students. After two decades of effort, only 17 percent of charter schools produce results that are significantly better than traditional public schools and 37 percent perform worse according to the 2009 Stanford University Center for Research on Education Outcomes (CREDO). Charter and magnet schools also provide more inconsistent learning and instruction methods. No charter school system has successfully managed an entire school district, and after 20 years of effort, the charter schools enroll only 4 percent of our students. Parents should not have to attend lotteries with the hope that their child will be selected for a better school. Every neighborhood school should be successful and every teacher should be successful as well.

Education reformers who believe large numbers of teachers and principals must be fired in order to achieve a dramatic breakthrough in student learning are simply on the wrong road and make great newspaper headlines for a couple of years. Eventually they quit or are fired like Michelle Rhee, former Chancellor of public schools in Washington, D.C. They always obtain some improvement, but never a major system-wide breakthrough in student learning. After 28 years, it is time to implement a new positive approach to our public school performance problem.

The Systems Approach For Academic Performance is the "tide that will raise all ships." Virtually all school administrators, teachers, and students could succeed if the federal government would invest less than a billion dollars over a five-year period in the 21st Century NCLB instructional, learning, and management systems. These funds could be obtained within the existing federal Department of Education budget through trade-off planning decisions.

A world-class public school education could become the 21st Century's civil rights issue, and it may be the most direct road to equal opportunity for minority groups in our country. President and Mrs. Obama should turn this issue into a personal and primary mission for their administration. In March 2011, the President asked Congress to rewrite the No Child Left Behind Law due to the fact that 82 percent of our public schools are in jeopardy of missing annual targets in reading and math, up from 37 percent last year.(9)

If President Obama does not step up to the challenge of making the No Child Left Behind vision and law a success, it could become one of the grand strategies for the Republican Party to differentiate itself from the Democratic Party in the 2012 election. However, the Republican Party cannot continue to sell the illusion of "choice." Instead, it must advocate the development of new instructional, learning, and management systems that will enable over 90 percent of American students to become successful learners during a 13-year public school education. These new systems must be implemented throughout the nation by 2020 to achieve the NCLB vision.

What Are the Three Challenges of Higher Education?

During the next ten years, the winds of change will sweep across American higher education institutions. Here are the three major challenges that our colleges and universities are currently facing:*(10)*

1. **Explosive Costs of a College Education**
   State and local governments are having severe budget
   problems due to the long-term recession. For the first time,
   budgets at institutions of higher learning are reduced. Only
   parents of upper middle-class or wealthy families can afford
   the traditional four-year college education on a campus
   away from home, without scholarships or financial aid.
   State and federal governments simply cannot afford another
   multi-billion-dollar entitlement program for millions of
   students.
2. **Demand For Quality Measurements For Learning**
   All across the spectrum of lifelong education programs,
   accountability is being mandated to justify the
   ever-increasing education costs that are fast approaching a
   trillion dollars. The high dropout rate must be replaced by a
   mastery of learning and performance system.
3. **Major Growth In The Number Of Qualified Applicants**
   If the No Child Left Behind Act is only partially successful,

hundreds of thousands of additional high school graduates will become motivated and successful students desiring a college education. This increase will require billions of taxpayer dollars to construct additional buildings on existing and new campuses and to hire thousands of professors and teaching assistants. This, of course, will mean major tax increases which are not feasible, but fortunately, the new paradigm will not require tax increases.

In 2005, President Bush (43) and his Secretary of Education established a Commission on Future of Higher Education which offered a rather ineffective report that failed to address the three key problems facing institutions of higher education. American institutions of higher education did not feel the extreme pain of insufficient operating budgets at first, so they continued to operate in the arrogance of success until 2009. Then serious budget shortfalls arrived on campus courtesy of the state governments. Now colleges are trying to figure out what to do to survive this deep and long-term recession. Clearly, higher education institutions require a new paradigm which addresses the three aforementioned challenges.

New Paradigm for Higher Education

Corporations started to create distance learning systems in the 1970s and, by the 1980s, had developed successful systems which saved them the millions of dollars that building additional education centers and staffing these centers would have cost. They also eliminated travel and living expenses associated with centralized education centers. Distance learning is now emerging as a successful instructional system within the pubic school system, and it has become the foundation for successful home schooling systems.

The design of a new paradigm should begin with a shared vision that will reduce costs, handle a major increase in the volume of students, and achieve a dramatic improvement in instructional quality. Within a college or university's professional college, a needs and task analysis should be conducted for potential careers of graduates. What do undergraduates in a certain profession need to know and be able to do as entry-level professionals? What will they need to know and do in order to advance in their careers? Instructional designers working with subject matter experts (professors) need to develop learning and performance objectives for an entire curriculum, not merely for one course. The latest information from research studies should also be included. Instructional designers can then develop common course assessments for each lesson to ensure that students learn a lesson and have the prerequisite knowledge to continue.

Instructional designers will also need to work with master teachers (professors) to determine which lessons can be successfully taught with distance learning and which ones would be better taught in a traditional classroom by a professor. Instructional designers can then determine which instructional methods and media will be the most effective way for a student to learn a lesson. Options could include a case study, a reading assignment, a required paper, interactive tutoring on a personal computer, a laboratory exercise, or a lecture. Lessons must be motivational and students must achieve mastery of learning and performance which means achieving an "A" or "B" grade.(11)

A curriculum is then broken up into courses. Distance learning courses become prerequisites for traditional campus classroom courses. Each professional college and each major area of study will have a different mix of distance learning and campus classroom courses. For example, electrical engineering might require one year of distance learning and three years of traditional classes on campus. An accounting major might require two years of distance learning courses and two years on campus, while a general business major may need only one year on campus with three years of distance learning. All courses would be available on campus for students from wealthy families who have $100,000 to $250,000 to invest in a four-year campus experience.

The economic breakthrough for families of our lower middle-class families will be the reduction in room-and-board and lower tuition rates resulting from distance learning courses. Some colleges are attempting to charge the same tuition for a distance learning course as they do for an on-campus one, but that approach is unfair to distance learning students. No one expects every state university to offer distance learning courses. However, if 10 or 15 state universities implement this paradigm, they would achieve real breakthroughs in lowering the costs for both students and universities.

For-Profit Universities Adopting Distance Learning Paradigm

A startling development in American higher education has been the emergence of for-profit universities that are using a combination of distance learning and classroom courses. They use centralized departments of course developers to design and create quality courses. The Department of Education has accredited over 700 for-profit schools as colleges and universities. Some of these schools are using national TV ads to promote the quality of their courses. These schools need to focus on providing high-quality courses at a lower price. Quality instruction and affordability are the keys to their future success to achieving the much-needed support of both state and federal governments.

Summary of Changes in Education

Education is an industry that resists change and acts as if there is no limit to the amount of taxpayer dollars it can obtain from local, state, and federal governments. Its goal is to provide free public education to American youth. During the past decade, college tuition and fees have increased by 92 percent compared to a 49 percent increase in medical care. Our country cannot afford this costly vision or strategy. Major changes and trade-off planning are absolutely essential to prevent explosive growth in education operating budgets. For example, the federal Head Start Program should include lessons that children of middle-class and wealthy families learn in pre-school so that all children will be prepared to be successful learners prior to attending kindergarten classes. Political leaders sell the concept that all Americans need a pre-school and college education. This concept is unaffordable. Today, 40 percent of college graduates work in jobs not requiring a college degree. Over 50 percent of all jobs do not require a college education. Our country needs to have over 90 percent of its students as successful high school graduates and approximately 45 percent as successful college graduates. Now is the time to develop an affordable education system that is the envy of the world.

It is a national disgrace that the United States cannot solve the 28-year old student learning crisis within its public schools. Neither political party has invested in a new instructional and learning paradigm. There have been over 200 governors elected during these 28 years, and none of whom have succeeded in solving their education problems. They just keep throwing money at the problems with a hope, and it is only a hope, that student performance will improve. The Chief State School Officers have not stepped up to design, develop, or implement a 21st Century instructional and learning system. Today, local school districts or states lack funds due to their law that they must have a balanced budget even during a severe recession. Unfortunately, the Deans at the Colleges of Education have not solved our student learning crisis either.

Only the Secretary of Education and the federal Department of Education can fund changes within education. Rather then send financial bailout money to states, the federal government needs to send new paradigms of instruction instead. In 2009, the stimulus legislation provided about $100 billion to education, including $48 billion in direct aid to states. This money saved 342,000 teaching and school staff positions. In 2010, the Department of Education asked for $23 billion more to save jobs in schools. $26 billion was approved to save jobs in schools and public safety.*(12)*

In the 1930s, state and local management of banks failed. The President and Congress implemented new organizations and new laws to ensure that banks protected the assets of their depositors. State departments of education have failed to control education quality or costs, so now is the time for the federal government to take a leadership role in all areas of education to control costs and improve student learning.

Education is by far the most feasible way for our government to show it can be both efficient and affordable. Improving education is far easier than restructuring health care, building a new nationwide energy system, downsizing the military, or recharging the private enterprise system for growth. Today, education is based on good intentions that guarantee bell curves of performance. China's debut in the international standardized test program offered a surprise. Chinese students are ranked number one, while American students are ranked 15th in reading, 23rd in science, and 31st in math. Many Americans are calling for a major government response which occurred in 1958 when Sputnik proved a surprise symbol that the U.S. was in second place in space.(13) It is time to manage education like other areas of society to ensure Americans become the most well-educated citizens in the world through the best practices of instruction. The Secretary of Education wants to get higher education out of remediation courses that are essential today.

If the United States would restructure its education systems along the concepts outlined in this book, our country would once again be the envy of the world. Using methodologies and technologies of the new systems, other countries could solve their literacy problems and build a foundation for educating their citizens. This would be the most effective foreign aid program in the history of our country. All the developing nations in Africa, Asia, and South America could benefit from such a program that would be affordable rather than just giving taxpayer dollars to another country.

Lesson 12 addresses the expanded role that the federal government will play in another vital sector of the economy: the development and implementation of a cost-effective and nationwide energy system.

NOTES FOR LESSON 11

1. EDUCATION WEEK, "Lessons Of A Century, A Nation's Schools Come Of Age," 2000, page 14
2. Page 13
3. Page 15
4. National Commission on Excellence in Education, "A Nation At Risk Report," April, 1983, page 5
5. "No Big Gains Seen in Reading, Math Scores, ASSOCIATED PRESS/SAN DIEGO UNION-TRIBUNE, March 25, 2010, page A5
6. *No Apology, The Case For American Greatness,* Mitt Romney, 2010, St. Martin Press, New York City, page 197
7. Mitt Romney, pages 213 and 214
8. "Why School Reform Fails: Student Motivation Is The Problem," Robert J. Samuelson, NEWSWEEK, September 13, 2010, page 21
9. "Obama Seeks Quick Action To Rewrite No Child Left Behind," THE WASHINGTON POST, SAN DIEGO UNION-TRIBUNE, March 13, 2011, page A7
10. "New Paradigm For Higher Education," Jack Bowsher, September 2005, pages 3-31
11. "New Paradigm For Higher Education, Jack Bowsher, September 2005, pages 40 to 87
12. "Prosperity-to-hysteria Two Step," George F. Will, SAN DIEGO UNION-TRIBUNE, June 6, 2010, page B6
13. "A Script For Sputnik," Jonathan Alter, NEWSWEEK, January 10, 2011, page 18

LESSON 12

IMPLEMENTING A COST EFFECTIVE NATION-WIDE ENERGY SYSTEM

Ever since the late 1970s when the Department of Energy was created by President Carter, Americans have heard a conflicting series of facts about what types of power sources they will use in future years and how much these new sources will cost. During the past 30 years, the United States has become more dependent on imported oil and no grand solution has evolved for alternative fuels. Today, our country imports roughly 50 percent of our oil which amounts to $200 billion a year. These imports are a huge drain on our economy because dollars sent overseas cannot be invested in our country.

In the 1950s, the United States started to build a national interstate highway system that no one could imagine not existing 50 years later. Yet, there were many conflicting opinions about how to build such a system and whether the country could afford such an expansive multi-billion dollar project. We seem to be in a similar situation today with the question of a national energy system.

What Are the Problems That Need To Be Solved?

There is constant and growing conflict between environmentalists and the oil industry. Sarah Palin wants to "drill, baby, drill" in the offshore areas and in the Arctic National Wildlife Refuge. John McCain was a "green" candidate, but now he is completely on the side of "drill, baby, drill." These folks have great doubts about the global warming issue.

Al Gore, who has done extensive research on the subject of global warming by sponsoring numerous summit meetings with the finest world experts, does not advocate particular sources for a nationwide

189

energy system. He grapples, instead, with the most complex theories and solutions, but he has a difficult time selling complexity. In a poll, 80 percent of CEOs and CFOs stated that they would not spend money to make their factories more efficient and save money in the long run if it hurt their next quarter bottom line.(1)

Today, 57% of Americans believe there is solid evidence that the world is warming, but that figure is down from 71% in 2008.(2) An estimated 36 percent of Americans believe global warming is caused by human activity, which is down from 47 percent in 2008. Gore blames this decline is due to boatloads of money that coal and oil industries have spent to muddy the science and confuse the public.(3) Al Gore writes, "Not too many years from now, a new generation will look back at us in this hour of choosing and ask one of two questions. Either they will ask, "What were you thinking? Didn't you see the entire North Polar ice cap melting before your eyes? Did you not care?" Or they will ask instead, "How did you find the moral courage to rise up and solve a crisis so many stated was impossible to solve?" Gore believes the Obama administration will eventually establish powerful incentives to begin the historic shift to new sources of energy.(4) He believes that this great transformation to a low-carbon economy will restore the economy to prosperity.

There is only so much oil and coal in the world. Forecasts since 1914 have predicted the United States would run out of oil in a certain number of years. Fifty years ago, there were predictions that our country would run out of coal when the vast majority of houses and buildings were heated by coal. Today, some experts tell us there are 1,258 trillion barrels of oil in the ground or under the sea, which is enough oil to last three centuries.(6) There now seems to be enough coal to last for several centuries.

Many political leaders and voters believe our growing dependence on foreign oil is a threat to our national and economic security. Canada supplies 19 percent of our imported oil, Mexico supplies 10 percent and Saudi Arabia provides 12 percent. Venezuela, Nigeria, Iraq, Angola, Brazil, Algeria, Kuwait, Ecuador, Colombia, Russia, Chad, and Libya (in that order) provide the balance of imported oil.(7) Since 1975, U.S. energy consumption has grown by 40 percent, while U.S. oil production has dropped 32 percent and oil imports have more than doubled. The world oil market is getting tighter, so tight that oil prices, which averaged $72 a barrel in 2007 reached $119 in 2008 and were projected to go higher in future years. Heating oil prices were 30 percent higher in 2008. Gasoline prices hit over $4 a gallon in some cities and were projected to reach $5, but the Great Recession prevented that price hike. A $10 increase in the price of oil is like a $42 billion tax on the American economy.(8)

In 2011, the nation once again felt the shock of increased oil and gasoline prices. The price of gasoline passed $4.50 in many cities and some experts predicted $5 a gallon prices or above. When it reached that level, President Obama stated he wanted to cut U.S. reliance on foreign oil by one-third by 2025. He approved 39 new shallow-water permits and seven deepwater permits since implementing new safety standards in response to the Gulf spill. President Obama continues to be interested in building new nuclear power plants in spite of the problems in Japan. He is also going to have the Justice Department investigate energy markets for evidence of manipulation of oil and gas prices. The President has established an Oil and Gas Price Fraud Working Group. Remember, it takes pain to create change and Americans suffered pain. Just as in 2008, the major oil companies had record and some called it indecent profits due to their monopoly on fuel oil and gasoline. Exxon had a first quarter profit of $10.65 billion in 2011, which was only exceeded by $14.83 billion in 2008. Many Americans want an excess profit tax or at least no more billion-dollar subsidies from Washington, D.C.

There are three major concerns that must be addressed as our country tries to build a consensus for a nationwide energy plan. First, our country must not run out of energy sources. Remember the long line of automobiles at gas stations in the 1970s. No one wants to repeat that situation. Rationing of gasoline, fuel oil, or electricity would do unbelievable damage to our economy and erode support for the government. Second, oil companies are capable of raising prices to a level where Americans cannot heat their homes sufficiently, cannot drive their cars as they would like to, and cannot turn on their lights or electronic equipment whenever they wished. Third, the failure of major oil companies could severely disrupt the economy because there may not be another company that could replace the missing energy flow. The good news is the fact that all the energy problems can be solved with good public policy decisions.

What Are Other Countries Doing for Energy?

China is planning to spend $600 billion over the next decade on its electrical network, especially on smart-grid technology to boost efficiency. As China's mainland economy surges, so do its requirements for energy. China is the number-two consumer of electricity behind the United States.(9) Ironically, American consulting firms and energy manufacturers are helping China reach its vision of having the world's finest energy systems.

While American automobile companies have resisted government efforts to raise the national average of miles per gallon, Japan has mandated that average new car mileage must reach 46.9 miles per gallon within the next five years and Europe has mandated 48.9 miles per gallon even sooner. Some experts believe a hybrid automobile can reach 75 mpg. However, passenger vehicles are responsible for only 16 percent of the total energy used. The majority of U.S. oil consumption comes from heavy trucks, airplanes, homeowners, manufacturers, and companies that produce products such as plastics, cement, and chemicals.(10) Of course, other major users are homes, apartment buildings, and offices.

Canada, China, Finland, France, India, Japan, Pakistan, Russia, South Korea, the United Kingdom, and Iran are building more nuclear power plants. If the United States does not develop a plan and implement a nationwide energy network in this decade, the nation will once again be first in expense, but third-class in another industry. A nationwide energy network has to be a priority in the next administration.

What Power Source Will Fuel Our Automobiles?

A big breakthrough in energy efficient cars during the past ten years was hybrids which use both an electrical and gasoline engine for an average of 45 miles per gallon. A number of manufacturers are now producing hybrid cars like the Prius which has an average cost of $22,000. The hybrid is simple to operate, uses existing service stations, and has unlimited driving range. Automobile manufacturers are also developing plug-in hybrid cars.

The electric car will be available during the next few years. Electric cars are quiet and require little maintenance. Detroit's first electrical car is the Chevrolet Volt. Chrysler, Ford, Mitsubishi, Nissan, and Toyota will produce plug-in cars. The challenge with these vehicles will be to reduce the price and increase their range. The price of a Tesla Roadster is currently $109,000. The hope is to get electric car prices down to around $30,000. The Roadster has a range of 240 miles before requiring additional electricity. Nissan has a car called the Leaf with a range of 100 miles and will cost around $20,000. Ford has brought out the Focus. Shai Agassi is the founder and CEO of Better Place, a company with plans to bring affordable electric cars to the United States by 2012. Better Place will work with Renault that will build the cars, and Better Place will build a network of 10,000 charging stations. Better Place is currently building charging stations in Denmark, Israel, and Australia where the cost of electricity is 3 cents per mile.

Hydrogen fuel cells are another potential source of energy for future cars. The majority of hydrogen is now derived from natural gas. BMW and Ford are developing test vehicles and trying to solve the technical challenges associated with this energy source.

Natural gas emits 95 percent less smog-causing pollutants and 30 percent less greenhouse gases than gasoline. One car that runs on natural gas is the Honda Civic GX which gets 24 mpg in the city, 36 on the highways, and costs $25,200. A gallon of natural gas ranges from 60 cents to more than $2.00.(11) There is plenty of natural gas in the United States. Today, although fleets of buses and trucks are using natural gas, fewer than one percent of vehicles in our country use natural gas as a primary fuel due to a lack of fueling stations. All of these alternative fuels have to be evaluated against the overall cost of a car. Customers most likely will not switch to a new fuel source if all other costs are much higher.

Future of Nuclear Energy in the United States

A consensus is building that more nuclear power will be used in future years within our country. Our nuclear industry was a casualty of the 1979 meltdown of the Three Mile Island reactor in Pennsylvania. The press labeled it a catastrophe even though no one was killed or wounded and there were no measurable health problems resulting from the event. The first American nuclear power plant was built in Tennessee where the Tennessee Valley Authority was the major energy project during the Great Depression. Senator Lamar Alexander from Tennessee wants our country to build 100 more nuclear power plants during the next 20 years. Today, 20 percent of America's electricity and 69 percent of its carbon-free generation of electricity comes from nuclear plants. However, it has been 30 years since our country started to build a nuclear power plant.(12)

France gets 80 percent of its electricity from nuclear power. China is starting construction of a new reactor every three months. The United States government has pledged $8 billion in loan guarantees that will enable two new reactors at the Alvin W. Vogtle Electronic Generating Plant in Georgia to provide electricity to 1.4 million persons by 2017. Currently, two dozen U.S. nuclear projects are going through the approval process with the Nuclear Regulatory Commission.

Fear-mongering about nuclear energy has put the United States 30 years behind other countries such as Japan and France, but our country could make great progress with a partnership between government and private utility companies. The federal government could help the nuclear power industry by developing standards for the design, construction, operation, and maintenance of new nuclear power plants. Of the over 100 existing nuclear plants, no two are alike. Having so many different designs cost billions of incremental dollars. We need an off-the-shelf strategy. Our government also has to move forward on a plan to handle nuclear waste, and ensure new nuclear power plants do not generate waste, which France has developed.

The United States has 102 operating nuclear power plants that provide 20 percent of our electricity.(13) The United States has a perfect safety record with the U.S. Navy submarines and aircraft carriers that are nuclear powered. There are 31 countries successfully operating hundreds of nuclear plants and 53 more plants are under construction. Nuclear power has proven to be a safe source for creating clean electricity.

Of course, the 2011 earthquake in Japan caused the alarm bells to ring once again on where to locate new nuclear power plants.

The United States will never reach its goal of energy independence and reducing carbon emissions without a sustainable nuclear industry. Nuclear power plants are expensive to build, but once in operation, they generate low-cost electricity. Nuclear power would help the United States become like France: completely free from importing

Middle Eastern oil which is becoming more important due to riots and protests in those countries.

Natural Gas Has Great Potential

Natural gas, which has fallen in price by over 50 percent due to abundant discoveries in recent years, also holds great promise. Natural gas produces 21 percent of the electricity in our country. In July, 2009, the Colorado School of Mines claimed the United States now holds 1,800 trillion cubic feet of natural gas, which is more energy than all the oil in Saudi Arabia. Another report stated there is 3.683 trillion cubic feet of gas. Many utilities are now debating whether to retrofit coal plants into power plants fueled by natural gas to reduce their operating expenses. This transformation would reduce our dependence upon foreign oil and would also reduce greenhouse gases. Natural gas is not as clean as nuclear power, but it still is a viable option. The cost to heat an average household is $778 using natural gas and $2,124 using heating oil.

Is Clean Coal An Option in the Future?

President Obama has devoted $4 billion to clean coal technologies, specifically carbon capture and storage (CCS) with the hope of making this energy source nearly emissions free. CCS separates carbon dioxide from the production process and stores it beneath the earth's surface. (14) One pilot project is being developed in West Virginia. The cost of coal will increase significantly to achieve clean coal, but with so much coal available, the United States needs to investigate this option. Our country has 600 coal fired power plants today, and 43 others are under construction.

Wind Energy Has Potential and Problems

Some people claim wind could generate 20 percent of power needed in the United States by the year 2030. Today, it provides about 2 percent. The United States is the leader in the utilization of wind power. To produce 20 percent of America's power by wind would require an estimated 186,000 tall turbines that would stand 40 stories tall, have flashing lights that could be seen for 20 miles, and cover an area the size of West Virginia. That same amount of power could be produced by four nuclear power plants occupying four square miles of land. Thousands of birds would be killed by wind turbines. Also, the weather would have a greater impact on when electricity is generated. (15) In 2010, the wind industry installed fewer turbines than any year since 2007.

Solar Power Has Similar Potential and Problems

Sunshine is a free and inexhaustible energy supply. Solar power is also clean, but it represents only a fraction (.02 percent) of worldwide energy production. Solar panels and mirrors mean more sprawl like wind power. The Florida DeSoto Next Generation Solar Energy Center has 90,000 solar panels that generate enough power to service 3,000 homes in the Sunshine State. Workers at a power plant must constantly perform maintenance to keep a solar power plant operational.(16) Costs need to come down by 25 to 50 percent for systems to be economical without subsidies. The upfront expenses including the installation of solar panels in a home create a non-level playing field for solar energy to compete with oil, coal, natural gas, and nuclear power which carry no upfront investment for consumers.

New Nationwide Power Grid

The National Academy of Engineering set about ranking the 20th Century's greatest technological achievements. They determined that it was not the Apollo program, the automobile, the splitting of the atom or computers. It was the electrical grid across the entire country. However, the nation's power grid has become antiquated, so the Obama administration has pledged $3.4 billion towards "smart grid" technology. The next generation of energy infrastructure must stabilize the grid in the event of failure, must incorporate green technology, and must vastly improve the grid's efficiency. This overhaul may eventually cost billions of dollars of public and private funds, but it is absolutely essential if solar and wind sources are going to be implemented on a large scale. Homes equipped with solar panels and areas equipped with wind turbines must be able to push power into the grid while homes, office buildings, and factories pull power out of the grid. A smart grid also must reduce the waste in transmission of power.(17) With new meters, consumers may save 5 to 15% on their electricity use. Smart technology will make our system more secure against an enemy by preventing cyberassaults. The new grid would, of course, solve the problem of moving extra power generated in the southwest to major cities in the midwest and northeast.

The Bloom Energy Company, headed by K.R. Sridlar, has invented small fuel cells powered by natural gas that are capable of generating electricity for a single home, a manufacturing plant, a large office building, a school, or a hospital, even an entire city. This new technology is now in a pilot test at a number of locations. Sridlar's invention could do to power plants what cell phones and networks have done to wires for the AT&T telephone network.

Offshore Drilling and the Environment

Keep in mind that wind, solar, and Bloom fuel cells only produce electricity for homes, office buildings, and factories. Oil and gasoline alone with electricity will continue to power transportation in the future. New energy projects require 5, 10, or even 15 years to bring them to the forefront. Oil and gas now provide two-thirds of American energy. With consumption growing nearly every year, the United States must continue to produce more oil and gasoline for at least the next decade. For this reason, the President advocates to Americans that we must continue to drill for oil, and create more jobs in the process. Improved exploration and production techniques such as drilling in deeper water, horizontal drilling, hydraulic "fracturing" (pumping liquids into fields to open up seams) have increased America's recoverable amounts of oil and natural gas.(19)

With the unbelievable spill in the Gulf of Mexico and the resulting 24-7 media coverage, every American is now hating "big oil:" Exxon, Chevron, and, worst of all BP. However, Americans must remind themselves that they want an unlimited flow of oil and gasoline at low prices and only "big oil" can make that happen in this decade. These companies also have major holdings in natural gas. They know there is a climate change problem and that alternative fuels will be used in the future, but Exxon has predicted that global energy demand will rise 35 percent between 2005 and 2030.

As for the giant spill in the Gulf of Mexico, the clean-up will cost billions of dollars, but BP has agreed to pay this bill. New safety procedures will be implemented in off-shore drilling projects, and new methods of clean-up will also be funded. The U.S. government will do a much better job of regulating "big oil" for safety and risky decisions as a result of what happened in the Gulf of Mexico. Our country cannot allow the January 1969 spill off Santa Barbara or the 2010 catastrophic spill to influence our decisions to the point where there is a severe shortage of oil and gasoline or a significant price increase.

Norwegian large rigs in the North Sea have operated accident free since they first started pumping oil in the 1970s. Their off-shore drilling produces more than $40 billion in revenues every year which has given Norway one of the world's highest standards of living. The U.S. and other countries will continue to drill for new oil sources. At $4 per gallon, polls show that 69 percent of Americans favor additional drilling. At $5 a gallon, it probably would be 80 to 90 percent. At $2.22 cents a gallon, only 42 percent favored additional drilling.

Transitioning From Hobby Shops To an Action Plan

After 30 years of reports, seminars, panel discussions, books, and pilot tests that have cost billions of dollars, the energy industry needs to partner with the Secretary and Department of Energy to develop a cost-effective energy plan just as Americans did in the 1950s to design a national highway system. Action plans require a vision and a strategy. There will always be many in Congress and across the country who claim that such a project is not affordable. Those persons never tell Americans if we do nothing the United States will be third-class behind European and Asian countries. This project may be one area of government that requires borrowed money during this decade as the national highway system required borrowed funds.

It is time to do nation-building within the United States. We need to shut down the "nice to do" projects and focus on the "must do" ones for real breakthroughs in energy. Even Mitt Romney has stated that the old strategy of "let the market work" by taking a hands-off approach has failed when it comes to energy. Markets cannot be expected to work their unique magic when they are controlled by oligopolies as the oil market currently is.(22)

It appears that the cap-and-trade concept is viewed by Republicans as an energy tax which will not pass. The President wanted to have an energy bill in 2010 whether it had a carbon cap or not. Republicans did not help the President even though it would annoy environmentalists if an energy bill was passed. The cap-and-trade section of the bill passed by the House is now a dead issue as the Senate refused to pass an energy bill in 2010. In recent years, our country avoids addressing major problems until they become a crisis. Energy is now a crisis and it could become a first-class crisis if the Suez Canal or the Suez-Mediterranean oil pipe line were closed.

Energy companies provide large contributions to both political parties. In the last election, they contributed over $16 million to Republican candidates and $5 million to Democratic candidates. Congress has approved billions of dollars in subsidies to oil companies over the years. This industry has the most profitable companies in our economy, but they still receive billions of dollars that are borrowed and add to the national debt. In 2011, with the spike in oil prices, Big Oil brought great damage to the U.S. economy just as they did previously with gasoline exceeding $4 a gallon. At that time, they helped send American automobile companies into a financial crisis. The President, Congress, and cabinet members need to reduce the system of speculation that is driving up the cost of oil and gasoline. Once again, Wall Street is inflicting great damage to our country.

Thomas Friedman of the NEW YORK TIMES wrote an excellent article on July 28, 2010 entitled, "We Will Regret Doing Nothing." Friedman stated, "Not one GOP Senator indicated a willingness to vote for a bill that would put the slightest price on carbon. Democrats appear to have given up on passing an energy bill that would cap greenhouse gasses. Once again, China is moving ahead with a new domestic carbon trading program to help it meet its 2020 carbon intensity target."(23) Our civil war in Congress continues to drag our country down from its former leadership role to one of "catching up" at some time in the future.

Like so many other aspects of our economy, energy requires a long-term successful partnership between government and the private sector. The climate change crusade has collapsed in the United

States, but our nation still needs a nationwide energy system for the 21st Century. Unfortunately, there is a group of political leaders who want to shut-down the federal Department of Energy as a symbol of reducing the size and cost of the federal government. Once again, if this happens, the United States will be third-class in the cost and use of energy compared to Europe and Asian countries. The CEO of Virgin Airlines, Richard Branson, stated he is a strong believer business should be a force for good, not just a money-making machine for its shareholders. Branson also believes if government were to set rules by which we all played, to incentivise industry to move in a particular direction, that would really help us get on top of the problem.(24) It is clear our country has a crisis in leadership with the civil war in Congress. We must free our country from being dependent upon Middle Eastern oil.

The next lesson explains something else we need now in this country: an efficient and affordable government.

NOTES FOR LESSON 12

1. "The Evolution Of An Eco-Prophet," Al Gore, November 9, 2009 NEWSWEEK, page 37
2. Same (page 38)
3. Same (page 39)
4. "The Plan That Saved The Planet," Al Gore, November 9, 2009, NEWSWEEK, page 40
5. Same (page 41)
6. "How Much Oil Lies In Reserve?" Peter Rowe, SAN DIEGO UNION-TRIBUNE, September 28, 2009, E1 and E3
7. "Foreign Oil Producers Have U.S. Over Barrel," Dan Calbreath, SAN DIEGO UNION-TRIBUNE, August 24, 2008, A1 and A 11
8. "Drake's Folly Becomes Washington's Folley," Jim Toedtman, AARP BULLETIN, October 2008, page 3
9. "A Power Plan For China's Electrical Grid," Bruce Einhorn, BLOOMBERG BUSINESSWEEK, January 4, 2010, page 100
10. *No Apology: The Case For American Greatness,* Mitt Romney, St. Martin Press, 2010, pages 234, 235, 237, 240
11. "The Power That Be," U.S. NEWS & WORLD REPORT, April 2010, pages 26 to 28
12. "This Nuclear Option Is Nuclear," George Will, NEWSWEEK, January 10, 2010, page 25
13. "Power Up," William Howard Arnold, SAN DIEGO UNION-TRIBUNE, January 4, 2009, page F1
14. "The Powers That Be," U.S.NEWS & WORLD REPORT, April 2010, page 26
15. "This Nuclear Option Is Nuclear," George F. Will, NEWSWEEK, January 10, 2010, kpage 25
16. "A Source Of Sunny Options," Alex Kingsburg, U.S. NEWS & WORLD REPORT, April 2010, pages 55 & 56
17. "A National Power Grid That Thinks," Alex Kingsburg, U.S. NEWS & WORLD REPORT, April 10, 2010, pages 37 and 38
18. "This Is Brand New," Fareed Zakaria, NEWSWEEK, May 3, 2010, page 44

19. "The Bias Against Oil and Gas," Robert J. Samuelson, NEWSWEEK, may 18, 2009, page 46

20. "The Evolution Of An Oil Giant," Kent Garber, U.S. NEWS & WORLD REPORT, April 2010, pages 39 and 40

21. "Offshore Drilling and The Environment," THE WEEK, August 22-29, 2008, page 13

22. *No Apology: The Case For American Greatness,* Mitt Romney, St. Martin's Press, 2010, page 232

23. "We Will Regret Doing Nothing," Thomas L. Freeman, THE NEW YORK TIMES, SAN DIEGO UNION-TRIBUNE, July 18, 2010, page 6B

24. "Richard Branson," Sharon Begley, NEWSWEEK, January 3, 2011, pages 58 and 59

LESSON 13

ACHIEVING AN EFFICIENT AND AFFORDABLE GOVERNMENT

Why Do Americans Want an Efficient and Affordable Government?

One of the six National Goals for the United States should be an efficient and affordable government. To succeed in the 21st Century, Americans must have the following services provided by their three layers of government:

- Professional foreign service organization
- A strong defense (not a war) organization for security
- Homeland security system to prevent terrorist attacks
- An economy that provides living-wage job opportunities
- Equal opportunity commission
- An affordable home, apartment, condo, or farm house
- A sound and safe financial system for savings and investments
- A successful public school (K-12) education
- An affordable college education for a large percentage of Americans
- An affordable life-time health care system
- Safe and affordable food system
- Local police, judicial, prison, and parole systems
- Fire department
- Emergency medical services
- Safe and decent neighborhoods
- Adequate road system
- Storm and solid waste sewer systems

- Clean and healthy water system
- Sidewalks, roads, and street lights
- Reliable transportation systems (bus, trolley, railroad, airlines)
- Safe pharmacy system
- Parks, community centers, athletic facilities
- Gas and electric services for buildings
- Gasoline and fuel oil services
- Effective zoning rules and building inspectors
- Pension benefit guarantees
- Old age pension system/Social Security
- Environmental protection system
- Good postal service
- Department of veterans' affairs and benefits
- Professional trade negotiators
- Administration to help small businesses
- Libraries and concert halls

This list of over 30 government agencies and support groups is probably not complete. The list could consist of at least 40 organizations and, perhaps, 50. When some Americans demand, "Get government out of our lives and let us have our freedom back," it is important to ask them which areas of government would they want to eliminate? Americans have the highest standard of living in the world because the United States has had for most of its history good and stable governments at all levels. Without our great government system, the United States would be a second or third tier country and our standard of living would be much lower. Failed countries have failed government systems. Truth be told, most Americans take the performance of our government for granted. The press works seven days a week, 24 hours a day, year after year trying to find fault with our political leaders. In addition, the civil war between the Republican and Democratic Parties has damaged the image and reputation of our government and negative ads during election times are not helpful.

Yes, performance problems exist within government agencies just as they do in corporations, small businesses, not-for-profit organizations, medical facilities, and educational institutions. Still, Americans could not have their standard of living without the successful departments of government. For example, some communities are cutting services to balance their budget. When a city tells their citizens they will no longer collect garbage, citizens are free of government, but they have to pay a monthly fee for garbage collection with no reduction in property taxes. It is simply wrong for political leaders to state, "Government is the problem." It is political leaders within government who are really the problem if they do not provide efficient government at affordable rates.

The three layers of government help Americans when natural disasters hit. It is always amazing to see local political leaders, who claim they need absolutely no state or federal assistance, plead for federal help and money when their area is struck hard by a tornado, earthquake, hurricane, oil spill, severe winter storm, or flood.

In reality, Americans have accepted the message from Abraham Lincoln that through government we should do together what we cannot do as well for ourselves. The Census Bureau reported in 2009 almost half (46.2 percent) of Americans received at least one federal benefit: 46.5 million are on Social Security; 42.6 millions are on Medicare; 42.4 million are on Medicaid; 36.1 million receive food stamps; 3.2 million receive veterans' benefits; 124 million have housing subsidies. Perhaps three-quarters or more Americans receive some sizable tax deduction such as home mortgage interest deduction or 43 percent have health care benefits that are not taxed.(1)

Most Americans want additional funds for education (74 percent), health care (60 percent), Social Security (57 percent), and many other areas of government such as better roads. Political leaders have sold voters that spending more money means a better life for citizens, so they always campaign on areas were they will support additional spending. Unfortunately, political leaders have also convinced Americans their taxes are too high.

This situation makes it extremely difficult to please voters, so they flip-flop back and forth between political parties hoping one will solve major issues facing our country. In previous lessons of this book, a reader now realizes that the two most important changes in government must be a focus on peace and prosperity which cause close to one trillion dollars of our annual deficits if these two goals are not achieved. There must be a partnership between government and senior business executives to create millions of jobs to drive up tax revenues and reduce the costs of unemployment by nearly $500 billion. The government must become more efficient in the operation of agencies such as defense, intelligence, education, energy, health care, etc.

Can Government Be Efficient and Affordable?

For years there has been a saying, "Good enough for government work," which implies that government employees are second-class, poor performers compared to company employees within the private sector. For decades, government employees were paid less than workers in private companies. In fact, up until the early 1980s, experienced senior executives within the civil service system who actually managed government agencies with multi-billion-dollar budgets were paid around $60,000. Presidential appointments, such as cabinet level and assistant secretaries of major departments, earned about $65,000 to $70,000. Government executives were working for the same wages that were paid to middle-level managers within the private sector. Top graduates at name universities and successful business executives rarely considered a government career.

All this has changed during the past 30 years. Senior Civil Service executives now command compensation in the range of $165,000 to $175,000. Cabinet secretaries earn around $185,000. Government employees enjoy great benefits such as health care, holidays, and vacation time that are superior to what in most of the private sector positions offer today. Ninety percent of government employees, compared to 18% of those in the private sector, have pensions. More important, they have a level of job security that is the envy of the American work force. Government now can attract many top high school and college graduates. An American cannot become a billionaire by working for the government, but they can enjoy a stable and good middle-class standard of living.

Job training in most government agencies is superior to that within the private sector. Career opportunities are also better because government has been a growth industry while the private sector has been downsizing and outsourcing.

Many universities now have a College of Public Policy and Government, so government agencies can hire outstanding students with graduate degrees. Our government has invested millions of dollars into management development programs to further its employees' education. By hiring outstanding candidates and providing them with great job and management training, government agencies should now be as capable and competent as private for-profit companies in managing their departments.

Downsizing of State and Local Governments

In the private sector, leadership has transitioned from growth strategies with increased employment in the decades of the 20th Century to downsizing and outsourcing with major increases in unemployment in the 21st Century. The same transition of leadership is taking place in the public sectors. Many mayors and governors are using machete techniques in budget cutting to achieve balanced budgets. They are elected to office for four, eight or more years and have time to make systemic changes over a period of years. During their administrations, they should do the same as the federal government or corporations by designing systemic changes for the major spending areas. Education, Medicaid, and prisons are usually the three largest areas of state budgets. Each of those areas can be reduced in expenses by making fundamental changes. For example, on a national basis, 43 percent of prisoners are returned to prison within three years because they usually have insufficient education, almost no social skills to obtain or hold a job, and few job skills so they become unemployed and resort to crime. All this can be improved by making sure every prisoner who is released from prison has at least some job skills, and has been trained on how to obtain a job as well as how to behave on a job.

Forty-four states and the District of Columbia have projected $122 billion in budget shortfalls for fiscal 2012 according to the Center on Budget and Policy Priorities. Statistics reveal 29 states have cut funding for older and disabled citizens and 34 states have cut public education. And 31 states have cut public health. All 44 states are firing employees, which is adding to the national unemployment rate.(2)

If governors and mayors would devote a great deal of effort to cost containment programs, they could handle much of the downsizing with retirements and attrition rather than laying off employees. In the past few years, over 400,000 Americans have lost jobs within state and local governments.

Many of the governors and mayors refuse to work with the Obama administration on stimulus programs for political reasons. In fact, some appear to be pleased to announce major layoffs with the hope the high unemployment situation will enable their political party to win the White House in 2012. Others are trying to do great damage or eliminate public employee unions to show they can be tough on the workforce. They really believe this will lead to their reelection campaign, but a recent poll tells another story. The ABC News/WASHINGTON POST poll in March, 2011 showed 89 percent of citizens opposed laying off firefighters, 86 percent opposed laying off police or school teachers, 76 percent opposed reducing the Medicaid program.(2) And, 62 percent oppose increasing or enacting new taxes which is a clear message to focus on cost containment strategies to reduce expenses as well as avoid major layoffs.

Michigan and a few other states are even going one further step with a takeover of financially troubled cities and towns as well as school districts. The new law enables elected government officials to be removed and to void union contracts by state appointed emergency managers. They can also hire private consultants and restructuring experts to help implement financial martial law that can cut pensions, benefits, and layoff large numbers of employees. The emergency managers' salaries and expenses which range from $150,000 to $350,000 come out of local government or school district budgets. Many people believe this new law is a "blatant unconstitutional power grab" that will be finally reviewed in the American court system.(3) It certainly is not a step forward in democracy and it is not in the U.S. Constitution. There are many political candidates who always claim state and local governments will be more effective and efficient than the federal government. The record of fiscal responsibility at the state and local governments has not been impressive during the Great 2008 Recession.

Leadership Is Key To Superior Performance

Leadership has the most impact on the overall performance of a for-profit company, a not-for-profit organization, or a government agency. Unfortunately, many management and executive development programs are weak and ineffective in communicating leadership methodologies. Such is the case for too many university programs as well. Leaders are not a special breed of people who have great leadership skills from birth. With the right training programs, an unlimited supply of middle managers can become successful executives.

In 2007, Lee Iacocca wrote a book, *Where Have All The Leaders Gone?*(1) Iacocca gave examples of weak leadership within corporations, government agencies, not-for-profit organizations, education institutions, and medical organizations. He asked, "Is it too much to ask our elected officials or senior corporate executives to actually solve a problem once in awhile?" Iacocca claims, "There is plenty of rhetoric, but little action. We have declared war on poverty, war on drugs, war on big governments, and war on crime; all in addition to our real wars." The United States has become a master at spending money and measuring poor performance. Iacocca wants stronger leadership.

The President should appoint a commission to review thoroughly how senior government agency executives and presidential appointments are trained for their leadership and management positions. After all, the government is spending over $3 trillion each year, so untrained senior executives can easily make multi-billion-dollar mistakes.

Growth of Federal Spending 2000 to 2010

During the past decade, federal spending grew by a shocking $1,668 billion, a 93% increase. The growth in defense, military medical, health care, Medicare, Social Security, veterans' benefits, and income security represent $1,545 billion or 93 percent of the total expansion in spending. All other government sectors have grown by $122 billion when spending in 2010 is compared to 2000. The time has come for the President and Director of Management and Budget to give four-year downsizing goals to almost every government agency in order to get spending under control.

Accomplishing More With Less (Smaller Budget)

This enormous spending problem will not be solved by merely freezing agency budgets for a few years or reducing budgets by a small amount each year. The first step is to determine if there are any programs that can be eliminated or downsized. Ranking the importance of all major programs is a good way to identify unnecessary ones. The second step is to request a reengineering study of all expensive programs. One government agency, such as the Office of Management and Budget (OMB), should develop the methodology for performing the reengineering studies. Nearly every organization has programs and processes that have not been changed significantly in decades. Reengineering studies need to be done to improve a process by increasing its quality and reducing its costs. These studies can also identify duplicate programs and expense at more than one level of government with the same objective. Education is a classic example of duplicate costs to improve student learning. When he was in office, Vice President Gore led reengineering studies that produced tangible results. As a result, the Clinton administration reduced the size and cost of government.

The third step is to do benchmarking and searches for best practices that lead to superior performance at lower costs. Benchmarking started in the private sector in the 1980s. Once again, a government agency like the GAO or OMB should develop the benchmarking training programs and methodologies that can be implemented in all federal government agencies. The following definition for benchmarking was developed by Michael Spendolini (5) (formerly with Xerox):

> *A continuous, systemic process for evaluating the services and work processes of an organization that are recognized as representing best practices for the purpose of organizational improvement.*

The fourth step is to institute a Presidential cost containment recognition program, such as the Baldrige Award, that rewards government employees for accomplishing more with less. Voters will support an administration that reduces government spending. Strategically downsizing an organization with their managers and executives leading the cost containment studies is far superior to Congress or any outside group taking a machete to hack away at an organization.

Develop Competitive Workforces Within Government

The President should direct the Office of Personnel Management to work with the ASTD (American Society for Training and Development) to implement a management system that raises the performance of all government employees to A and B levels. The Systems Approach for Workforce Performance outlined in Lesson 10 is an example of what must be implemented, while the Director of Personnel Management phases out the old bell-curve of solid C performers. The President must be able to state that training and performance systems have been implemented in every government agency to ensure outstanding employee performance.

Budget Process for Accomplishing More With Less

Political candidates who are out of government often tell voters that there is so much government waste because of duplicate, useless, and outdated programs that it will be easy for them to reduce spending once they are elected. When elected, though, these politicians never seem to find the waste and vote instead for billions of dollars in additional spending. Downsizing government agencies is not easy; a few emotional speeches on the subject are not sufficient. There must be a formal process for reviewing every agency so the government can accomplish more with a smaller budget.

The Director of Management and Budget must issue spending objectives over a four-year period that phase down spending in almost every government agency. Each government agency should submit budgets that identify programs (In-Plan) and programs which will have to be reduced or phased-out (Out-Plan). In corporate finance, some department heads try to play games during the budget cycle by placing their most important programs in the Out-Plan with the hope that the less important programs will also be funded. This type of game-playing ends whenever senior executives agree to eliminate entire Out-Plans. The shocked department heads usually respond by asking for an opportunity to reprioritize their In-Plans and Out-Plans. Smart senior executives should agree to their request, but should also penalize anyone who resorts to such game-playing during the budget cycle.

Bring Earmarks Under Control

Earmarks are usually pet projects for Congressional Districts which send a strong message to voters that a member of Congress can deliver special funds to their area of the country. The Republican Party during the two Bush administrations carried this earmark program to new heights in both the quantity and cost of earmarks. Democrats were also users of earmarks. Washington lobbyists often use campaign donations to achieve generous earmarks for their projects which, of course, justify their large salaries and expenses.

Both political parties are trying to show that they are against earmarks in this federal government financial crisis, but secretly they are playing games to reinstitute earmarks as soon as any election is over. The Senate is having a difficult time giving up or even limiting earmarks. Many Congressional members claim earmarks are beneficial because a Senator or Congressperson can identify worthy projects that sometimes escape the attention of Congress, the Pentagon, or the White House.

One way to control earmarks is to ban any campaign donation from officers or an organization that receives an earmark. Another way is to ban all earmarks for profit-making companies. The political reality is that voters have lost confidence in Congress to police itself on earmarks. In 2006, Congressman Randy "Duke" Cunningham from the San Diego area pleaded guilty to conspiracy and tax evasion after admitting to taking $2.4 million in bribes in an earmarking scandal that revolved around defense contracts. Cunningham is now serving over eight years in prison, a giant fall from grace for a former Navy air ace during the Vietnam War from a predominantly Republican Congressional district. Unfortunately, both parties have contributed to a long list of questionable earmarks.(6)

In the May 31 to June 6, 2010 issue of BLOOMBERG BUSINESSWEEK magazine on page 51, a poll by the Pew Research Center stated that Congress has a low rating compared to these other institutions:(7)

- Congress: 24% (recent surveys state it is 11%)
- Banks: 22%
- Corporations: 25%

- Mainstream media: 31%
- Hollywood films: 33%
- Obama administration: 45% (other surveys are over 60%)
- Church/Synagogue: 63%
- Small businesses: 71%

For some reason, members of Congress do not care how low their ratings are with the American public as long as they are reelected. The nearly 10,000 earmarks in 2009 representing $16 billion was less than one half of one percent of spending, but they help explain why Americans have such a low opinion of Congress. The civil war between the political parties has also contributed to this low approval rating.

Case Study for Stop Throwing Money and More Employees at Problems

Americans get upset with government when systems are not fixed and more money is the government's only solution. Too many political leaders are believed to be good representatives when all they do is spend more money with just a hope that it will solve problems. Billions of dollars have been wasted with this response to large national problems. Constant pressure from the 24-7 mainstream media promotes spending sprees that pass for an attitude—spend any amount so it looks like the government is actually doing something. The media gets our citizens to believe that the government can fix any problem if it just spends millions or billions of dollars. In the great 2010 oil spill, a private sector company had the tools and talent to stop the oil leak. Government was helpful in the cleanup, but it did not have the knowledge or the technology to stop the oil leak. However, for weeks, the media interviewed experts and government persons who demanded that the government drown the situation with money and more personnel. Everyone is a capitalist until a private company makes a catastrophic mistake. Then, everyone wants the government to take over the situation.

Another classic example of uncontrolled spending is our immigration problems. With a bipartisan Congressional effort in 1986, President Reagan passed a new immigration reform bill that was supposed to eliminate the mass influx of illegal immigrants. Unfortunately, his fellow

Republicans wanted cheap labor for small businesses in construction, farming, gas stations, retail stores, landscaping, and custodial services, so they never enforced the law that prohibited hiring immigrants who had no papers. Millions of illegal immigrants poured into our country for those jobs.

An estimated 12 million persons are living illegally in the United States at a time when there are more than 15 million Americans seeking employment. Comprehensive immigration reform is required to protect jobs for Americans. Mexico is a failed country because it has a small class of wealthy citizens who have absolute control over its majority population of poor people. The country's small middle-class population has little-to-no influence over the weak and ineffective government that has ruled for decades. The Tea Party should look at Mexico when they scream about tearing down the U.S. government. If Mexico comes apart at the seams in future years, the United States could become one giant refugee area.(8) A fence may be required to secure our border because an army of border patrol guards and thousands of National Guard troops are not able to control the borders. Controlling the Mexican border without a fence requires an army of border agents trying to stop hundreds of thousands of Hispanics from illegally entering the United States each year. In one area, San Diego, agents arrested about 65,000 persons and there are probably thousands more who make it safely into our country. This clearly tells us the current border control system is a failed one. Something must be done to control the border at an affordable cost. Immigration experts claim the number of deportations in 2011 will probably top 400,000 which is a record number. Think of the cost to operate our immigration system which has almost doubled in the past ten years. Is our country going to wait until we have 25 million illegal immigrants before Congress can agree on a comprehensive system to fix this crisis? A "do nothing" Congress is extremely expensive. A fence can be removed in the future when Mexico has a stable government and economy. Step one is to have comprehensive immigration reform.

Democrats want Hispanics as voters because, between 1993 and 2010, the number of House districts where minorities are at least 30 percent of the population nearly doubled from 109 to 205.(9) Many areas of our country could not operate without Hispanic employees who accept low wages for tough jobs that most Americans avoid. In future years, Hispanics will wield significant political power and will have tremendous influence over future elections. Some estimates claim by 2050, Hispanics will comprise one-third of the U.S. population. Republicans do not want these people to be voters, so they demand: "no amnesty for illegal immigrants."

The United States has grown by welcoming immigrants for over 200 years. People from around the world come to study in U.S. universities on temporary visas and millions have stayed to become productive citizens. Our high-tech companies have pleaded with Congress to increase the annual allotment of H-1B visas for highly skilled workers. In 2010, about 65,000 such visas were granted.

Over the years, almost 12 million immigrants have been classified as illegal, but a majority of these workers are not undocumented. Nearly 4 million Mexican citizens have matriculas identity cards issued by a Mexican consular office. Millions more have individual tax identification numbers issued by the Internal Revenue Service to foreigners who are ineligible to receive a Social Security card, but can still hold jobs or possess assets that make them liable for taxes within the United States. Many American businesses are accepting these documents for identification purposes in the transaction of goods and services.

When will Congress pass a comprehensive immigration reform bill? President George W. Bush told Americans that he was going to fix the broken immigration system in 2001. The 9/11 attacks delayed his first effort. In 2006 and 2007, a bipartisan effort by President Bush, Senator John McCain and Senator Ted Kennedy attempted to pass a comprehensive immigration reform bill, but it lacked the 60 votes in the Senate. President Obama has pledged to try again. Fixing the current system will improve our economy by removing any incentive employers have to exploit immigrant workers. It will also enhance national security by identifying each person in our country. It will send a clear message to all potential immigrants that they can gain employment in our country only by legal means, and it will help preserve our national identity as a country of laws abided by legal immigrants.

Most important, it will stop the flow of billions of dollars that fund the army of border patrol (24,000 and growing) personnel who chase illegal immigrants through fields like they were animals with many being killed or dying due to a lack of food and water. It should also stop dramatic gestures such as President Bush sending 6,000 National Guard troops to our border, President Obama sending 1,200 more troops, and local politicians demanding tens of thousands of troops. Border states will not have to pass laws to ask any Hispanic-looking individual to prove he/she is an American citizen. When Arizona passed such a law in 2010, hundreds of protests were held across our country by tens of thousands of protesters.

On immigration, our country is again divided by the two political parties and their civil war. The basic question should be "What is best for the American way of life and standard of living in future years?" It should not be "What is good for a political party to win votes in the next election, and what impact will immigration have on future voting patterns and our nation's spending requirements?" Since 1992, the Border Patrol budget has increased ten-fold, but all this money has not solved the problems. Our country must have a comprehensive immigration reform law to solve these problems.

Concerns About the Way Budgets Are Being Reduced

A number of journalists are concerned about the way deficit cutting is being discussed. David Brooks wrote, "The country's future greatness will be shaped by whether we cut wisely or stupidly." Brooks is concerned that young Americans will suffer the most by major cuts in education. Too many legislators and administrators are cutting on the basis of what is politically easy and not programs that are ineffective. (10)

James Surowiecki in the NEW YORKER wrote, "It's hard to make a case for investing more when everyone believes we should be spending less, but there's never been a better time. Interest rates are historically low, so borrowing is cheap, and the weak economy means that there is less competition for labor and resources.(11) As stated previously, the government has funded many excellent projects and research raising the standard of living as well as being the foundation for economic growth.

Are Governments Essential or Evil?

This is a question being raised by some political leaders within the United States and other countries. When one looks at various countries around the world, it is clear affordable and efficient governments are the ideal situation. In this complex world of global economies, global financial systems, expensive computer and communication systems, every country requires an affordable and efficient government that has a great impact on how well a country's economic system performs and how good the standard of living is for its citizens. Only the most extreme libertarians believe there should be little or no government, and they cannot point to successful libertarian governments or countries that have a high standard of living due to almost no government.

On the other hand, it is true some political leaders are evil. There are the autocratic, oppressive, and corrupt dictators as well as benevolent and progressive dictators. In democracies, there are the well run governments that benefit from bipartisan politics and the grid-lock democracies that barely function with a declining standard of living for their citizens. Unfortunately, there are some political leaders who implement damaging strategic programs resulting in dysfunctional democracies.

All of this tells Americans, they should become more involved in the political process to be certain outstanding candidates run for political office and are elected to lead the country. The solution to American problems is not to have a massive downsizing of government, but to improve the leadership quality within government at the local, state, and federal levels. Our country cannot afford to have incompetent leaders in key political offices. This is also true in other countries. Top performing countries all have great leaders who are raising the standard of living for their citizens.

Major Challenge for Two Political Parties

The federal government is in the same position as the American automobile industry: its spending is out of control compared to revenues. Senior executives at the three automobile companies could never bring themselves to do the major surgery needed to reduce spending. As each year passed and the auto companies' financial positions worsened, automobile senior executives made a few small changes and hoped that somehow their revenues would increase. Finally, after General Motors and Chrysler went bankrupt, the federal government told them how to reduce spending. Simultaneously, Ford brought in a new chief executive officer who made bold decisions to save that company from bankruptcy. Will the Cabinet Secretaries and federal government senior executives have the courage to make major changes prior to the complete meltdown of the federal financial system? Only time will tell. Hopefully, voters will support the political party that is willing to make major spending changes.

One major difference between leadership and management in the private sector from the public sector is the multi-billion-dollar budgets of lobbyists who work every day trying to either create change or resist change. In 2000, the total spending for lobbyists was $1.6 billion. In 2010 the spending was up to $3.5 billion and growing. Financial firms, utilities, pharmaceutical and health care companies, business associations, oil and gas companies are the big spenders for lobbyists. Lobbyists also provide millions of dollars in campaign funding. Because of them, sweeping legislative fights over health care, financial reform, energy, climate change, and defense will be well-funded as the United States moves towards a balanced budget.(12) Many lobbyists are former members of Congress from both Republican and Democratic administrations.

The Great Recession of 2008 created one major change in government at all three levels—federal, state, and local. No longer can each agency expect to receive an annual increase in their operating budget with the belief an increase will be funded with a tax increase or funds will be transferred from another government agency. Elected officials and senior executives in each area of government must now focus on how to achieve productivity and performance improvements to contain costs. Public sector union leaders must also work with elected political leaders to improve workforce productivity and support an affordable government.

Now that a reader has a basic understanding of the history of how our government evolved from sound financial management to reckless and excessive spending as well as knowledge pertaining to the major issues causing the runaway spending, the next lesson will provide a blueprint on how the federal government could return to balanced budgets in this decade like the ones it had in the 1990s.

NOTES FOR LESSON 13

1. "Big Government Stands At The Brink," Robert J. Samuelson, NEWSWEEK, SAN DIEGO UNION-TRIBUNE, April 11, 2011, page B5

2. "Going Broke," Marsha Mercer, AARP BULLETIN, May, 2011, pages 14, 16 and 18.

3. "Financial Martial Law," Susan Berfield, BLOOMBERG BUSINESSWEEK, May 2, 2011, pages 4 and 5

4. *Where Have All The Leaders Gone?*, Lee Iacocca, Scribner/ Simon & Schuster, 2007, pages 1 to 263

5. *The Benchmarking Book,* Michael J. Spendolini, American Management Association, 1992, page 9

6. "Congress Gets Serious About Curbs On Earmarks," Dean Calbreath, SAN DIEGO UNION-TRIBUNE, March 4, 2010, pages A1 and A13

7. "Americas Most Trusted," Pew Research Center, BLOOMBERG BUSINESSWEEK, June 6, 2010, page 51

8. *Killer Politics,* Ed Schultz, Hyperion/Harper Collins, 2010, pages 110 and 111

9. "Latino Power And The Census," David S. Broder, THE WASHINGTON POST, SAN DIEGO UNION-TRIBUNE, April 5, 2010, page B5

10. "Time For Austerity—After Evaluation," David Brooks, THE NEW YORK TIMES, SAN DIEGO UNION-TRIBUNE, March 2, 2011, page B5

11. "Sputnikonomics," James Surowiecki, THE NEW YORKER, February 14, 2011, page 44

12. "Washington Bubble, Tight Budgets Favor Lobbyists," TIME magazine, April 24, 2011, page 19

PART IV

ACHIEVING GOALS AND A BALANCED BUDGET BY 2020

With the six national goals as the vision for the 21st Century, political leaders in this decade can achieve the goals and a balanced budget by 2020.

President Clinton achieved a balanced budget in the 1990s. Realizing a balanced budget in this decade will be a much harder challenge due to the excessive spending that took place in the previous decade. Slogans and illusions will not help in this effort to regain fiscal responsibility. The President, cabinet officers, and members of Congress will need to exhibit superior leadership skills rooted in a thorough understanding of all the major issues and all the proven change-management methodologies to achieve both the national goals and a balanced budget.

The theme of the next eight years should be "Rebuilding America" as our national political, business, education, and medical leaders solve the major problems and barriers that have created our current financial crisis and performance problems within the global economy. This leadership crisis must be solved.

LESSON 14

REQUIREMENTS FOR INCREASED REVENUES & DECREASED EXPENSES

Financial Management Meltdown in Federal Government

The federal government's financial condition changed drastically from 2000 to 2010.(1)

Receipts	Expenses
2010—$2,163 billion	2010—$3,457 billion
2000—$2,025 billion	2000—$1,789 billion
Growth $138 billion	Growth $1,668 billion
7% Increase	93% Increase

It is hard to believe that so much damage could have been inflicted on the government financial system during a ten-year period. In 2000, the federal debt was $5.6 trillion and the cost requirements for interest charges were only paid on $3.4 trillion of public debt. The U.S. government had surpluses in 1998, 1999, 2000, and 2001 that totaled $560 billion. The excessive spending of President Reagan had been brought under control. President Bush (41) had implemented a tax increase and a pay-as-you-go law in the early 1990s which President Clinton continued throughout his eight years. President Clinton with only Democratic support in Congress passed another tax increase in 1993 to reduce the size of the annual deficit. The second President Bush, on the advice of Vice President Cheney and with the support of a Republican Congress, eliminated the pay-as-you-go (PAYGO) requirement in order to add expensive government programs without eliminating other expensive government programs. This fiscal policy enabled Bush and Cheney to spend and borrow record sums during their eight years. Remember, Cheney said repeatedly during all this spending, "Reagan told us deficits do not matter."

This spending rate has been accelerated by two preemptive wars, ten years of occupying Islamic countries, billions of dollars in overseas nation-building projects, an expanded Medicare prescription drug benefit that was not fully funded with fees, a meltdown of the economy resulting in the 2008 Great Recession, bail-out funds to save Wall Street, insurance companies and the auto industry, as well as stimulus funds to prevent a long-term depression similar to the 1930s. There were also trillions of dollars in tax cuts that were supposed to increase revenues. Three Chairmen of the Federal Reserve, who were all appointed by Republican Presidents, have agreed that tax cuts do not always increase tax revenues, but they do increase the growth of the economy. The practice of spending all the surplus funds ($2.4 trillion) of the Social Security and Medicare Trust Funds over the years to pay for General Fund expenses has also contributed to the financial debacle. During the past 30 years, one political party has constantly sold the idea that tax cuts will force our government to spend less. This concept sounds good in theory, but it has proven to be a complete failure over the past 30 years. The same political party has been the big spender for these 30 years as well. In addition, there has been excessive spending in many federal agencies. This overspending has led to a national debt that is forecasted to be $16 trillion by 2012, and $20 trillion by 2016 with interest costs of over $500 billion by that same year.

Avoiding an Overreaction To Financial Crisis

After the terrorist attack on 9/11/01, there was a gross overreaction with a War on Terror being one of the major reasons why our country is in a serious financial crisis. It is important ten years later for our political leaders to not make another gross overreaction to solve the financial crisis leading our country into a long-term and deep economic depression. Clearly, the country has both revenue and spending problems to be solved in the next administration.

When a country is borrowing over 40 cents for every dollar spent, there is an immediate requirement to raise more revenue and to reduce spending. The statement that our country does not have a revenue problem, only a spending problem, is another illusion that has contributed to this financial crisis. For decades, Grover Norquist and his Americans For Tax Reform organization have convinced Republican lawmakers they cannot raise taxes. If a Republican votes for any law even resembling a tax increase, they will have a challenge in the Republican primary during the next election. This has resulted in 233 House Republicans out of 240 to sign a pledge that they will not raise taxes. Mr. Norquist has two House Democrats and Senator Nelson of Nebraska signing the same pledge. In addition, there are 1,252 state legislators who have signed a similar pledge. Unfortunately, there has been no pledge by the Republicans to limit spending to achieve a balanced budget in our nation's capital. Mr. Norquist does not feel responsible for the trillion-dollar annual deficits or the mountain of debt, but he has made a major contribution to the potential meltdown of the federal government.

To avoid inflicting severe financial pain on Americans with a series of tax increases and loss of important tax deductions, political leaders must fully understand what areas of the General Fund far exceed affordability which is the fundamental problem causing our financial crisis. The War on Terror, healthcare, unemployment, education, tax cuts, and the creeping expansion of most budgets within government agencies must be contained with the action plans discussed in previous lessons of this book. Then and only then will the federal government begin to move on a road to financial stability and affordability. Before a political party takes a machete to the federal government and causes terminal damage, a strategic plan must be developed to reduce the size and cost of government. Until this is accomplished, Americans will resist giving up their major tax deductions or accepting large tax increases. Senior citizens, who are a large voting block, will not forfeit their Social Security and Medicare benefits to bailout the mistakes of our political leaders over the past 30 years. Information in this lesson explains how cost containment can be the most important strategy to solve our financial crisis. Eventually, there may be a requirement for some tax increases and/or reductions in tax deductions, but let's first try controlling spending with superior management by our political leaders.

Break Up the Unified Budget and Focus on the General Fund

It is imperative that the President and Congress, who are elected in 2012, return our federal government to sound financial management with the goal of having a balanced budget in this decade like the one achieved in the late 1990s. One of the first steps to financial sobriety is the breakup of the unified federal government budget into three financial statements based on the three major sources of revenue:

1. Social Security based on payroll taxes
2. Medicare based on payroll taxes
3. General Fund (All revenues and expenses other than Social Security and Medicare) based on personal income and corporate taxes

This approach will help voters and taxpayers understand which areas of the government are far exceeding budgets. It will also stop the transferring of funds from Social Security and Medicare Trust Funds to camouflage excessive spending in the General Fund. In the future, if a President leads this country into another no-win and long-term civil war with no end in sight, Congress will need to enact a surtax to pay for the massive cost of our involvement in that war. Future political leaders and members of Congress must be held accountable for excessive spending and irresponsible tax cuts that create record deficits, a mountain of debt, and hundreds of billions of dollars in interest expenses to service the debt.

Only Fund Tax Cuts With Reductions in Spending

During the past 30 years, both political parties have been guilty of buying votes with tax cuts which is one of the fundamental causes of our runaway national debt. David Stockman, the Budget Director under President Reagan, stated in an April 22, 2011 WASHINGTON TIMES article that the President cut taxes too much in the early 1980s. The President later signed 11 tax increases that nearly recovered 50 percent of the loss revenue. No President in the 21st Century has signed tax increases to recover revenues that are no longer affordable due to the wars and the 2008 Great Recession. Tax cuts are only legitimate when spending is reduced to the same level as the proposed tax cut. The PAYGO law should be modified to enforce the rule that tax cuts cannot be used to stimulate the economy because they reduce revenues for future years without any additional votes by Congress. If the economy needs to be stimulated, a stimulus bill must be approved by Congress. This approach will also bring a greater focus on expense control because any tax increase will, no doubt, become permanent. Of course, an annual surtax can be authorized by Congress to pay for an increase in revenues in the event of a temporary crisis.

Debt ceiling laws of previous years have been totally ineffective. Both political parties have no problem raising the debt ceiling and voters do not punish a political party for raising the debt ceiling. However, voters always respond negatively to the need to raise taxes or to impose a temporary surtax on their income tax.

The federal debt at the end of 2008 was about $10 trillion which was ten times greater than when President Reagan took office in 1981. Keep in mind, at one percent, the cost of interest to service this debt would be $100 billion; at two percent interest, it is $200 billion; and at three percent, it is $300 billion. At ten percent, the cost of interest is one trillion dollars. That is one reason why the Federal Reserve tries to maintain very low interest rates. However, the two major problems with low interest rates are they become a silent tax on all senior citizens and others who save for their retirement, and they de-value the dollar to the point where Americans feel like third-class citizens when they travel to other countries in Europe and Asia. Interest is a tax on Americans, but they receive no government services for paying this tax.

Summary of Recommendations By the Deficit Commissions and Committees

Following the 2010 midterm election, a few groups attempted to develop a plan to reduce the size and cost of government as well as reduce the trillion-dollar annual deficits. Dr. Alice M. Rivlin, the grande dame of budget politics, and former Senator Peter Domenici (Republican of New Mexico), developed a plan sponsored by the Bipartisan Policy Center, a think tank created by former Democratic and Republican majority leaders and partially funded by the Rockefeller and Peterson Foundations. This report was entitled "Restoring America's Future."

They had 17 other budget hawks working with them to devise a plan they hoped would serve as a model if the President's commission deadlocked.

The second report was published by The Committee For A Responsible Federal Budget sponsored by the Peterson and Pew Foundations. These budget reform members consisted of 36 former government executives including the Chair of the Federal Reserve, two Comptroller Generals of the GAO, Director of the Congressional Budget office, Directors of OMB (Office of Management and Budget), Cabinet Secretaries, Members of Congress, and the Presidents of Foundations. Their report was entitled "Getting Back In The Black." The third report was entitled "A Thousand Cuts: What Reducing the Federal Budget Deficit Through Large Spending Cuts Could Really Look Like," written by Michael Ettlinger and Michael Linden from the Center for American Progress.

The Peter G. Peterson Foundation held a Fiscal Summit in May 2011 which was based on the reports of the following six organizations:

AEI: American Enterprise Institute
Bipartisan Policy Center
Center for American Progress
Economic Policy Institute
The Heritage Foundation
Roosevelt Institute/Campus Network

Two of these organizations strongly support the Paul Ryan plan that was passed by the House of Representatives. Two groups support rebuilding the middle class by investing in America's economy. Another organization presented the "Budget for Milennial America" representing the thinking of the "grandchildren" of our society which was for rebuilding our country with numerous investments. One group presented a more "middle of the road" solution.

The Peterson Summit in 2012 hopes to review solutions that have been passed into law. Hopefully, this information has been forwarded to Vice President Biden and his group that is trying to reach a compromise solution to the debt.

President Obama created the National Commission on Fiscal Responsibility and Reform after Republican members of Congress refused to approve a Congressional Commission. The National Commission on Fiscal Responsibility and Reform consisted of 18 members, nine from each political party. Republicans sent 9 members once there was agreement that all recommendations had to have 14 agreement votes out of the 18 members. Former Senator Alan Simpson was a co-chairman for the Republicans and former chief of staff to President Clinton, Erskin Bowles, was the Democratic co-chairman. This commission's document was the most widely read report on how to reduce the federal budget.

All these groups had the best of intentions, but they failed to build a consensus for the following reasons:

1. They did not build a consensus on the key national goals that Americans want their President and Congress to achieve in this decade. Therefore, all these task forces tried to balance the budget without a roadmap to a vision that would enable Americans to maintain their standard of living.

2. They continued to view the deficit from the perspective of the Unified Federal Budget which led them to the wrong conclusion that entitlements such as Social Security and Medicare were responsible for the financial crisis. Truth be told, Social Security and Medicare Trust Funds had accumulated surpluses of $2.4 million in 2010 and the General Fund had a cumulative national debt close to $14 trillion. It is clear that Social Security and Medicare programs have not caused the financial crisis. It is the General Fund that has this distinction.

3. No doubt for political reasons, the Commission did not identify the crisis in leadership as the fundamental cause of excessive spending, the annual trillion-dollar deficits, and the mountain of debt accumulated in recent years. Political parties fail to discuss the cost of all their proposals. For example, it is hard to believe how little discussion there has been about the true cost of the War on Terror and how inaccurate these costs have been reported in various presentations. The same is true of tax cuts. The original justification for the 2001 tax cuts was the fact there had been four years of budget surpluses and the

country should lower taxes to reduce the surplus. As soon as
the wars in Afghanistan and Iraq were started, there should
have been a surtax on the income tax.

4. None of the various organizations that have studied the
   deficit and debt issue have approached the problem with the
   assumption that the revenues of Social Security can be solved
   in the near future and that the runaway costs of health care can
   be solved based on the 12 areas of cost containment outlined
   in Lesson Six. If they had made those two assumptions, they
   would have realized the General Fund continues to have a
   serious cash flow problem of over a trillion dollars a year that
   must be solved in the next four years or certainly by 2020. If
   the public policy personnel who staffed the commissions and
   committees had focused on the General Fund by comparing
   the 2000 budget to the 2010 one, it would have become clear
   there are major spending areas out of control. First, is the fact
   the country loses billions of dollars in tax revenues due to the
   economic debacle caused by deregulation, mismanagement
   of financial institutions, sub-prime loans, and meltdown of
   the stock market investments. Second, there was a rapid rise
   in employment security expenses due to high unemployment
   and underemployment levels. Third, hundreds of billions of
   dollars were lost due to tax cuts that are not affordable. Fourth,
   when expenses of Defense, Intelligence, Homeland Security,
   Veterans' Benefits, Medical Costs of active duty and retired
   military personnel plus interest on debt had increased to over
   a trillion dollars, it is clear a 25 percent surtax on income
   tax was required from 2003 to 2014 (presumed end of the
   Afghanistan Civil War), but never proposed or acted upon
   by Congress. Fifth, explosive growth of health care, besides
   Medicare, which was led by Medicaid, is another major cause
   of the annual trillion-dollar deficits. This growth should have
   motivated the commissions and committees to strongly urge
   Congress to focus on building quality measurements and
   strategies that have been proven in several leading medical
   centers to reduce expenses by over $100 billion per year.
   Sixth, education is yet another area of the General Fund
   that has had explosive growth between 2000 and 2010. New

paradigms of instruction and management are required for the K-12 public schools, institutions of higher learning, and workplace training.

5. A number of studies want to claim the current payroll taxes for Social Security and Medicare as revenue to the Unified Federal Budget. They will then reduce the benefits through means testing and use many billions of dollars of payroll taxes for the General Fund expenses such as defense and interest or tax cuts. Middle-class voters simply do not realize how they will lose their pension and health care benefits with tax reform proposals. Once the press starts revealing this story, voters are going to rebel against tax reform.

Bond holders of U.S. Treasuries are not interested in long-term projections of savings. They want to know how the deficit will be substantially reduced in the next few years. The focus must be on major reductions in the General Fund and accounts during 2013 to 2016, which have been outlined in this document. Americans want the President and Congress who are elected in 2012 to stimulate the economy to reduce unemployment by 50 percent. This means a drop from 10 percent to 5 percent. This reduction would reduce the annual deficit by several hundred billion dollars. Americans much prefer ending the two pre-emptive wars in Iraq and Afghanistan and a downsizing of the Defense, Intelligence, and Homeland Security organizations to an affordable peacetime level, thus reducing the overall expenses by $300 billion. Our citizens do not want additional tax cuts that are based on borrowed money. Americans also want the federal government to ensure affordable health insurance from the day they are born to the day they die, and in addition, they seek the government to increase the quality of health care to reduce insurance costs. Finally, our citizens want real breakthroughs in the student learning crisis and a reduction in the cost of education.

The public needs to be educated on the overall financial crisis. In a November 22, 2010 article in NEWSWEEK, "Truth or Consequences" by Evan Thomas, the sub-headline stated, "Obama's only real hope to be an effective President and secure his legacy: talk straight about the looming economic disaster facing the country." Hopefully, this book will help him achieve that objective. Voters are not going to accept tax increases based on misleading statements that Social Security and Medicare caused the mountain of debt and the annual trillion-dollar deficits.

On December 3, 2010, only 11 members of the 18 voted to send the report to Congress, which was three short of the required 14. This could be viewed as a defeat for fiscal responsibility, but it may be the beginning of a process for eventually developing a realistic plan to reduce the size and cost of government. Both the Presidential and Congressional candidates in 2012 will be forced to address this potential financial crisis in 2012. Frankly, it should have been addressed in the 2004 and 2008 general elections as well as the 2006 and 2010 midterm elections. Some people believe that the Deficit Commission report will have the same "do nothing" results as the 1986 Grace Commission that recommended changes to reduce inefficiencies and waste in the federal government. There is one major difference. Today, we will have a $16 trillion debt by 2016 and a forecasted debt of $20 trillion in 2020 that will lead directly to a "bond crisis" with higher taxes and interest rates, so the potential financial crisis cannot be ignored.

There is no question that many members of Congress will want to keep their heads in the sand to avoid being lopped off by various interest groups who will finance their opponents' campaigns. However, voters can ask penetrating questions in 2012 that will force each political party to give a detail plan how they will aim for a balanced budget by 2020. It is a mistake to state the country can have a multi-decade effort to get its finances in shape. Our country cannot borrow hundreds of billions of dollars every year for decades.

If no bipartisan agreement is reached in 2011 or 2012, the President in 2013 needs to appoint someone to work on a grand strategy to achieve a balanced budget by 2020. This balanced budget administrator, who could be the Director of OMB, needs to assemble seven teams each working on a major area of expense control and quality performance.

- Social Security revenues
- Health care (including Medicare and Medicaid)
- Military, VA, Intelligence, Homeland Security, Medical
- Education (K-12, higher education, workforce training)
- Energy (reduce the cost and prevent supply interruptions)

- Commerce (recharge the Free Enterprise System)
- Most other Federal Agencies must phase down their costs

The study should start with a spending target in each of these government areas leading to a balanced budget by 2020. The goal of each study team would be to develop a plan to operate one government area at an affordable level. For example, the Military, Intelligence, and Homeland Security would be told they must accomplish their operations for X amount of dollars by 2020. There must be a phased implementation plan to achieve that spending level by 2020.

In his NEWSWEEK article, "Wake Up, America: Why We Must Balance The Budget," Robert J. Samuelson stated, "The virtue of balancing the budget is that it forces people to weight the benefits of government against the costs. It is a common-sense standard that people grasp. If the deficit commission is serious, it will set a balanced budget in 2020 as a goal. Consider. In 2020, the deficit will be $1.254 trillion on spending of $5.67 billion according to the Congressional Budget Office. And $916 billion of the deficit would represent interest payments. The message from Europe (and Greece) is that this approach ultimately fails. Lenders retreat from buying treasury bonds or insist on punishing interest rates." Interest could soar to two trillion dollars. Mr. Samuelson is against all the mumbo-jumbo about stabilizing debt to GDP because voters cannot understand nor influence excessive spending with that type of measure or goal.(3)

Some people believe the road to a balanced budget is through the elimination of tax deductions that are now called tax expenditures or tax earmarks. Every American who loses a tax deduction will consider it a tax increase which will reduce their ability to spend. For example, if interest on primary homes is limited to $500,000, this will be a major tax increase on middle-class and wealthy Americans who drive the economy with consumer spending. It would also reduce the value of their homes. No doubt, there are some tax deductions that could be reduced or eliminated and these should be added to the overall deficit reduction plan.

Reducing the Defense, Intelligence, and Veterans' Benefits Budgets

Expense areas that are no longer affordable are defense, veterans' affairs, homeland security, and intelligence. For a number of years, our country has borrowed over half a trillion dollars annually ($500 billion) to conduct the War on Terror. This is not sustainable. The United States cannot pay for the War on Terror unless the President and Congress can convince voters and citizens to accept a 20-to-25 percent surtax on income tax. The defense expenses alone have increased by 160 percent from $294 billion in 2000 to $768 billion in 2011. To this number you need to add almost $100 billion in health care costs, the $50 billion cost of homeland security, the $90 billion cost of veterans' benefits, and $100 billion for interest on debt. The total military and security budget of $1,108 billion is nearly equal to the total amount of income taxes and corporate taxes leaving no cash for any other part of government. In the last ten years, the United States has raised the cost of conducting a war to the level where no country can afford to wage war—not even the richest country in the world without new taxes.

In his July 25, 2010 article entitled "Pentagon Pressured To Cut Back On Budget Requests," Thom Shanker stated, "After nearly a decade of rapid increases in military spending, the Pentagon is facing intensifying political and economic pressures to restrain its budget, setting up the first serious debate since the terrorist attacks of 2001 about the size and cost of the armed services. Defense Secretary Robert Gates has sought to contain the budget-cutting demands by showing Congress and the White House that he can squeeze more efficiency from the Pentagon's bureaucracy and weapons programs and use the savings to maintain fighting forces. Gates is calling for the Pentagon's budget to keep growing in the long run at 1 percent a year after inflation plus the costs of war. Next year they want a 10.7 percent increase."(4) This data indicates that Pentagon planners continue to support the current military strategies of being policemen of the world operating in over 70 countries, being involved in preemptive wars, occupying hostile countries, and implementing multi-billion-dollar nation-building projects. These strategies are unaffordable without at least a 25 percent surtax on income tax which Congress and voters will never approve. The large surtax on income tax would motivate voters to pressure the military to downsize its current wartime budget to a peacetime budget like the one that existed in 2000. A surtax could be imposed: 25 percent in the first year, 20 percent in the second, 15 percent in the third, and 10 percent in the fourth to emphasize a phased downsizing strategy.

Two-thirds of Pentagon spending is on personnel costs. The volunteer military is not affordable for extensive wars. Lesson 8 described a breakthrough in the reduction of personnel costs by having non-career volunteers who serve only two years. This breakthrough would also stop the growth in veterans' benefits that are projected to be close to $164 billion by 2016 and the growth in medical costs of both active duty and retirees that now exceeded $100 billion. This change in staffing would not reduce any benefits to veterans who fought in World War II, Korea, Vietnam, Iraq, or Afghanistan, but it would save tens of billions of dollars in future years. The overall cost of the defense, veterans' affairs, intelligence, and military budgets now exceeds a trillion dollars if interest on borrowing for these budgets during the past decade is added. This overall trillion dollars in cost must be reduced by $300 billion if a balanced budget is to be achieved in this decade. With a $500 billion Department of Defense budget, our country will remain the most powerful nation in the world just as it was at $300 billion in 2000, before the excessive spending started due to a change in our foreign policy (*you are either with us or against us*), and the shift from being a defense organization to an aggressive war machine.

The major areas of expense that must be considered to decrease spending are:

- Phase out of Iraq and Afghanistan Wars.
- Major reduction in overhead recommended by Secretary Gates.
- Reduction in weapon systems.
- Reduction of troops in Europe, Korea, Pacific, Middle East.
- Phase down Army and Marine levels within our country.
- Convert to two-year enlistments rather than lifetime service.
- Stop building aircraft carriers and a few other ships.
- Reduce number of carrier battle groups.

- Reduce civilian personnel and contract employees.
- Reduce medical expenses due to ending of the wars.
- Consolidate intelligence programs to become more efficient.
- Reduce the growth of veterans' benefits with 2-year enlistments.

There are many Americans and political leaders who never look at the budget as they constantly support increases in defense spending and veterans' benefits. To them, a declining defense budget sends a message that our country is in decline. Some people believe that a reduced defense budget would undermine our ability to project power which enables us to be the policemen of the world. These people have to be educated that Americans will not support a major tax increase to be the policemen of the world.

During his final speech in office in 1960, President Eisenhower warned Americans not of an external enemy but of a more insidious threat. "This conjunction of an immense military establishment and a large arms industry is new in the American experience. The total influence-economic, political, even spiritual is felt in every city, every State house, every office of the Federal government . . . we must guard against the acquisition of unwarranted influence whether sought or unsought . . . the potential for the disastrous rise of misplaced power exists and will persist. We must never let the weight of this combination endanger our liberties or democratic processes."(5) The military has not taken over our government, but budgets and interest costs consume all of our income and corporate tax revenues which is not sustainable in future years.

Reverse the Loss of Taxes and Cost of Unemployment

Many political leaders and economists believe the economy will soon come alive with millions of new jobs if we have low interest rates and tax cuts. We have had low interest rates and tax cuts for years and the country has plateaued around 9 percent unemployment which translates to 15 million Americans. The length of our severe unemployment could be 5 years by 2012 and 9 years by 2016. It is a depression, not a recession, for unemployed Americans. By embracing the national goal of prosperity and reducing the unemployment rate to 5 or 6 percent by 2016, tax revenues will increase by $250 billion and unemployment cost support (food stamps, Medicaid, unemployment insurance) will decrease by $250 billion for an overall reduction of $500 billion (half a trillion dollars) in the annual deficit. How does the President achieve prosperity when most business leaders are upset with him because he tried to end the tax cuts for wealthy Americans who experienced record increases in their income during the 2001 to 2010 decade? The President needs to establish a commission of Chief Executive Officers who embrace a social responsibility to return this country to prosperity and full employment. Large corporations have $1.8 trillion of cash on their balance sheets. A certain percentage of that cash must be invested in the expansion of companies to create jobs. Not only do large corporations have cash, but they also have considerable excess capacity for more production, and many companies have record profits. Corporations must invest in new products and services as well as new marketing programs to increase demand which creates new jobs. If business leaders continue to stonewall the President, Congress, and their fellow citizens by using cash to inflate stock and by downsizing and outsourcing employment to foreign countries, the President and Congress will have every right to implement a "Rebuild America" program for infrastructure projects and to create jobs within the public sector to reduce unemployment.

In recent history, every economic system adopted by a country, whether it is socialism, state capitalism, or free enterprise, must create jobs for the vast majority of the adult population. If there is a large amount of unemployment or underemployed citizens, there will often be severe unrest or even serious demonstrations like those which occurred in Middle Eastern countries in 2011. Eventually, voters will change the system as England did when their citizens voted for a socialist labor party in the 1930s and after World War II.

The American economy is based on near full employment with income taxes at both the state and local levels. Corporate taxes are based on having a high-level of prosperity. Sales taxes at the state and local levels are again dependent upon high employment within a free enterprise system. The cost of providing support to unemployed, underemployed, homeless, and citizens who are listed as the working poor required hundreds of billions of dollars in 2010.

The United States must have a robust middle class in order to provide adequate tax revenues to support local, state, and federal governments. For those Americans and institutions who cheer when there are layoffs, payroll reductions, pension cancellations, reduced health benefits, broken union contracts, etc., it is important to remember when taxes go down and unemployment costs rise, a declining standard of living forces government to reduce services.

Improve Health Care Quality and Reduce Costs

The Affordable Care Act of 2010 finally ensured that the vast majority of Americans have health care insurance from the day they are born to the day they die. Medicare is a successful program because it is simple to understand, administer and manage. The President and his Secretary of Health and Human Services have already implemented programs to improve Medicare quality and cost for Americans 65 years and older. It will take six years, 2011 to 2016, to achieve these programs' objectives. Lesson 6 articulates potential changes in Medicaid that could reduce at least $100 billion in costs. Working Americans currently deal with a hodgepodge of insurance companies with expensive marketing, administrative, executive compensation, and quality problems that may never be solved. In addition, corporations now want to unload the burden of providing health care benefits for their employees just as they unloaded company pension plans. At some point in the future, the United States will probably phase into "Medicare For All," a single-payer, government plan, which is not socialized medicine because citizens select their doctors and hospitals. Every other major country operates such a plan today, making their companies more competitive. Such a plan would require a VAT tax or a payroll tax that would be funded 50 percent by employees and 50 percent by employers. The President and Congress should plan for this health care funding system because Americans and their employers are not going to accept large annual increases in health care premiums from insurance companies forever.

Improving Financial Management for Education Systems

For over 30 years, the Secretaries of Education have measured their performance on how much money they have convinced the President and Congress to spend on education. In 2001, the federal budget for elementary, secondary, vocational education, and higher education was $32 billion. In 2010, expenses were $128 billion which included a major increase due to the stimulus bill.(6) With the recommendations outlined in Lesson 11, the education budget could be phased down by $20 billion. The federal government should use the multi-million-dollar research budget to develop researched-based and validated learning systems and management systems like the ones discussed in Lesson 11. The federal government should not pay for operating expenses within public schools or institutions of higher education. This expense is the responsibility of state and local governments. If schools suffer financial cutbacks in the next few years, they will be more willing to adopt national learning standards, common course assessments, and professional development programs for teachers. They will also be more open to learning systems provided to them from the federal government at no charge, which would be financed within the existing budget. If Congress eliminates the federal Department of Education, they are institutionalizing the 19th Century instruction and management systems providing American children with a third-class public school system. Only the federal government has the power and finances to develop No Child Left Behind instructional and management systems for the 21st Century.

Reduce Almost All Federal Government Budgets By 20 Percent

Lesson 13 articulated a plan to make it reasonable to reduce all other federal agency budgets by 20 percent over a four-year period, or 5 percent per year. By 2016, attrition alone could reduce spending in most agencies by approximately $90 billion. Federal government employees, including the military, have received several wage increases during the past decade. These cost-of-living increases are simply unaffordable based on current tax revenues. The private sector discontinued giving cost-of-living increases in the 1980s when inflation came under control. The Director of OMB could determine if some government agencies could achieve 30 percent reductions over four years while other departments could only reach a 10 percent objective, but the average program of cost containment would be around 20 percent. Keep in mind, it takes four years to accomplish this; not a one-year budget cycle. Another area needing to be questioned is the continuous borrowing of funds to subsidize profitable agribusiness. Producing food is now a profitable business and there could be a reduction in the Department of Agriculture. In his July 19, 2010 NEWSWEEK column entitled "The Center Holds: In Britain Even Pain Is Popular," Fareed Zakaria explained, "Prime Minister David Cameron of the Conservative Party has come down firmly on the side of their debate which is reduce spending by 25 percent including the military. The British finance minister (Chancellor of the Exchequer), 39 year old George Osborne, presented a budget that promised to get Britain's fiscal house in order with sharp cuts in spending coupled with tax increases."(7) If Europeans put their finances on a sound basis with China, Japan, Korea, and Singapore, the United States will have no choice but to adopt Option 3 as outlined in Lesson 1. If the United States continues to have record deficits and $20 trillion of debt with nearly a trillion dollars of interest expense, investors will stop purchasing U.S. Treasury bonds.

The Government Accountability Office (GAO) offers an excellent case study on how to strategically reduce the size and cost of government. In the 1990s, the GAO reduced its staff from 5,200 employees to 3,500 for a 30 percent decrease. After the downsizing, which took four years, the GAO produced more studies, reports and Congressional testimonies with a smaller staff. Comptroller Generals at the GAO have been sending reports to both the executive and congressional branches of government for 25 years warning our political leaders that our spending and borrowing were not sustainable. In fact, even if the economy returns to a prosperity level, the United States cannot achieve a balanced budget without major systemic changes in several government areas. Whenever there is a new Congress, the GAO sends them a list of high-risk programs and which government agencies cannot be audited due to incomplete accounting systems as well as which agencies have qualified audits. Top agency officials and the Office of Management and Budget are working with the GAO on the high-risk list to improve the performance of federal government agencies.

Stabilize Social Security

The recommendations by the bipartisan National Commission On Fiscal Responsibility and Reform that were outlined in Lesson 7 will probably be passed with some modifications by Congress and signed by the President. In 2010, former Senator Alan Simpson was quoted in PARADE magazine, "We are not going to cut Social Security—we are going to stabilize it. None of the ideas that have been presented will affect anyone over age 58. But we are going to make the system work."(8) Social Security should not be part of the deficit reduction program because it should have a separate budget and financial statements.

Another Source of Additional Revenues

One other key question to ask is: Why should Americans earning more than $25,000 (the poverty line), but less than $50,000, not pay any income taxes for all the services that they receive from the federal government? It is estimated that 47 percent of American households do not pay one cent of income tax. People living below the poverty line simply cannot afford to pay income tax. Americans who work for minimum wages cannot pay income tax. In fact, people who work two minimum wage jobs are barely reaching the poverty line. They already pay taxes for Social Security and Medicare, and they pay real estate taxes whether they rent an apartment or own a home. However, millions of Americans have household incomes in the $25,000 to $50,000 range. They could also afford to pay a 5 percent income tax ($1,250 to $2,500) for all the services they receive from the federal government.

Are Americans Paying Too Much or Too Little in Taxes?

Most middle-class Americans pay plenty of money to the various levels of government through the following taxes:

- City income taxes
- City sales taxes
- Property taxes

- State sales taxes
- State income taxes
- Vehicle license fee
- Federal income taxes
- Taxes on utilities
- Excise taxes, such as gasoline taxes
- Payroll taxes for Social Security and Medicare

If you total all these taxes, most middle-class citizens are paying 25-to-40 percent of their earnings to various government agencies. Wealthy people pay far more cash in taxes, but the total percent of their taxed income is lower.

Increase Taxes on Wealthy Americans

From 1979 to 2005, incomes for the top 5 percent increased 81 percent while incomes for the bottom 20 percent, American workers, declined 1 percent. The richest one percent of U.S. households now own 34.3 percent of the nation's private wealth, more than the combined wealth of the bottom 90 percent.(9) If tax cuts for people earning more than $250,000 are cancelled sometime in the future and the capital gains tax returns to 20 percent, $100 billion more in tax revenues will come in from citizens who can afford to pay more tax. The truth is the Bush tax cuts were not affordable based on the excessive spending in his administration and all of them should be allowed to expire in 2012. However, to prevent a double-dip recession, the tax cuts for the middle class must remain until the Great Recession is over. However, all tax cuts from the year 2001 may not be extended after the year 2012. On the April 16, 2011 *Meet The Press* TV program, Alan Greenspan advised putting the tax rates back to the Clinton level and balance the budget with spending reductions after the Bush tax cuts expire in 2012. President Clinton agrees with this tax strategy.

Additional IRS Agents To Collect Taxes

The IRS estimates the tax gap for Americans failing to pay the correct amount of income and corporate taxes is $345 billion.(10) Hiring 16,000 new IRS agents could produce $145 billion in additional revenues owed to the United States. As long as we are going to have a tax system, we may as well make sure we are all paying our share. Between 1995 and 2003, the IRS enforcement division lost 36 percent of its staff. No one likes to be audited, but the government has to collect sufficient revenues to pay all of its expenses. If some Americans are cheating, honest Americans are paying more than their fair share. Republicans have successfully made "taxes" a dirty word for 30 years, but taxes are a vital necessity. It is a matter of paying your dues as a member of this club we call America.(11) Tax collection are also not dirty words.

Recap of General Fund Reduced Spending and Increased Revenues

The following estimates that could be saved on an annual basis by 2016 are based on a four-year phase-down of expenses and a phase-up of revenues which is based on the information provided in previous lessons to achieve a balanced budget.

Return Country to Prosperity	
Increase tax revenues from higher employment	$246 B
Decrease in unemployment expenses	<u>254</u> B
(Assumes an unemployment of 5 percent)	$500 B
Reduce the cost of defense, intelligence, veterans' benefits	$300 B
Reduce the cost of Healthcare (Medicare and Medicaid)	$100 B
Reduce the cost of all other government agencies/departments	$100 B
Better tax collection	$130 B
Reduce Earmarks	$ 10 B
Restore tax on $250,000 incomes and above on capital gains back to 20%	$100 B
Restore tax on $50,000 to $250,000 earnings	$135 B
Increase tax on earnings of $25,000 to $50,000	<u>$ 25 B</u>
Total with increase revenues and lower expenses	$1,400 B

Although some Republicans and Democrats have tried to demonize Washington, D.C., the new Congress and the President who are elected in 2012 must contend with the fact that most government programs remain enormously popular with voters. A new study in late 2010 by THE WASHINGTON POST, the Henry J. Kaiser Foundation, and Harvard University shows that most Americans who say they want more limited government also claim Social Security and Medicare "very important." They want Washington to be involved in schools, and help reduce poverty. Nearly half want the government to maintain a role in regulating health care.(12) And a vast majority of Americans look to government as a positive force to return our country to economic prosperity and high employment levels.

Raising the Debt Ceiling

Something had to be done in 2011 to raise the debt ceiling because our debt was at the $14.3 trillion level in May. Even with unconventional financing methods, the debt ceiling has to be raised by August. President Roosevelt raised the debt ceiling six times during his 13 years in the 1930s and World War II in the 1940s. President Truman is the only President who never raised the debt ceiling. This means in the most turbulent times of 1933 to 1952 (20 years), the debt ceiling was only raised six times. With peace and prosperity in the 1980s, President Reagan raised the debt ceiling 18 times in eight years as he created more debt than all the other Presidents in the history of our country. President George Bush (43) raised it seven times in eight years.

Some political leaders want voters to believe they can refuse to raise the debt ceiling to show support for a reduction in spending. Not true. The government must raise the debt ceiling or default on the existing Treasury bonds which would drive up interest rates by potentially hundreds of billions of dollars. That action would require a major increase in income taxes. No political party will actually refuse to raise the debt ceiling once the country reaches that point.

The United States cannot become a "dead beat" nation. Once the House and Senate have sufficient votes to raise the debt ceiling, there will be a number of Senators and over a hundred House members who will be able to vote "no" which will help them get reelected, but their vote is merely symbolic: not a deciding vote. Many of these symbolic voters will state they will not vote yes unless there are comprehensive, dramatic, effective, and broad-based cuts to federal spending, including changes to Social Security and Medicare. These politicians sound like real fiscal conservatives, but they truly are going along with an increase in the debt ceiling. The debt ceiling has been raised nearly 100 times since 1917 when it was first established.

Real Tax Reform: Flat Tax, VAT Tax, and Fair Tax

For many years, various groups and professors have proposed the United States scrap the Internal Revenue Code and the IRS. These people often discuss the $30 billion paid by taxpayers to professionals to fill out the complicated forms, the $110 billion of labor by taxpayers either to complete their own tax forms or to fill out organizers for tax firms, and the $345 billion that taxpayers cheat the government out of on their tax forms.

The two most discussed alternative taxing methods have been the VAT (national sales tax) and the Flat Tax. The Commissions on Deficit Reduction appear to favor the FLAT tax. Some people make it sound as if everyone will be paying less tax if the government changes to one of these alternative taxes. Articles and lectures on this subject make these alternatives sound too good to be true. It would be more helpful if professors and consultants would do an in-depth study that reveals how much people will actually pay under these alternative taxes. Some Americans are going to pay more tax while others will pay less. More importantly, the new proposed method of collecting federal taxes must bring in as much in revenue as the government is spending, not just what the current income tax collects, which makes this a difficult time to change tax systems. In other words, Americans will pay more tax because there is excessive spending in the General Fund. Many tax deductions will be eliminated under the Flat Tax. The new tax system must collect 40 percent more if expenses are not reduced. Voters will probably not buy into a new tax system until they are convinced that taxes will not increase for the vast majority of Americans.

The Fair Tax has been conceived by business executives and economists over the past 14 years. Today, 76 economists support the Fair Tax as well as a number of House and Senate members. The Fair Tax would eliminate:(12)

– All federal income and corporation taxes

- – All payroll taxes for Social Security and Medicare
- – All estate and inheritance taxes
- – All capital gains taxes
- – Eliminate the IRS Department

The Fair Tax is a national sales tax with few deductions. Americans would receive a monthly check to refund their taxes that were paid for their necessities of life. There would be no way to cheat on taxes. Even illegal immigrants would pay taxes on everything they purchased. Political office holders would not be able to offer tax deductions to special interests or people who give large campaign contributions. No doubt, the Fair Tax would be a revolution in government financing and must be studied in great detail before it would pass the Congress. The major opponents to Fair or Flat taxes are state and local governments who do not want the federal government to have a sales tax. The Fair Tax might have a better chance of being approved if it would not replace payroll taxes of Social Security and Medicare, which should be funded separately.

The one outcome that could truly increase taxes for Americans would be a VAT tax on top of our current income tax. In the future, Congress could raise both income and VAT taxes as it continues its excessive spending year after year. This worst-case scenario would reduce consumer spending and drive the United States into a long-term economic depression. Americans would be willing to change to a different taxation method, but only after realistic and accurate proposals are developed for Congressional approval. It will require great leadership by the President, Congress, and the Secretary of the Treasury to sell an entirely new tax system, which is really a separate decision than reducing the size and cost of government.

Tax Cut Law for 2011 and 2012

After intense negotiations between leaders of the Republican and Democratic Parties, an $858 billion tax plan was approved in December by the House, Senate and the President approximately six weeks after the midterm election. President Obama and the Demorcratic Party asked for elimination of tax cuts for single taxpayers with gross incomes over $200,000 and married couples with incomes over $250,000.

Republicans wanted the Bush tax cuts renewed for everyone, including very wealthy Americans. Due to the large victory of Republicans in the 2010 midterm election, President Obama compromised to ensure there would be no tax increases on everyone in January 2011, which economists forecasted would cause a second (double-dip) recession. In this compromise, Republicans agreed to an unemployment insurance extension for 13 months, a new estate tax exempting estates under $5 million per person and would tax estates over $5 million at 35 percent. In addition, there would be a one-year reduction of two percent in Social Security taxes for most workers which would, hopefully, stimulate consumer spending creating many jobs and increasing the economic growth rate.

All this action made sense from the viewpoint of trying to recover the economy from the 2008 Great Recession. But from the viewpoint of reducing government deficits and debt, it must have been a real shock to members of the committees and commissions who were trying to increase tax revenues and decrease the size and cost of government. In round numbers, an extra trillion dollars will be added to the national debt, so by 2012 the debt could be $17 trillion rather than $16 trillion. Once again, Congress and the President made an Option One decision to keep spending and borrowing rather than developing and implementing major change in military, health care, education, and economic development programs as outlined in Option Three. This is, of course, the result of a deadlocked Congress who voters elected in 2010. Options Two and Three appear to be on the shelf for two years like the deficit and debt reduction reports from committees.

Some pundits and columnists believe this tax law would put pressure on the President and Congress in 2011 and 2012 to implement major tax reforms such as the Flat or Fair Tax. An illusion of 2010 was the idea billions of dollars could be taken from Social Security and Medicare tax receipts through means-testing the middle-class benefits which appears to have died with the 2010 tax cut bill. A 2011 and perhaps 2012 illusion may be tax reform will balance the budget. Voters do not focus on annual deficits or national debt. They do focus on "take home" pay after taxes are paid. Due to trillion-dollar-deficits, very few Americans will pay lower taxes under the Flat or Fair Tax when the goal is to achieve a balanced budget by 2020. Therefore, tax reform will be just as difficult to sell to voters as reduced benefits for Social Security and

Medicare. In fact, it will be a greater challenge because nearly all tax payers, who are voters, will pay more tax even if tax rates are lower. As the all-important general election approaches in 2012, do not expect tax reform to be passed until 2013 or later.

The 2011, 2012 and 2013 Budget Debates

After the 2010 midterm election, a number of Republican governors are attempting to eliminate their public employees' unions. The state budgets are being reduced by laying-off thousands of government employees, including teachers. With demonstrations taking place by workers, union members, families, and supporters, thus bringing large crowds to state capitols, there is a growing conflict between working citizens in the United States and the Tea Party and Republican leaders who want to tear down major government agencies. In the meantime, the two political parties in Washington, D.C. are gridlocked over the 2012 federal budget.

The 2011 federal budget was not approved until April 14, 2011 with only six months of the 2011 fiscal year remaining. In other words, the approval was six months late due to the civil war in Congress that delayed the approval due to a threatened Republican filibuster in the Senate before the mid-term 2010 election. After the election, Republicans took control in the House of Representatives and agreed to the $38 billion in spending cuts before they approved the 2011 budget.

When the 2012 budget was published in January, Republicans claimed it was "dead on arrival" because it did not reduce entitlement spending. In April, Paul Ryan unveiled the "Pathway To Prosperity" plan which was the proposed 2012 Republican budget. On April 15, 2011 all but four Republicans in the House passed the Ryan/Republican budget and sent it to the Senate. One hundred percent of the Democratic House members voted against the Ryan/Republican 2012 budget. The Senate did not pass the Ryan/Republican 2012 budget.

There will be great debate between the two political parties on the 2012 budget throughout the balance of 2011. The 2012 budget may not be approved in 2011 and the country will operate with a series of continuous resolutions during 2012. Also there is the possibility the federal government will be shut down sometime in late 2011 or in 2012 because Congress cannot even approve a continuous resolution to keep funding the government at the 2011 spending level. This is what happened in 1995 when a Republican Congress would not pass a budget that President Clinton would approve. How far apart are Republicans and Democrats from approving the 2012 budget? On health care, they are miles apart.

The Democratic Party also supports increases in revenues by taxing Americans with $250,000 incomes or greater at the level they paid in the 1990s when there was a balanced budget. The Ryan/Republican plan gives major new tax breaks to wealthy citizens which causes the annual deficits to be in the trillion-dollar range adding to the national debt.

The Democratic Party also believes they can fix Social Security revenue requirements by making adjustments to when early retirement and full retirement start as well as lifting the caps on large incomes providing more revenue from six percent of the workforce. The Ryan/Republican plan does not address a solution for Social Security, but seniors and middle-age Americans are nervous because if Ryan is willing to completely change Medicare, they believe he could quickly produce a plan to reduce Social Security benefits.

The Ryan/Republican plan also ignored meaningful reductions in defense spending. The Democratic Party definitely plans to phase out of the two long-term civil wars and phase down defense spending. The Ryan plan would require a 25 percent surtax on income to continue the War on Terror for an indefinite period.

With these major differences, the 2013 budget document President Obama and OMB will publish early in 2012 will be his 2012 campaign budget. He does not require congressional approval for this document. Republicans will once again state "dead on arrival." There is a good chance the civil war within Congress will reach to higher levels during the 2012 campaign season. This could result in no approval for the 2013 budget until after the general election in November 2012. The winning political party will then approve the 2013 budget early in 2013 after the President is installed. Therefore, it will be voters who decide which budget and financial strategy they want for the 2013 to 2016 years.

In the meantime, neither political party has solved the unemployment crisis. American workers and their families will be most upset with all the political parties as the 2012 election heats up. Workers are concerned that some corporate and political leaders want to downgrade the vast majority of Americans from the middle class to the working poor. The 2012 election year may well be a year of major demonstrations and numerous conflicts between voters and political leaders. That is why political leaders should think about a positive vision of "Rebuilding America" with six national goals rather than a vision of inflicting severe financial pain and unemployment on millions of Americans who already are experiencing a decline in their standard of living.

Summary of the Overall Fiscal Plan

Keep in mind that, under Option 3 (documented in Lesson One and recommended by the author), no large tax deductions will be taken away from Americans. Social Security and Medicare benefits will be fully funded. The military will be fully funded as a defense organization and will remain, by far, the most powerful defense organization in the world. No VAT tax will be required. The business community will not be assessed additional taxes, nor will there be additional taxes on gasoline or fuel oil. The country will have universal health care. The financial system will have been stabilized. The economy will be recovering and Americans will be going back to work. There will be no double-dip recession in the near future, and education systems will have returned to being the finest in the world. The six national goals will have been achieved:

1. Peace with homeland security protection from terrorists
2. Prosperity with full employment
3. Adequate and Affordable Health Care
4. Superior and Affordable Education System
5. Efficient and Affordable Government
6. Decent Retirement

As stated in the introduction of this book, the following four areas want no limits on their spending:

- Health Care
- Education
- Military, Intelligence, Homeland Security
- Federal government agencies

In order to achieve the six national goals, these four areas must be managed within affordable budgets as outlined in this book. Again, the great hope is the President and Congress elected in 2012 will not implement a tragic overreaction to the deficit and debt by taking a machete to many important government programs which are the foundation for our standard of living and the American way of life. The budget can be balanced in this decade just as it was in the 1990s with great leadership by our elected political leaders.

Needless to say, the United States needs a great leader in the President's job for the next four years and a large majority in Congress to support the President. The next President and his/her Cabinet will need to mount an overpowering story on why the federal government must reduce spending and services, as well as increase taxes, to pass laws that will solve our financial crisis. The next lesson will address these topics and will discuss whether both political parties are capable of saving the federal government from a financial meltdown in this decade.

NOTES FOR LESSON 14

1. "Receipts, Outlays, and Surpluses or Deficits by Fund Group:1934-2015," 76 U.S. Treasury Department, 2010, pages 28 and 29

2. "Debt Commission Cites Need For U.S. to Take Drastic Actions," Glen Johnson, Associated Press, SAN DIEGO UNION-TRIBUNE, July 11, 2010, page A6

3. "Wake Up, America," Robert J. Samuelson, NEWSWEEK, May 31, 2010, page 21

4. "Pentagon Pressured To Cut Back On Budget Requests," Thom Shanker, NEW YORK TIMES Service, SAN DIEGO UNION-TRIBUNE, July 23, 2010, page A3

5. *Econned: How Unenlightened Self Interest Undermined Democracy and Corrupted Capitalism*, Yves Smith, Palgrave MacMillan, 2010, page 306

6. "Outlays By Function, 2001 to 2015," U.S. Treasury Department, 2010, pages 68 and 69

7. "The Center Holds," Fareed Zakaria, NEWSWEEK, July 19, 2010, page 20

8. "Can These Men Fix The Dificit?" Steven Beschloss and Janet Kinosian, PARADE magazine, July 4, 2010, page 8

9. *Killer Politics,* Ed Schultz, Hyperion/Harper Collins, 2010, page 3

10. "The Tax Man Should Cometh," Ezra Klein, NEWSWEEK, April 26, 2010, page 21

11. *Killer Politics,* Ed Schultz, Hyperion/Harper Collins, 2010, page 48

12. *Fair Tax: The Truth And Answering The Critics,* Neal Boortz and Congressman John Linder, Harper, 2008

13. "Government Gets Mixed Reviews In New Study," THE WASHINGTON POST, SAN DIEGO UNION-TRIBUNE, October 10, 2010, page A5

LESSON 15

REQUIREMENT FOR STRATEGIC AND BOLD LEADERSHIP

Vision Based on the Six National Goals

Americans want to live in peace and support themselves financially throughout their adult years. During their lifetime, they will need affordable health care and excellent education systems. They want an honest, efficient, and affordable government that is dedicated to improving their standard of living. Also, they need a decent retirement with the support of a Social Security pension and Medicare insurance. This vision is based on the six national goals which both parties should promote. Voters must determine which candidates have the leadership skills to move our government in the direction of an improved standard of living for all its citizens. They should be voting with a basic understanding of the key issues that will improve their standard of living. All the problems facing our country resulted from decisions made by political leaders in past administrations, so they can be solved by political leaders in future administrations. Voters must select competent and honest political leaders who will continue our recovery from the 2008 Great Recession and who will mitigate the financial crisis currently faced by our government.

The Most Powerful and Challenging Job in the World

The President of the United States lives and works in the White House where a staff of over 200 people try to make his/her life more comfortable each day. The first family can entertain several times a week without cooking a meal or serving a drink because the White House staff takes care of all the necessary logistics and service. The staff also coordinates glamorous state dinners and recognition events. No one has a larger or more well-equipped private plane than the President, and advance personnel plan all the events whenever he travels on Air Force One. Secretaries and executive staffs prepare the President for every meeting. Camp David is available for weekend retreats. A communications system enables our President to talk to anyone in the world and an expense account allows the President to travel to anywhere in the world. When the job is over in four or eight years, the President has a lifetime pension, an office and staff, and the ability to earn millions of dollars in speaking fees and by writing books. No wonder so many Americans have the ambition to become President of the United States. But to be elected, an individual has to raise hundreds of millions of dollars for campaign expenses and work night and day, seven days a week for 18 months. The majority of men and women who try to win this great position fail and have only a pile of debts to show for their efforts.

Once elected, the President must manage approximately 35 major government agencies with millions of employees and over $3 trillion to allocate annually. There is no other job like it in the world. Few, very few, persons are qualified to run for this position. A winning candidate must have supreme intelligence, significant contacts with domestic and world leaders, superior communication and persuasion skills, great organizational capabilities, and above-average stamina. This person must also be an outstanding student of history, government and the economy.

The President must select several hundred qualified executives to serve in presidential appointed positions to lead his/her agenda from concept to implementation. Some Presidents merely maintain the status quo with a few minor changes in a limited number of government agencies. Presidents who inherit or become involved in wars, depressions, recessions, and large national issues such as equal opportunity must be visionary and strategic leaders.

Barack Obama was elected to be such a visionary and strategic leader because a majority of voters were unhappy with the two unnecessary wars, the failed occupations of Islamic countries, the number of Americans killed or seriously wounded in Iraq and Afghanistan, the waste in nation-building projects, the meltdown of our financial institutions, the massive decline in housing values, the over-50% decline in the stock market, the unemployment of nearly 15 million

Americans, the 2008 Great Recession, the escalating cost of health care, the mismanagement of federal disasters such as the floods in New Orleans, and the poor performance of our public schools.

Unfortunately, the press and many citizens expected all these problems to be solved in less than two years. History clearly indicated it would probably take at least six-to-eight years to solve all these problems, as well as our out-of-control illegal immigration situation and our nationwide energy system. To compound matters, our federal government needs to cut back on spending because our national debt has increased to the point where we can no longer live on borrowed money.

Time for Scaling Up Presidential Leadership

When a new President is sworn into office, many members of Congress have an attitude that they will be here long after this President leaves so Congress will set the agenda. It takes months and sometimes two years for a new President to assert leadership to a level where the White House takes charge of the agenda. Military, intelligence, and state department personnel often plan to continue with their existing strategies and plans. As it does with Congress, it takes months or years for a President to install new strategies and goals. Leaders of the largest corporations and Wall Street often want no government interference. Crises such as a recession, a meltdown of the stock market, or the collapse of financial institutions enable a President to establish his/her leadership of the economy. State and local party chairpersons only seek a working partnership with a new President after they experience losses in the first midterm election.

President Clinton Accomplished Four Goals

After a slow start in 1993 and after the Democrats lost their majorities in Congress in 1994, President Clinton achieved a remarkable record for his years in office:

- The 1992 federal deficit, which was nearly $300 billion at the end of the first President Bush's administration, became a surplus of $200 billion at the completion of President Clinton's administration.

- Plans were in place to repay the trillions of dollars borrowed from the Social Security and Medicare Trust Funds.
- Unemployment fell from 7% to 4% with 20 million new jobs created in the private sector.
- GDP grew at an average rate of 3.4% with low inflation.
- Poverty rates declined significantly.
- The cost of welfare and safety nets were reduced.
- The stock market reached an all-time high.
- Iraq's military expansion was contained.
- Israelis and Palestinians were peacefully discussing a two-state solution.
- All world leaders, including those in China and Russia, respected the United States.

The Clinton years were a significant period of peace and prosperity, and citizens began to believe their federal government could be both efficient and affordable. Senior Americans continued to have a decent retirement with Social Security pensions and Medicare benefits. President Clinton accomplished four national goals, but he was not able to pass health care reform or achieve a real breakthrough in the student learning crisis.

President Bush Failed To Achieve Any National Goals

No national goals were achieved during the eight years that President Bush and Vice President Cheney were in power:

- The decision to respond to the 9/11 attack with a War on Terror cost five trillion dollars of debt and the lives of over six thousand service personnel. Tens of thousands were wounded, and al-Qaeda is still operating in many countries.
- Terrorist attacks within the United States were not prevented by the decisions to invade and occupy Islamic countries.
- The national debt doubled during these eight years. With the two wars continuing for 9 and 13 years, plus the impact of the 2008 Great Recession, the national debt

will be close to $16 trillion by 2012. It had been only $5 trillion in 2000.

- Millions of Americans lost their jobs due to the 2008 Great Recession.
- The meltdown of financial institutions in 2008 required a $700 billion TARP bailout of troubled assets.
- Millions of American families lost their homes and much of their net worth.
- Very wealthy Americans lost billions of dollars.
  Rich Americans lost millions of dollars.
  Upper middle-class Americans lost thousands of dollars.
- The Bush-Cheney administration failed to solve the problems associated with Social Security revenues, immigration, clean energy, and student learning.
- The relief efforts for the Hurricane Katrina disaster were severely mismanaged.
- The stock market lost 53 percent of its value.
- The national poverty rate rose to 13.2%. 39.8 million Americans are living at or below the poverty line.
- Corporate profits dropped by 80 percent in 2008.
- Construction of new homes and buildings almost stopped.
- Government spending increased by 66 percent.

President Bush and Vice President Cheney made the recovery from the Great Recession nearly impossible due to their ongoing wars, their commitments to nation-building in Iraq and Afghanistan, and their mountain of debt that resulted in record deficits for ensuing White House administrations. They also failed to reign in the runaway costs of health care and the inhumane rationing of health care coverage by the HMOs. They claim only two achievements. One being that there were no more attacks like 9/11 and they reduced taxes, which were not affordable.

On the other hand, President Bush and his team were masters at getting elected. Bush's first elected position was Governor of Texas, a big job. His next successful election was President of the United States because he promised tax cuts. President Bush was reelected four years later by delivering on his tax cut promise and rallying the nation to a War on Terror. President Bush also produced a spending machine based on the two wars and the 2008 Great Recession which made it difficult for whoever was elected in 2008 to look successful with excessive spending and high unemployment resulting in a major victory for the Republican Party at the 2010 midterm elections. Of course, it was helpful to the Republicans that the Democratic Party made many mistakes both in Texas and in the 2000 and 2004 presidential campaigns as well as the 2010 midterm election.

President Obama's Accomplishments in Three Years

Many Americans are unhappy with the recovery pace from the 2008 Great Recession. Others are not pleased that comprehensive immigration reform did not become law in President Obama's first three years. Clean energy advocates were expecting a comprehensive energy bill. However, President Obama can still point to the following positive actions with Congress that have improved the economy and standard of living for the vast majority of Americans:

- The country has returned to growth in GDP.
- Consumer confidence rose to the highest level in three years.
- Over two million Americans have been hired rather than millions being fired.
- The housing market is starting to rebound
- The stock market has substantially rebounded.
- Financial institutions have been restructured and re-regulated to protect deposits and to restore credit.
- Almost all Americans will have health insurance.
- Passing student loan reform has made college more affordable.
- With health care reform, millions of Americans will no longer have to live in fear of an injury or illness bankrupting them.
- Working with our allies, the United States' image as a country of peace has been restored.

– The American Recovery and Reinvestment Act pulled America back from the brink of another Great Depression and saved thousands of jobs.

– The American auto industry was saved by loans that were paid back with interest, thus protecting tens of thousands of jobs.

– Both farm and industrial exports are growing rapidly, up 22 percent and 18 percent.

– The trade deficit that peaked at $759 billion in 2006 is now $496 billion.

– Individual savings have grown from 1 percent to over 5 percent.

– Household debt has decreased by $1.1 trillion.

In the closing weeks of 2010, President Obama was able to end the "don't ask, don't tell" practice in our military services, and Congress and the Senate passed the nuclear reduction START Treaty negotiated with the President of Russia. Another important bill was the measure providing medical care to ailing police and fire fighters who had responded to the 9/11 bombings that Congressional Republicans had resisted as another federal bailout. Most important, there was a bipartisan agreement on maintaining the Bush tax cuts for two more years and a new Inheritance Tax bill. President Obama signed into law the first major overhaul of the nation's food safety infrastructure since 1938. The tax bill included over $200 billion for what some people call Stimulus II which is directed to creating new jobs. Most important, the economy finished in 2010 with an upbeat Christmas season, a GDP growth of 2.5 percent, a projection for selling many more automobiles in 2011, and a stock market that passed the 12,000 mark early in 2011.

Losses at the Mid-Term 2010 Election

With the results of the 2010 mid-term election, President Obama will not accomplish in four years everything that all citizens wanted. Neither did President Roosevelt who had to implement an eight-year recovery program for the Great Depression, or Presidents Clinton and Bush (41) who needed twelve years to correct the fiscal problems created by President Reagan. President Obama should have told Americans that our nation was at the start of an economic depression in 2009 and his objective was to prevent a long-term and deep depression. Therefore, he would need to make major changes and offer bold new programs to reduce unemployment.

Communications from the White House in 2009 and 2010 failed to convince a large majority of Americans that Obama's recovery program would be successful, costing the Democrats numerous seats in the House and Senate. Neither did President Obama tell voters that if Republicans took over the management of either the House or the Senate there would be a "do nothing" Congress for 2011 and 2012 that would halt recovery of the economy. President Roosevelt was more successful in 1934 when Democrats increased their already large majority in both the House and Senate by nine seats even with unemployment being in excess of 15 percent. President Roosevelt and his communications personnel never let Americans forget it was President Hoover who did nothing to stop the cash runs on banks, the stock market meltdown and the poor economy that triggered the Great Depression and massive unemployment. A vast majority of Americans believed in Roosevelt's vision and Four Freedoms as national goals. In 2010, the Republican Party ran a national campaign on issues that affected the entire country while the Democratic Party ran one based on local issues. A famous quote from Speaker Tip O'Neill that all elections are based on local issues is no longer accurate, which helped cause the Democratic defeat.

In 2008, 130 million Americans cast their votes in the Presidential election. In contrast, in 2010 only 75 million voted which was a decrease of 55 million voters. The Democratic Party should have run a national campaign on how the ship of state was sinking when they took office in 2009. Their campaign should have shown how they were focused on the following:

1. Damage control to save Americans from a long-term economic depression and major plans to increase employment in 2011 and 2012.
2. Stabilizing the financial system with the TARP Program which was a bipartisan effort between President Bush, candidate Obama and Congress.

3. Saving the housing market from a depression.
4. Geting control of the War in Afghanistan with a new management system and phased-down strategy.
5. Gaining control of a runaway health care system, so millions of additional Americans could be insured.
6. Saving the stock market from a free fall and creating a growth market.

The national campaign should have convinced voters that Democrats saved the ship and millions of Americans from drowning in the massive problems that existed in early 2009. Communications failed and a majority of voters decided that a grid-locked Congress that would accomplish little or nothing in the 2011-2012 years was the right direction for our country. Republicans won a stunning victory without a new charismatic leader or any major plans to solve the problems of the economy, unemployment, or the trillion-dollar deficit. Unfortunately, excessive spending will continue for at least two years due to a grid-lock Congress which is Option One for our country which was described in Lesson 1. Republicans want to spend two-or-three years to repeal the healthcare reform bill which will return the United States to the most expensive healthcare system in the world with 20-to-25 percent of our citizens uninsured. Only 39 percent of voters want to repeal or scale back the health care reform bill and that number is decreasing.(1) Voters wanted a focus on job creation and economic growth.

President Obama made the same mistake that President Clinton made in 1994. Obama did not articulate a vision with a set of national goals that Americans could rally around for his entire four years. Speaker Newt Gingrich outsold Clinton and the Democratic Party with his Contract With America in 1994. In that year, Americans were not anti-government according to Gingrich. Voters simply wanted a smaller government, and with major reductions in spending, they hoped to receive tax cuts as well. Republicans failed to deliver on the vision of the Contract With America, so President Clinton was re-elected in 1996 and eventually Mr. Gingrich left Congress. Before 1994, except for three two-year periods in 1946, 1958 and 1981, House Republicans had not been in the majority since 1930. Since their large losses in the 1930s, Senate Republicans had only been the majority party for two years (1981-82) before 1994. Senator Phil

Gramm told Speaker Gingrich, "I am astounded on how much easier it was to be in the minority. The majority has to think through an issue, translate it into legislations, make the compromises necessary to build a majority for the bill, and manage the committee, the House floor, and the conference with the Senate. In other words, they actually have to govern. The minority party simply has to vote no."(2)

Lessons Learned at 2010 Midterm Election

The top one percent of Americans who are multi-millionaires or billionaires are so wealthy they can fund campaigns both in primary and general elections in order to place their candidates into Congress. Candidates can possess little knowledge of the major issues facing our nation, be inadequate communicators and they can avoid the press, but they still get elected. A $4 billion midterm election in 2010 produced a Congress more beholden than ever to special interests. There is no focus on achieving the national goals and little attention on reducing unemployment. With the current finance campaign laws, these same people may even be able to determine who runs for President in 2012. In his final speech as a Senator, Christopher Dodd stated, "Powerful financial interests, free to throw money about with little transparency, have corrupted the basic principles underlying our representational democracy."

Two Political Parties Are Miles Apart on the Budget

To reduce the General Fund annual spending by over a trillion dollars, there are three areas of expense driving up the annual deficit by over a trillion dollars. First is the increase in unemployment by over 100 percent plus millions more being underemployed which is around $500 billion of extra expense and loss of tax revenues. Second is the two unfunded wars and the almost unbelievable increase in the defense, intelligence, veterans' affairs, military health costs over the past ten years which is another $500 billion. Third is the continuous cost in health care of several hundred billion dollars.

Just to remind all of us how large a trillion is; if someone spent $1 million dollars per day since the time of Jesus until now, the spending would not have reached a trillion for another 730 years. Neither political party has developed a grand strategy to reduce unemployment by at least 50 percent over the 2012 to 2016 time period. Only one political party has a plan to end the two wars by 2014, but neither political party has a realistic strategy to reduce the defense, intelligence, VA, military medical expenses by several hundred billion dollars per year which can be accomplished if the United States would change its foreign policies and defense strategies. Only one political party has a strategy to reduce the cost of health care while providing health insurance to the vast majority of Americans. And one party will not increase taxes. Therefore, the two political parties are miles apart on how to balance the budget in this decade.

Let's review two budget plans that are now on the table within the halls of Congress to reduce the annual deficit against the six national goals.

President Obama submitted several budgets in 2011. The first one was in January, which Republicans rejected because it did not reduce entitlements. In April, he gave a speech at George Washington University with a concept budget of reducing the deficit $4 trillion by raising taxes on high-income Americans, reducing the defense budget, lowering health care costs, and reducing the size of government agencies. In the debt ceiling crisis during the summer, Obama discussed other budgets with various groups who were trying to reduce the deficit. All of these efforts were rejected by the Republican Congressional leaders. Obama was willing to make some changes to both Social Security and Medicare, but he would not reduce senior Americans to a life of poverty. His budgets were compatible with the six national goals.

The Republican Party is endorsing the Paul Ryan plan, "The Path to Prosperity." There are no tax increases. As discussed in Lesson 6, it eliminates Medicare by replacing it with a voucher system for all Americans under 55 years old. The plan is silent on Social Security, but many Republicans want to convert Social Security to a personal account system like a 401k rather than the current payroll tax. The plan also supports means testing the Social Security system. There would be large additional tax cuts for citizens who are high earners. The Bush tax cuts would become permanent for all citizens. The Affordable Health Care law of 2010 would be repealed which would drive up the cost of health care for all citizens, but it would reduce the cost of health care for the government. The plan supports the $178 billion in savings identified by Defense Secretary Gates, but $100 billion is reinvested in higher military priorities, so a net $78 billion is insufficient for achieving a balanced budget in this decade. The plan assumes a growth rate that would reduce unemployment to 2.8 percent, but there are no real plans to achieve this growth objective. Therefore, it truly is a continuation of the policies of 2001 to 2008 that created a mountain of debt due to the continued strategy of being the policemen of the world in a continuous war, no plans to reduce unemployment, and unrealistic plans to reduce the cost of health care for citizens. President Obama called Ryan's budget proposal an effort to slash government programs to preserve and expand tax cuts for the wealthy. Nancy Pelosi called it the "Pathway to Poverty" for most Americans.

Once again, the two parties are miles apart. The national goals could be used to try to bring the two political parties back together for a bipartisan solution to the annual trillion-dollar deficits and the growing mountain of debt. But being realistic, Democrats and Republicans will probably not agree on a bipartisan solution in 2011 nor during the campaign season of 2012. Voters can decide in 2012 which political party they want to have solve the financial problems in 2013 to 2016 by electing a President with a large majority in both the House and Senate.

What Must Republicans Do To Be Elected?

First, they need to find a new leader as they did in 1952 when they selected General Eisenhower. "Ike" had no ties to President Hoover and he never participated in the negative responses from Republican leaders to the recovery program that President Roosevelt sold and implemented in the 1930s. Eisenhower was also a war hero. He became a successful President with peace, prosperity, and an efficient and affordable government. He also supported Social Security and sponsored the very successful, but expensive national highway system. He kept the country out of potential wars in Vietnam and the Middle East. The Republican Party barely remembers or comments about President Eisenhower, who governed from the center rather than from an ultra-conservative agenda. In fact, over a 100-year period, the Republican Party today is only proud of one President, Ronald Reagan, who accomplished three out of the six national goals: peace, prosperity, and an affordable and decent retirement for seniors. He never achieved a smaller and affordable government, nor did he address the student learning crisis or health care concerns. He did solve the Social Security revenue problems. During the Reagan administration, the federal government grew by more than 60,000 employees in contrast to 373,000 fewer employees with President Clinton.(2)

The new Republican Presidential candidate should have no ties to the failed Bush-Cheney administration or to the Republican Congressional leaders from 1994 to 2008 who supported excessive spending. This will require the party to select a mayor or governor who is new to Washington, D.C. politics.

The Republican Party has many worthy goals and principles that appeal to millions of Americans:

- Reduce the size and cost of government
- Lower taxes
- Support for a strong defense organization
- Minimize government interventions and regulations
- Urge Americans to be self-sufficient
- Support for traditional values

To achieve these goals and objectives in future years, the Republican Party must make major changes in its political strategies and must obtain a majority of votes in the 2012 election. Below are the changes the party will need to make:

1. Transition from foreign and military policies of regime changes, preemptive wars, occupations, and nation-building to a policy of containment and peace that will reduce the defense budget by $300 billion.
2. Support a new comprehensive immigration law that will appeal to Hispanic voters and solve the immigration problems.
3. Provide the detail implementation plan to create more jobs, to preserve existing jobs and to reduce unemployment.
4. Support a practical fix for the Social Security revenue problem that does not involve high-risk investment decisions like 401(k) plans.

5. Support new regulations for financial institutions that will avoid failures such as the S & L crisis in the 1980s and the meltdown of financial institutions in the 4th quarter of 2008.
6. Present a plan that gradually reduces the operating budgets for all government agencies and departments over a four-year period.
7. Promise no tax cuts until there are surpluses.
8. Develop a detail plan to increase quality and reduce health care costs.
9. Develop a detail plan to achieve a balanced budget by 2020.
10. Develop a successful implementation plan for the No Child Left Behind Act that solves the student learning crisis within the pubic schools.

These changes are far different from those articulated by Senator Mitch McConnell who stated, "The American people want us to put aside the left-wing list of changes. The single most important thing we want to achieve is for President Obama to be a one-term President. If our primary legislative goals are to repeal and replace the health-spending bill, to end bailouts, cut spending, and shrink the size and scope of government, the only way to do all these things is to put someone in the White House who won't veto any of these things."(3) Senator McConnell's statement mentioned nothing about returning the country to prosperity or reducing the unemployment rate by 50 percent. In fact, there was no focus on any of the six national goals except a general statement to downsize government.

The Republican Party is in serious trouble on the subject of employment. Many American workers hold Republicans responsible for the millions of lay-offs in 2008 and 2009. The Republican congressional leaders in 2009 and 2010 never offered a realistic plan to create new jobs. After their success in the 2010 election, Republicans still offer no specific plan to create millions of jobs. To the contrary, the party seems to be focused on laying-off tens of thousands of government employees at the federal, state and local levels. It is estimated that well over a million jobs have been eliminated at state and local governments since the Great 2008 Recession started. Thousands of private sector jobs have also been lost due to the reduction in state and local budgets. When House Speaker John Boehner was asked about all the potential lay-offs at a press conference in February 2011, he stated, "Since President Obama has taken office, the federal government has added 200,000 (a totally incorrect number) new federal jobs, and if some of those jobs are lost in this, so be it." With the Republican governors trying to destroy unions and the Congressional Republicans being against unemployment insurance, the Grand Old Party appears to becoming the party of unemployment. Not a good image for 2012.

Many members of the press and the Republican Party will claim that it is impossible to bring this much change to the Grand Old Party. Keep in mind though, that the Republican Party during the World War II years and the post-war period changed from being the party of NO and calling the American President a socialist, a communist, and a dictator to being a responsible minority party working in a bipartisan manner with the Democratic Party. This dramatic shift enabled President Eisenhower to be elected President in 1952.

President Reagan brought great change to the Republican Party. President Clinton convinced the Democratic Party to govern from the center. Margaret Thatcher changed her party so much that England turned away from socialism. Tony Blair persuaded the Labor Party to govern from the center and to forget about nationalizing major corporations. Today, David Cameron has returned the Tory party (Conservatives) to power by making major strategic changes. When a political party has suffered a series of defeats, change is always possible. However, it takes an outstanding new leader which is exactly what the Republican Party needs now.

David Brooks wrote an article for the NEW YORK TIMES entitled "A New Malaise Befuddles The Nation." Brooks stated, "70 percent of Americans think the country is on the wrong track and nearly two-thirds believe the nation is in decline. The U.S. has experienced nine straight months of slow economic growth. The public mood is darkening. At this point, we could see changes that are unimaginable today. A semi-crackpot like Donald Trump could storm the gates and achieve astonishing political stature."(4) In the future, leadership mistakes are going to inflict severe financial pain on Americans because the financial blunders cannot be covered by borrowing billions or trillions of dollars. The key message to voters in 2012, 2014, and 2016 is—be careful who you elect to Congress and the White House. Your standard of living can be raised or greatly reduced for you, your children, and your grandchildren if you elect incompetent political leaders. Don't let the press or a political party's propaganda machine influence your vote with side issues such as where the President was born or is he really a Christian.

Pledge To America and Contract With America

In September, 1994, more than 300 GOP candidates stood on the steps of the Capitol to endorse the "Contract With America." Republican candidates made it the centerpiece of their national campaign and sold it to voters. That has not been the case with the "Pledge To America" which was announced in a lumberyard in September, 2010. Some Republican candidates view the pledge as an a la carte menu of good intentions and policies from which to select, not a manifesto to be endorsed.(5) It is not a vision with national goals.

The pledge does not provide a detail plan to bring quality improvements and lower health care costs for all Americans. It provides no plan to increase Social Security revenues. There is no comprehensive plan to reduce government spending. In fact, the national debt will increase at a faster rate due to the pledge's proposed tax cuts. It calls for more deregulation which caused the Wall Street and free enterprise system meltdown. Defense spending will continue to escalate as the War on Terror goes on for many years. The "Contract With America" was never achieved and the "Pledge To America" will never be implemented. They simply helped the Republican Party gain votes.

Some Republicans want to continue selling the vision of smaller government, small businesses, additional tax cuts for hard-working Americans, only small incremental changes in the status quo, more defense spending, and more deregulation of businesses and financial institutions. After all, they won the White House 28 out of 40 years with this vision and they believe it will sell again in 2012, because they were so successful in the 2010 midterm election. The vision was never implemented in these 28 years and, if the White House operates under it again from 2013 to 2016, it will surely trigger a financial meltdown of the federal government in this decade.

If the Republican Party nominates a candidate in 2012 who endorses:

- The Bush-Cheney performance record
- The Paul Ryan Pathway to Prosperity
- Calls for more military spending
- Promotes the reduction of Social Security and Medicare benefits
- Demands major reductions in women's health programs
- Promises nothing more than border security rather than comprehensive immigration reform
- Has no realistic plan to create millions of jobs
- Sides with oil companies the way Cheney did

Republican Party will most likely lose the 2012 election.

Potential Impact of the Tea Party

Voters have another choice. They could vote for Tea Party candidates who want to take a machete to the federal government. There are approximately 80 Republican members of Congress who identify with the Tea Party.

The Tea Party had a golden opportunity to take over the Republican Party after their major losses in the 2008 general election. To accomplish that they needed a visionary and charismatic leader like President Reagan who would have offered a rebuild America vision with national goals. They could have offered a grand plan to phase down the War on Terror to reduce the annual deficit by several hundred billion dollars. They could have offered a new comprehensive plan to recharge the free enterprise system with a goal to reduce unemployment by 50 percent which would have reduced the deficit by half a trillion dollars. In addition, the Tea Party could have supported a strategic plan to reduce the cost of health care by implementing new quality programs, and they could have offered a national program to fix the student learning crisis within the public schools. All of this would have led to a balanced budget in this decade.

Unfortunately, no visionary and charismatic leader has emerged. The Tea Party has endorsed the Paul Ryan budget plan and are now selling the concept they can inflict more financial pain on Americans than the Republican Party by slashing Social Security and Medicare benefits, eliminating important tax deductions, reducing government services, and providing no assistance to American companies that are on the verge of going out of business. All of this leads to major increases in unemployment, and lower take-home pay for citizens who do have jobs. A Tea Party candidate must be against bailout funds and similar packages even if the economy sinks into a depression, which it will under their leadership. They also want to starve the revenue flow to the federal government with more tax cuts that are not affordable. While there are three or more Tea Party factions, the overall Tea Party objective is to return the federal government to the way it operated during President Hoover's administration; a small government that does not get involved in the economy or welfare of its citizens.

E. J. Dionne of the WASHINGTON POST wrote an article in April, 2010 entitled "The Populism of the Privileged." The article stated that the NEW YORK TIMES and CBS News did a careful study of just who is in the Tea Party movement. They claim it is the reemergence of an old anti-government far right group that accounts for about one-fifth of our country. Tea Party members tend to be Republican, white, male, married, and over 45 years old. They represent the populism of the privileged and they are very conservative. The article stated that 73 percent of the Tea Party believes that providing government benefits to poor citizens encourages them to remain poor. Only 17 percent believe the federal government should spend money to create jobs, and 63 percent claim they watch FOX News for information about politics and current events. A 2010 poll conducted by the nonprofit Public Religion Research Institute showed that half of Americans who consider themselves part of the Tea Party movement are also part of the religious right (conservative Christian) movement. They believe the United States has always been and is currently a Christian nation.(6)

Sarah Palin is one of the Tea Party leaders, and like most members, she never gets specific on what areas should be eliminated to reduce the size and cost of government. She, of course, wants to cut taxes and let small businesses grow, thrive, and prosper. At the Boston Tea Party event on April 14, 2010, she stated, "Just give us our constitution, our guns, and our religion. Washington, D.C. can keep all their ideas for change which we do not need." If Tea Party candidates take over the Republican Party, they could do significant damage to the American standard of living or they could improve our lifestyle.

Listed below are the non-negotiable core beliefs of the National Tea Party:

- Illegal aliens are here illegally
- Pro-domestic employment is indispensable
- Stronger military is essential
- Special interests must be eliminated
- Gun ownership is sacred
- Government must be downsized
- The national budget must be balanced
- Deficit spending must end
- Bail-out and stimulus plans are illegal
- Personal income taxes must be reduced
- Business income taxes must be reduced
- Political offices must be available to average citizens
- Intrusive government must be stopped
- English must be the nation's official language
- Traditional family values must be encouraged
- Common sense constitutional conservative self-governance must be our country's mode of operation

What we need now from the Tea Party candidates are detail plans on how these objectives and implementation plans will be sold to Congress and enacted by the President without sending the country into an economic depression.

Morton Kondracke, a conservative columnist, wrote on May 1, 2010, "While the GOP is on tract to score big victories in 2010, it's in grave danger of committing long-term suicide unless it's rescued from right-wing madness. With consistent—sometimes ugly opposition to immigration reform, resistance to climate and energy change remedies, hostility towards gay rights, including shocking language at Tea Party rallies and waging primaries as ideological purification rituals all represent long-term threats to the party." Kondracke could also have added negative opposition to health care reform and regulations of Wall Street financial institutions. "The party of no-hell-no without constructive ideas for national problems will never become the majority party." Kondracke also wrote, "Ideology that is extreme never sells 50 percent. You have to be relevant to people's lives. You have to solve problems that people deal with every day."

On the other hand, based on what happened in 2010, the joint efforts of the Republican and Tea Parties might achieve a major comeback victory in 2012 if the President and Democratic congressional candidates communicate as poorly in 2012 as they did in 2010.

Where were Tea Party members in the 1990s when President Bush (41), President Clinton, and Vice President Gore were trying to solve the financial problems from the Reagan administration? No one remembers any large group of conservatives carrying signs in praise of these three political leaders who created the financial miracle of converting annual deficits into annual surpluses. President Bush (41) and Vice President Gore each lost their elections due to a lack of voters who appreciated their accomplishments. It is no wonder then that President Bush (43) decided to follow the Reagan strategy of borrowing and spending trillions of dollars, rather than be a fiscal conservative like his father. He wanted to be reelected in 2004 and his spending helped him accomplish this objective.

What President Obama Must Do To Be Re-elected

First, President Obama has to educate Independent voters and, if possible, some Republicans that "liberal" is not a dirty word. From 1932 on, the Democratic Party has a long record of raising the American standard of living:

- Supported the growth and expansion of the middle class with good jobs, good wages, good benefits, and a growing economy.
- Twice regulated and stabilized financial institutions to protect bank deposits and investments for Americans.
- Created Social Security pension for retirees.
- Created Medicare benefits for retirees.
- Passed universal health care with a goal to improve quality and reduce costs.
- Passed laws for women and minorities to have equal opportunity and equal pay in the job market.
- Passed civil rights for minorities.

- Desegregated the American public school system, universities, military, housing, hotels, public recreation facilities, and restaurants.
- Supports civil rights for Americans who are born gay.
- Provided a safety net for the unemployed.
- Supports a clean environment and a solution to climate change problems.
- Supports instructional improvements and access to good public schools and institutions of higher education.
- Supports freedom of religion.
- Converted large annual deficits into a balanced budget.

Second, Obama has to sell his vision and national goals to achieve a complete recovery from the 2008 Great Recession that he inherited from President Bush. His vision will need to focus primarily on job creation. He must have a realistic plan to create millions of jobs in the second administration.

Third, he has to end the wars in Iraq and Afghanistan, which he is scheduled to do in 2012 and 2014. In the second term, he also needs to downsize the wartime military organization to a peacetime one that is affordable.

Fourth, Obama has to convince Americans he has a plan to reduce the size of the annual deficits. He must develop a plan to achieve a balanced budget in this decade.

Fifth, he has to promise to pass important laws such as comprehensive immigration and energy bills which eliminate dependence on hostile nations.

Sixth, he needs to implement major changes within the Departments of Education and Energy in this second administration.

Seventh, he should sponsor a nationwide training program for all Democratic candidates to expand their knowledge of the issues and on how to manage a successful campaign. Too many Congressional candidates in 2010 were unable to sell his accomplishments to voters because they failed in the art of communications and persuasion as well as managing a successful campaign. Obama can make the 2012 election a national referendum on "Rebuilding America" by reducing the size and cost of government as well as achieving the six national goals.

President Obama's speech on April 13, 2011 at George Washington University surprised Democrats as much as Republicans. In 40 minutes, he outlined a plan to reduce the deficit by $4 trillion by raising taxes on the rich, shrinking the defense budget, protecting Social Security and Medicare, continuing to improve health care at lower costs, regulating big business, and reducing the size of government. Two weeks later, he approved a plan to kill Osama bin Laden and within 30 days his approval rating was at 60 percent.

In the meantime, the Republican Party was having a difficult time defending the Paul Ryan plan because senior citizens and baby boomers do not want to give up their Social Security checks and Medicare benefits to finance a never ending War on Terror or more tax cuts for the rich. In fact, only 11 percent of baby boomers are convinced they will have a decent retirement due to the loss of company pensions. A recent survey claimed 64 percent of boomers see Social Security as the foundation of their retirement earnings.

Eventually, wealthy Americans are going to have to pay more taxes because they elected the biggest spenders in the history of our country with President Bush (43) and Vice President Cheney who created a mountain of debt. There are consequences when voters elect political leaders who state they are fiscal conservatives, but establish new records for spending and borrowing. In the Obama administration, Republican leaders of Congress have called for more defense spending, no stimulus programs to reduce unemployment, no programs to create new jobs, as well as resisting all efforts to reduce the cost of health care. All of this guaranteed record trillion-dollar deficits from 2009 to 2012. Very wealthy Americans did receive tax cuts (current actual rate of payment is now 17 percent), but they lost large sums of money in the meltdown of the stock market and in their real estate investments. It was fortunate that the public and private sectors were able to create a record rebound of the stock market.

Finally, like President Truman in 1948, Obama must convince voters in 2012 that the 2010 midterm election produced a "do nothing" Congress in 2011 and 2012. Republicans in Congress are not improving economic growth or creating millions of jobs. In fact, with the Republican threat to not approve the debt ceiling, business executives and financial institutions are hoarding cash which is reducing the growth in the economy causing the stock market to decline, the job creation system to falter, and the real estate values to once again decline. Without a Democratic Congress, the President has not been able to continue his programs of recovery from the 2008 Great Recession. The Republican Congress could be leading the nation into a double dip recession in 2012.

If President Obama has a Democratic Congress with a large majority in his second term of office, he might be able to implement a $7 trillion reduction in deficits during the remainder of this decade. This reduction would enable the President, who is elected in 2016, to achieve a balanced budget before 2020. This approach will require an aggressive implementation of systemic changes outlined in this book that accomplish the financial plan on page 243 in Lesson 14, requiring additional revenues and major reductions in spending.

American Voters Must Decide Between Two Strategic Roads

Some Presidential and Congressional candidates in 2012 want to significantly reduce the services and benefits of the federal government. This group created the debt ceiling crisis and was willing to do major damage to the American and world-wide economies because they voted against raising the debt ceiling. This approach would have caused much higher interest rates and a national default on U.S. Treasury bonds. This faction was not upset with the downgrade of the U.S. credit rating from AAA to a lower rating. The same persons appear to support a Lowering the American Standard of Living strategy for our country's future with the hope of winning both the White House and Congress in the 2012 general election.

If these candidates had been in power in 2008, they would not have saved the American financial system from a complete meltdown. They would never have approved any stimulus programs as Presidents Bush (43) and Obama did to save the country from an economic depression. These members of Congress were greatly disappointed when the Congress and President did raise the debt ceiling and vowed if they are in the majority in 2013 there will be no more increases in the debt ceiling even if the world and U.S. economies collapse because of their votes. This group promises to not bail out any American corporations or industries. If elected in 2012, this group of candidates will stand by as President Hoover did in 1929 and watch the country sink into a long-term economic depression with unemployment exceeding 15 or 20 percent. Americans must understand they are voting for a Lowering of the American Standard of Living strategy rather than Rebuilding American strategy.

In the heat of battle over raising the debt ceiling, many members of Congress insisted that the federal government must pass a balanced budget amendment to the U.S. Constitution with a requirement of a two-thirds vote for tax increases. Even Senator John McCain stated this legislation was a waste of time and energy because the states and citizens would never approve such an amendment. A majority of state governments have balanced budget amendments within their constitutions, which have caused a serious financial crisis during the Great 2008 Recession. If such an amendment where passed at the federal level, there would be millions of letters going to citizens as well as state and local governments informing them that the federal government was eliminating or reducing many programs essential for our standard of living. When great floods, hurricanes, tornadoes, etc. happen within our country, there would be no support from the federal government. This amendment could also be used to greatly reduce Social Security and Medicare benefits. During the years it would take to achieve a balanced budget amendment, our country would drift along under Option One with record trillion-dollar annual deficits.

With Option One (Continue Spending at the Current Rate) that leads to Option Two (Major Tax Increases and Benefit Reductions), the United States will continue to move in the direction of more deficits and debt and eventually an economic depression. Our nation will try to be the policemen of the world with a defense, intelligence, homeland security, veterans' benefits, and military medical costs that require almost a trillion dollars of personal income tax. This strategy means a 20-to-25 percent increase in taxes. The free enterprise system will continue to be motivated by the stock market which means more layoffs of American workers as jobs are outsourced to low wage countries reducing tax revenues and driving up the cost of unemployment services. All of this leads to an economic depression and very high unemployment. The Departments of Education and Energy will be closed. This guarantees the American public school system will remain third-class behind European and Asian countries because there is no central leadership or funds to develop new 21st Century learning and management systems. The famous American universities will be unaffordable to a majority of Americans. Without national leadership, the energy system and costs will also be third-class. The health care system will regress to being controlled by HMOs and will be unaffordable by millions of Americans, including senior citizens who have reduced Medicare benefits. Most Americans will work for 50 years and retire to a world of poverty for their senior years because Social Security checks will be smaller or not available due to means testing, and in most situations the 401k accounts will be too small.

In 2011, it became clear that some candidates for President and a number of political leaders in Congress want to solve the potential financial crisis by inflicting severe financial pain on Americans with Option Two with a Lowering American Standard of Living strategy. They believe they can convince voters that Social Security and Medicare are the causes of the financial crisis, and not the excessive spending for the War on Terror, the job-killing 2008 Recession, and the runaway cost of health care during the past ten years. They believe their propaganda system can sell this illusion because Americans really do not understand the real causes of the financial crisis.

The alternative road for voters to select is best described as the Rebuilding America (Option Three) strategic direction. It is built on the foundation of peace and prosperity that are absolutely essential to accomplish the six national goals as outlined in Lesson 5. The United States replaces the policemen of the world foreign policy strategy with the successful containment strategy that is affordable and protects our nation. The government and business leaders form a working partnership to develop a realistic strategy to reduce unemployment by at least 50 percent which provides a major increase in tax revenues and reduces unemployment costs. These two fundamental changes for peace and prosperity reduce the annual deficit by nearly a trillion dollars in four years. This enables Social Security and Medicare benefits to be available to future generations of Americans. Some adjustments must be made to increase Social Security revenues. There must be a laser focus on reducing health care costs in this decade. All major federal government agencies, on average, must reduce their budget by 20 percent over a four-year period. The major challenges of our country must be solved such as the student learning crisis in the public schools and affordability of education. A new national strategy for energy must be developed and implemented. Comprehensive immigration reform must be passed. All this is feasible as documented in this book. All six national goals and a balanced budget can be achieved in this decade. The fundamental question for the 2012 election is: will at least one political party adopt the Rebuild America strategy to avoid a potential financial crisis and severe financial pain for citizens.

Voters Have To Ask Penetrating Questions of Candidate Statements

How do voters cut through the flood of information that may or may not be accurate prior to an election? Voters must seek the truth by reading numerous publications and listening to various news programs on television. They need to ask penetrating questions, such as the ones listed below, on what the candidate says at campaign rallies or in print or state on TV interviews on what he or she will do if elected.

–   What are your detail plans to reduce the overall spending to achieve a balanced budget in this decade?
–   Will you reduce our military budgets to a level of a defense organization rather than keep it at a wartime budget?
–   Will you support changes in the Social Security program to ensure adequate benefits for all Americans in future years? How will you accomplish this objective?
–   Will you support changes in health care that will improve quality and simultaneously lower costs for an affordable health system with health insurance for all Americans?
–   Will you support adequate financial institution regulations to protect our deposits and investments? Will you protect citizens from unreasonable interest charges on their credit cards?
–   Will you support government programs that will create new jobs and promote job security programs? If the private sector does not create jobs, will your party create jobs in the public sector?
–   With there being virtually little job security in the private sector, will you support programs that enable citizens to keep their homes, health insurance, automobiles, appliances, and furniture during reasonable time periods between jobs?

–   Will you support a nationwide energy system that makes our country truly independent of foreign oil? How will you accomplish this goal?
–   Will you support comprehensive immigration reform laws and programs?
–   Will you support major changes to solve the student learning crisis within our public schools?
–   What will you do to contain or lower costs for attending institutions of higher education?
–   Do you support the six national goals?
    1. Peace With Strong Defense and Homeland Security Systems
    2. Prosperity and a Rising Standard of Living With High Level of Employment
    3. Adequate and Affordable Health Care System
    4. Superior and Affordable Education Systems
    5. Efficient and Affordable Government
    6. Decent Retirement

Some political consultants and communication specialists will also select a goal such as five percent growth rate or three percent unemployment for their candidate that solves the deficit problem. These numbers are just picked out of thin air unless there is a detail plan of action to achieve the goal. For example, in 2002, with bipartisan support, President Bush established a "No Child Left Behind" goal for public schools that stated all students must achieve an A or B grade in math, reading, and science at all grade levels. There was no plan of action or implementation plan to achieve the goal except to rank and shame teachers and principals into achieving the goal with the same learning and management systems that have existed for100 years. Today, the vast majority of public schools are listed as failures. Voters must ask detail questions of candidates to be certain political goals and pledges are not just mere words that can never be achieved. The press should also ask penetrating questions.

Bipartisanship Did Not Succeed During 2009 to 2012

In the November 22, 2010 NEW YORK TIMES, Paul Krugman wrote an article entitled "There Will Be Blood." He started with a quotation from former Senator Alan Simpson, one of the co-chairman of the Deficit Reduction Commission, "I can't wait for the blood bath in April . . . . when debt limit time comes, they're going to look around and say: What in the hell do we do now? We've got guys who will not approve the debt limit extension unless we give 'em a piece of meat, real meat, meaning spending cuts."(7) "Republicans will probably try to blackmail the President into policy concessions by, in effect, holding the government hostage."

Krugman went on to state, "You might think that the prospect of this kind of standoff, which might deny many Americans essential services, wreak havoc in financial markets, and undermine America's role in the world, would worry all men of good will. The fact is that one of our two great parties has made it clear that it has no interest in making America governable, unless it is doing the governing. The same party is trying to bully the Federal Reserve into giving up completely on trying to reduce unemployment. President Obama is still talking about bipartisan outreach, but the G.O.P. is just not interested in helping a Democrat govern."(7) High unemployment and a stagnant economy helped Republicans win a large number of seats in Congress in 2010 and they believe high unemployment and a slow growth economy will help them win the Senate and the White House in 2012.

The debt ceiling was a classic example of a dysfunctional government that embarrassed our government leaders and political parties. It led to a reduction for the first time in the credit rating of our triple A score, and more important, it greatly damaged the overall image and reputation of the United States. The Part One spending cuts of $907 billion over ten years was a minimum amount that impressed no one. The Part Two cuts of $1.2 trillion beginning in 2013 that will be based on the recommendations of a new super congressional committee could also be unimpressive. This, course, means over a trillion dollars of deficits and borrowing will continue in 2012. The President and Congress who are elected in 2012 will have major decisions to make in 2013. One decision will be the extension or expiration of the Bush tax cuts. Another major decision involves raising of the debt ceiling by several trillion dollars, and the third decision, hopefully, will result in a responsible and large reduction in government spending in the 2013 to 2016 budgets. Our government cannot continue to borrow nearly $3 billion a day. Voters in 2012 must not let the gridlock situation in Congress continue during the 2013-2016 administration because it could trigger a long-term economic depression and meltdown of the federal government's financial system.

Sometime in the 2011 and 2012 timeframe, the government may shut down which Republicans made happen when President Clinton tried to govern from the center. This time, however, it will be a significant step towards a "bond crisis" when the financial markets of the world finally decide the American federal government cannot reduce the size and cost of its government nor is there any hope for the United States to have a balanced budget. With that, the United States will be forced into a deep and long-term economic depression because banks and other countries will no longer supply borrowed money for our large annual deficits and massive payments of interest on debt.

If the high rate of spending continues by both political parties through 2016 with some additional tax cuts, there will be no soft landing for this financial crisis. There could be riots in city streets, on college campuses, in state capitols, and in Washington, D.C. over the allocation of funds from a greatly reduced budget because Americans and foreign financial institutions will no longer purchase U.S. government bonds. The United States will struggle through a difficult period as the Soviet Union did when its citizens stopped their government from spreading Communism throughout the world and began nation-building projects within their own country. Our military services and veterans would suffer the most just as their counterparts did in Russia. Our senior citizens would also suffer from significant reductions in Social Security and Medicare benefits.

The 2012 election will be one of the most important elections in the history of our country. Our future standard of living could be substantially reduced by a meltdown of the federal government financial system if political leaders make the wrong decisions during the next four years. For example, at this time, it is possible to bankrupt the federal government with a series of tax cuts.

In Lesson 1, we learned the first option for our country was "Continue The Civil War Between Political Parties," which is how our national debt grew from less than a trillion dollars in 1980 to a forecasted $16 trillion in 2012 and $20 trillion in 2016. Only voters can ensure that Option One is not continued in 2012 by electing a large majority in both the Senate and the House who support the goals and strategies of the elected President. Democrats and Republicans now vote against each other more than at any time since the Civil War, giving us little hope for a bipartisan solution to our financial crisis and the major issues facing the United States. Another grid-locked Congress for four more years will probably result in an economic depression and certainly a lower standard of living for a majority of Americans. President Roosevelt saved the capitalist system and the American way of life in the 1930s because the country gave him large majorities in Congress and supported his economic recovery programs. Both presidential candidates should ask for a large majority in Congress based on the major changes they plan to implement if they are elected.

Conclusion and Recommended Actions by Educated Voters

It would be ideal for our nation if both political parties supported the vision and national goals as outlined in this book. The election could then be between two Presidential candidates who would both offer their positive plans and programs to accomplish the vision of Rebuilding America with the six national goals. But if one political party cannot accept the goals or the vision, voters must decide not to vote for that Presidential candidate and the Congressional candidates of that political party if Americans want to rebuild America. Political leaders who want to slow the pace of change or merely maintain the status quo will, by default, contribute to leading our nation into a financial debacle. In Washington, D.C., politics may be a game to some people, but ineffective leadership clearly lowers the American standard of living. Politics is now about survival for the American way of life. Political consultants will, no doubt, try to sell their candidates with negative advertisements and a slick communications strategy which will not focus on the national goals. Voters must not be influenced by misleading slogans and ads.

Simply put, Americans get the government they vote for. Far too many people do not take this responsibility seriously. Millions of citizens do not even bother to vote. Others just do a quick vote without becoming knowledgeable about the real issues and challenges facing our nation. Only a minority of Americans are involved in our political process which, in this upcoming election, will determine whether the United States remains a great country with the highest standard of living or becomes a struggling nation with a lower standard of living, economic stagnation, and high unemployment.

Now that you have invested a few hours to become knowledgeable about the national goals, federal financial system, the national debt, the ever expanding annual deficits, and the major areas of government that caused the financial crisis, you are probably asking: What should I do as an informed citizen to help solve the crisis? The answer is simple: vote for qualified candidates and share your knowledge with friends so they too can make good voting decisions. Everyone's vote will be crucial in 2012.

A reader of this book is not going to agree with every message in the document. A reader should first decide on whether he or she wants to modify the six national goals described in Lesson 5. Based on the revised list of national goals, modify the questions that are in Lesson 15. Decide which Presidential candidate and which political party in Congress will be able to rebuild America. Also, ask yourself which political party will protect and enhance your standard of living as well as your family's (children and grandchildren) standard of living. If you do not need your Social Security or your Medicare in your senior years, and you are not concerned about yourself or any member of your family having adequate health insurance throughout their lifespan, then you can vote for either political party. If you do have concerns, be careful which political candidate you decide to vote for. It is important that elected candidates for Congress and the White House are from the same political party because a split government where the President is from one party and the Congress from another results in a "do nothing" government eventually leading to an economic depression and a financial meltdown of the federal government in this decade.

Keep in mind, if voters elect a "do nothing" government in 2012, partnered with a free enterprise system that is "dead in the water," they are truly voting for a long-term and deep economic depression that will greatly reduce the American standard of living for decades. The Dean of Singapore's Lee Kuan Yew School of Public Policy and author of *The New Asian Hemisphere: The Irresistible Shift Of Global Power To The*

East, made the following comments in his NEWSWEEK article "Asian Wisdom." "For most of the 20th Century, Asia asked itself what it could learn from the modern innovative West. Now the question must be reversed: what can the West's overly indebted and sluggish nations learn from a flourishing Asia? Both China and India now balance capitalism with judicious government direction. If Americans could only free themselves from their antigovernment strait-jackets, they would begin to see that U.S.'s problems are not insoluble. Americans will have to put aside their attachment to the rhetoric of smaller government and less regulation. There are good taxes and bad taxes. Asian countries have embraced this wisdom, and have built sound long-term fiscal policies as a result."(8)

Fareed Zakaria's article in TIME magazine on June 27, 2011 included the following quote, "In fact, right now any discussion of government involvement in the economy, even to build vital infrastructure, is impossible because it is a cardinal tenet of the new conservatism that such involvement is always and forever bad. Meanwhile, across the globe, the world's fastest growing economy, China, has managed to use government involvement to create growth and jobs for three decades. From Singapore to South Korea to Germany to Canada, evidence abounds that some strategic actions by the government can act as catalysts for free-market growth." Of course, this is exactly what happened in the United States prior to 1980.

Voting to end the civil war in Congress, ending the financial crisis by reducing the size and cost of government and committing to the six national goals is the way to rebuild America. As a reader of this book, you are to be congratulated on being an educated voter for rebuilding America. Voters can return our nation to growth and prosperity as it was in the 1990s if they elect qualified candidates. Americans must forget which political party they voted for in previous years, and decide in 2012 which candidates will rebuild America and save our country from another Great Economic Depression like the 1930s.

NOTES FOR LESSON 15

1. "Poll: Public Mixed On Republican Tax, Health Plans," Alan Fram, ASSOCIATED PRESS, SAN DIEGO UNION-TRIBUNE, November 12, 2010, page A4

2. *Real Change,* Newt Gingrich, Regnery Publishing, Washington, D.C., 2008 page 17

3. "Election Dissonance," Hendrik Hertzberg, THE NEW YORKER, November 15, 2010, page 31

4. "A New Malaise Befuddles The Nation," David Brooks, NEW YORK TIMES, SAN DIEGO UNION-TRIBUNE, April 27, 2011, page B5

5. "Pledge Fails to Find Role In GOP Campaign," Ben Pershing, THE WASHINGTON POST, SAN DIEGO UNION-TRIBUNE, October 6, 2010, page A7

6. "Poll Shows Overlap Between Tea Party and Religious Right," Michel Boorstein, THE WASHINGTON POST, SAN DIEGO UNION-TRIBUNE, October 6, 2010, page A7

7. "There Will Be Blood," Paul Krugman, THE NEW YORK TIMES, November 22, 2010, Opinion Page

8. "Asian Wisdom," Kishore Mahbubanic, NEWSWEEK, December 2, 2010, page 34

OPPORTUNITY TO ASSESS KNOWLEDGE
AFTER READING THE BOOK

Now that you have read the book, use another piece of paper or your electronic reader to answer the following 25 questions which will show you how much you have learned as an educated voter prior to your decisions on which political party to support in 2012.

1. What should be our country's national goals?
   1.
   2.
   3.
   4.
   5.
   6.

2. Which political party or are both political parties spending and borrowing to the level where there will be a financial meltdown of the federal government in this decade?

3. Do you have a better understanding of the overall federal budget?

4. Which political party is mostly responsible for the mountain of debt created during the past 30 years?

5. Are the entitlements of Social Security and Medicare responsible for the mountain of debt?

6. What major areas of the General Fund have caused growth in spending?

7. Do you believe the federal government should be able to create and implement systemic changes within this decade to achieve a balanced budget?

8. What adjustments would you support within the Social Security System to provide adequate funds for benefits to all Americans through 2050?

9. What changes would you support to reduce the cost and improve the quality of healthcare?

10. Do you support the concept that every American must have healthcare insurance from the day they are born to the day that they die?

11. Do you believe the United States should phase out of civil wars, occupation of hostile nations, and multi-billion-dollar nation-building programs?

12. Do you believe spending for military services, homeland security, and intelligence can be significantly reduced during the next eight years and still maintain an effective defense against all potential enemies?

13. What action programs do you believe the federal government should implement to accelerate economic growth and reduce unemployment to less than 5%?

14. Do you believe the federal government should regulate the "Too Big To Fail" institutions?

15. Would you support a national curriculum of courses with 25 percent local lessons and new instructional and management systems to achieve the No Child Left Behind Vision?

16. Do you believe the federal government should motivate institutions of higher learning to have a more affordable education system for obtaining college degrees?

17. Do you believe the federal government should develop a national energy system that would reduce the cost of energy as well as the threat of hostile nations cutting-off our oil supply?

18. What percent of the budget reduction should be implemented in all government agencies over a 4-year period?

19. What areas of the General Fund must be reduced to achieve a balanced budget in this decade?

20. Do you believe our nation can achieve a balanced budget in this decade?

21. Do you feel more qualified and comfortable to discuss major issues facing our country and the national goals with members of Republican, Democratic, and Tea Parties?

22. Will you attend campaign rallies and meetings as well as town hall meetings to further your knowledge of the issues facing our country?

23. Will you ask candidates a series of penetrating questions to further qualify them with your vote?

24. Do you feel the information in this book has helped you make a better selection of qualified Congressional and Presidential candidates?

25. Will you recommend this book to your family members and friends prior to the election?

ACKNOWLEDGMENTS

This book is based on my work over several decades, during which time I have had the opportunity to interact with literally hundreds of senior executives both in the private and public sectors. From them, I learned management methods and various leadership styles enabling organizations to become extremely successful. I also studied why organizations fail and decline over the years. Various leaders of management development programs and seminars have also contributed to my knowledge of what must be accomplished to develop successful visions and strategies.

Numerous clients have enabled me to review the success of best practices in almost every industry. In the field of education, I have worked with many leaders in the school reform movement, some of the great leaders of famous universities, and training directors of our major corporations. All of these people have contributed to my knowledge enabling me to write three books on the subjects of how to improve the American public school systems, challenges facing institutions of higher education, and a management system to develop a competitive workforce.

This book would not have been possible without journalists who write important columns in our daily newspapers and weekly magazines. In addition, books have been written by political leaders, potential presidential candidates, economists, historians, and others who have been helpful in providing many facts that appear in this book.

The financial facts in the book have been provided by the annual financial reports and statements published by the Secretary of Treasury which are available to all citizens. I also wish to acknowledge the assistance and advise from my twin brother, Charles Bowsher, who was a partner at one of our major auditing firms and later one of the internationally known management consulting firms. He also was appointed to serve as the Assistant Secretary of the Navy for

Financial Management by both Presidents Johnson and Nixon from 1967 to 1971. Later, President Ronald Reagan appointed him to a 15-year term (1981 to 1996) to be the Comptroller General of the United States in charge of the GAO which included working with the administrations of Presidents Bush (41) and Clinton. Since then he has served on many corporate boards and government commissions. He was helpful in directing me to various official public documents the federal government issues in regard to the budget and other financial reports of various programs.

With all the sources of information, unless otherwise specifically attributed, all the messages and opinions in the book are my own. Any mistakes or inaccuracies in the book are mine alone. Of course, there is so much inaccurate information published in many documents, it is a challenge to ascertain which facts to utilize from so many conflicting numbers.

I want to thank a number of people from various political parties and organizations who read early drafts of the manuscript and who contributed many successful and important facts to me. The North County chapter of the San Diego World Affairs Council and the Rancho Bernardo Lunch Bunch organization provided speaking opportunities enabling me to review some of the key messages in the book. My son, Rob Bowsher, did an outstanding job editing the book and made the document more readable than it would otherwise have been. My other son, David, works with me on my Power Point presentations summarizing the key messages of the book. The personnel at iUniverse, my publisher, were also most helpful in the entire process of converting the manuscript into the finished product. Most important, I wish to thank my wife, Charmian Bowsher, who worked with me on an almost daily basis to create the book. This book simply would not exist without her computer skills and editorial advice.

ABOUT THE AUTHOR

Jack Bowsher has had four careers. He started with an accounting degree from the University of Illinois and an MBA with a major in finance from the University of Chicago. He practiced accounting during his tour of duty with the U.S. Army and the U.S. Steel Corporation. Later he changed careers by joining IBM where he studied and sold the utilization of advanced computer and communication systems. He served as the Director of Large Account Marketing after ten years of working with customers.

In his 33-year career with IBM, Jack became known as an educator where he redesigned the curriculum for customer executive education, sales training, marketing education, industry education and management development. Eventually, he was responsible for the overall education strategy for training over 400,000 employees and millions of customer personnel in 130 countries. During this period, Jack worked with several leading business and management graduate schools.

After retiring from IBM, Jack had a successful consulting career with two major management consulting firms in the areas of education, executive leadership, and the management of systemic changes. He consulted with corporations, government agencies, not-for-profit organizations, and a number of education institutions over a ten-year period. He was also a member of the Comptroller General's Advisory Board at the the Government Accountability Office (GAO) from 2002 to 2006, and he is currently a board member on the World Affairs Council in San Diego. Mr. Bowsher has had a life-time interest in politics and government. He has worked with the Republican, Democratic and Tea Parties in recent years as he did research for this book.

Jack Bowsher has previously authored three books:

Jack E. Bowsher

- *Educating America: Lessons Learned In The Nation's Corporations*
- *Revolutionizing Workforce Performance: A Systems Approach To Mastery*
- *Fix Schools First: Blueprint For Achieving Learning Standards*

INDEX OF SUBHEADINGS